Mission Improbable

Mission Improbable

Using Fantasy Documents to Tame Disaster

LEE CLARKE

The University of Chicago Press * Chicago and London

LEE CLARKE teaches sociology at Rutgers University. He is the author of *Acceptable Risk? Making Decisions in a Toxic Environment* (1989) and *Organizations, Uncertainties, and Risk* (1992, with James F. Short, Jr.).

The University of Chicago Press, Chicago 60637
The University of Chicago Press, Ltd., London
© 1999 by The University of Chicago
All rights reserved. Published 1999
08 07 06 05 04 03 02 01 00 99   1 2 3 4 5

ISBN: 0-226-10941-0 (cloth)

Library of Congress Cataloging-in-Publication Data

Clarke, Lee Ben.
    Mission improbable : using fantasy documents to tame disaster / Lee
  Clarke.
    p. cm.
    Includes bibliographical references and index.
    ISBN 0-226-10941-0 (cloth : alk. paper)
    1. Emergency management.   2. Risk management—Social aspects.
  3. Preparedness.   I. Title.
  HV551.2.C53   1999
  363.34'7—dc21   98-40808
                                                                      CIP

For Charles Perrow,
mentor and friend

Humpty Dumpty growled out, ". . . Why if I ever *did* fall off—which there's not a chance of—but *if* I did—" Here he pursed up his lips, and looked so solemn and grand that Alice could hardly help laughing. "*If* I did fall," he went on, "*the King promised me . . .*"

"To send all his horses and all his men," Alice interrupted, rather unwisely . . .

"Yes, all his horses and all his men," Humpty Dumpty went on, "They'd pick me up again in a minute, *they* would! . . ."

Lewis Carroll, *Alice through the Looking Glass*

The great enemy of truth is very often not the lie—deliberate, contrived, and dishonest—but the myth—persistent, persuasive, and unrealistic.

J. F. Kennedy

I make coffee one early Saturday morning at a friend's house, then sit down to read for a few minutes while it brews. After a while I realize it isn't plugged in, so I do so, and Chick says, "Not plugged in?" "No," I replied, "it's Brown's Ferry all over again." There are laughs all around and Edith says, "A quick response is worth a thousand contingency plans."

Contents

Acknowledgments

A number of people helped me make this book, or helped me make it better. Jo Ann Kiser was a terrific copy editor. Ruth Simpson did excellent research assistance in the early part of the project. Eviatar Zerubavel helped me reconceptualize the project when I got bogged down in it. The Divine Doug Mitchell showed patience and grace in the production of this thing, though he must have wondered at times whether the book was itself a fantasy document. The National Science Foundation, the Natural Hazard Center, the Disaster Research Center, and Rutgers University provided some grant support but are absolved from responsibility.

Lisa Adams, Carol Heimer, Allan Mazur, and Scott Sagan reviewed the book and provided many, many pages of useful comments. All of them saved me from factual errors, pushed me to be more clear, and were generous with their very penetrating criticisms, not all of which I could attend to. Carol was even kind enough to let me use some of her words.

James Jasper, my sweet, sharp critic, didn't let big disagreements between us prevent him from generously commenting on the entire manuscript. His friendship and intellectual insight have been indispensable to me and to this book. I have no closer comrade.

Patricia Roos was extremely generous with her thoughts, and much else too. Dear Pat has borne with me through much more than just this project, and for that deserves something far beyond this mere acknowledgment. In public at least, it's the best I can offer.

Charles Perrow read the entire manuscript. He reads all my manuscripts, and indeed has been my main critical reader for twenty years. During that time Chick's critical appraisals of my work have been the yardstick by which I've judged my success. He hasn't always agreed with what I've done with his comments, but then no one can be right all the time. He has never failed to produce pages and pages of sometimes scathing remarks, usually well reasoned, and always ending with something like "Love, Chick" or "My usual sensitive self." When I first got to graduate school, I was advised by other students to "take Perrow's class. He's difficult but you'll learn a lot." Massive understatement, that. What I began to learn during that first class are the same things I continue to learn from Charles Perrow: how to think and how to write, which, he has always rightly insisted, are inseparable. My father once advised Chick to tell me that he had taught me everything I know but not everything he knew. I fear that's more true than my father realized. As important as the mentoring has been to me, Chick and I successfully made the transition from professor-student to friend-friend. It is as deep a personal relationship as I have, and I cherish it. But for all that, Professor Perrow remains a mentor. There is none better at that, and that is why, with love and admiration, I dedicate this book to him.

1

Some Functions of Planning

Planning Is Prosaic

Everyone plans. We lie in bed in the morning and plan to get to work. We get to work and plan for the next meeting or whom to have lunch with or how to get home in the evening. We plan to make supper, we plan how to spend the night, we plan for the next day's work. Adults who don't plan are considered unstable.

Larger social units plan too. A youth organization plans to ask for money, a church plans to save souls, a corporation plans an expansion, a country plans a foreign invasion. Large social units that don't plan are judged ineffective, poorly managed, irresponsible, or sometimes just plain dumb.[1]

Planning is not bounded by history or culture. Certainly the range of things for which people in modern times plan has widened. As social life gets more complex so does the variety of phenomena that demand forethought. Still, the great structures and conquests of Antiquity required extensive planning. Obvious examples are the Crusades, the pyramids, Stonehenge.

So planning is a prosaic, and ubiquitous, fact of life. It is always with us, in one way or another, because either we are constantly doing it ourselves or we are part of someone else's plan. Perhaps planning's mundanity is the reason it seems uninteresting. At best, we tend to think of planning as a fairly low-level activity that might warrant attention from policy analysts or perhaps from industrial psychologists trying to fit people to organizational needs. As well, when scholars and commentators write about plans they most often see their work as an exercise in increasing organizational effectiveness, as a way to increase profit margins, or as a way to decrease job dissatisfaction. Such exercises can be quite important—who doesn't want more effective organizations?—but often aren't intellectually exciting.

This book is premised on quite the opposite view. I think there are many interesting things about planning, if we turn our gaze to the symbolic, in addition to the functional, aspects of it. The book's theme is that *organizations and experts use plans as forms of rhetoric, tools designed to convince audiences that they ought to believe what an organization says. In particular, some plans have so little instrumental utility in them that they warrant the label "fantasy document."*

We will see that the production of fantasy documents always results from interaction between two or more players. This is important to know because an easier way to think about the issue is that actors confront problems and try to reason out possible solutions; from a list of such solutions, decision makers pick the one they think is best. Academics know this way of thinking as the rational model of decision making, and it concentrates so heavily on the instrumental aspects of people's behavior that it is mute about symbolism.

It will be tempting to conclude that fantasy documents are self-conscious lies, deliberately designed by powerful executives and cunning experts to hide their true interests, and to dupe the public into believing things that aren't true. It will be tempting to come to that conclusion because the production of fantasy documents often looks just like that! But in fact the message is more disturbing. As powerful as organizational leaders can be and as cunning as experts sometimes are, the more frightening truth is that they are often unmindful of the *limits* of their knowledge and power. We have more to fear from organizations and experts overextending their reach, propelled by forces endemic to modern society, than from conniving conspiracies.

We will also see the influence of complex organizations on the production of plans and on how people behave. This is important to know because most of us are used to thinking in either individualistic or institutional terms. An example of the former is when we assume that the U.S. President actually controls the government; an example of the latter is when we assume that The Government is a unitary actor. We don't usually see how forces that are intrinsic to complex organizations shape how people think and act. Of course, there is always a lot of negotiation, social conflict, and disagreement behind the face of any organization. But organizational forces can be so strong that it often makes good sense to speak of organizations as if *they* were unitary actors. When I talk as if organizations act I will be using a shorthand language that emphasizes the strength of those forces.[2]

To focus on symbolic planning is to neglect what is perhaps the predominant model of planning in organizational social science. That model, which usually goes by the name of rational actor theory, argues that the conduct, character, and creation of plans follow the demands of the task. Such an argument—that the character of the problem determines the solution—has a long history in social science. We have a lot of research on better planning, more efficient planning, or more participatory planning, depending on an author's practical or political commitments. The usual presumption in social science is that the first step in an adequate planning process is to assess fairly completely what the problem is; the second step is to write a plan that addresses, and hopefully will solve, the problem; the final step is to implement the plan. In this sequence it isn't hard to see common sense lurking in the background, which perhaps explains why so much writing on planning is so dull.

I think that such rational, common-sense planning is possible under conditions of relatively low uncertainty. When information about problems can be easily gathered, and when that information can be trusted, then it is possible to create plans that might be reasonably expected to work. When uncertainty is relatively low, it is easier to gather good empirical knowledge and to develop good theories that will make sense of that knowledge. Good data and good theories, in turn, enable better prediction and thus better planning for the future.

Of course, there are problems that are *moderately* uncertain. Consider the following issues, all rife with uncertainty, all characterized by good science on all sides of the arguments, and all of which entail considerable political disagreement:[3]

- Will environmental change create imbalances of power between developed and developing societies? And if so, in what direction?

- Will burgeoning populations in poor countries create massive numbers of environmental refugees to rich countries?

- Will global warming create terrific food shortages and attendant Malthusian horrors?

Predicting how environments change, and how environmental change will affect political organizations, requires taking account of a large number of variables. The same goes for arguments about global warming. The problems are exacerbated because the science for each of the issues isn't hard and fast, and besides, the problems are just *so big* that planning and prediction for them are nearly Herculean. Herculean but not impossible. It *is* possible to get evidence on deforestation, degradation of agriculture, types of social conflict, and flooding. These are *moderately* uncertain issues because directly relevant data, and relatively good theories, are available, or conceivably could be available, with sufficient amounts of scientific and political attention, and money.

Under conditions of *high* uncertainty, however, the nature of planning changes in major ways. Under highly uncertain conditions rational planning becomes more difficult. Concomitant visions of the future will likely be distorted by inadequate or corrupt data, and by the poor conceptual scheme brought to bear on those data. When important aspects of the future are not or cannot be known, planning is shorn of its most functional aspects (knowing what "important" means is part of effective planning). This is not to say that planning under high uncertainty can't in principle *be* effective. It is to say that the ability to know what constitutes effectiveness is terribly low or nonexistent. The importance of planning's symbolism then increases, relative to a plan's likelihood of being realized. In fact, under conditions of high uncertainty the promise and apparatus of rational planning itself becomes mainly *rhetorical*, becomes a means by which plans—independently of their functional relevance to the task—can be justified as reasonable promises that exigencies can be controlled. When uncertainty about key aspects of a task is high, rationalistic plans and rational-looking planning processes become rationality badges, labels proclaiming that organizations and experts can control things that are, most likely, outside the range of their expertise. Planning then becomes a sign that organizations hang on themselves, advertising their competence and forethought, announcing to all who would listen, "We know what this problem is and we know how to solve it. Trust us." Thus do organizations try to control the uncontrollable.

The Relevance of Organizations

I place organizations at center stage in planning dramas, even though other social actors obviously plan. This is not incidental. The main stories I use to explore the themes outlined above concern nuclear power generation, oil spills, and nuclear war. Organizations, and not other social units such as nations, classes, networks, or publics, have been the key actors shaping actions, ideas, and policies about these topics.[4]

Few would dispute the central roles that organizations play in all these cases, or indeed organizations' roles in other aspects of modern life, if they paused to consider the matter. Yet only recently have we made much real progress in understanding how organizations create and respond to situations that involve actual or potential peril. More generally, the biggest advances on understanding and explaining uncertainty have been in economics and psychology, and organizations rarely appear in writings from those fields. This is unfortunate, because it is in fact organizations, and the elites who try to run them, that make the crucial choices concerning what technologies will be developed and put in place, and that develop new social forms in response to those technologies. It is also organizations, and not the detached, rational, asocial individuals of psychology and economics, that we must depend on to respond to the risks, and catastrophes, they create. There simply is no choice, when a big oil spill happens, but to call out the Coast Guard, the Environmental Protection Agency, corporations, and so on. In these responses, of course, organizations can fail us, and sometimes quite badly. Modern organizations bear us fruits unimaginable to our ancestors, but they can also create tragedy unparalleled in history. It is organizations that create technologies and production processes that give us modern disasters. It is organizations that construct the most important plans for responding to disasters. It is organizations that socially construct risk, danger, and safety.

I want to develop this view a bit. A signal feature of modern existence is the prevalence of organizations in nearly every aspect of social life. From birth to death organizations shape our choices and are, often enough, even the great creators of much of culture. This simple fact, which is so institutionalized that it tends to be taken for granted, also applies to technology and the capacity for catastrophe that organizations and technology can bring. The savings and loan industry meltdown in the early 1990s could not have happened if the industry's organizational structure had been simpler and more open to outside scrutiny. We looked, as well, to organizations for the response to that catastrophe. When Chernobyl turned itself into a molten, radiating mass, observers with the clearest vision looked to the organizations behind nuclear technology for blame, and again we looked to organizations for rescue. That individuals were involved—as causal agents and as victims—in these social, economic, and technical breakdowns does not gainsay the central role of organizations in them. Indeed the effects on individuals of organizational failures show mainly that most of us, most of the time, are at the mercy of organizational action. After all, an argument that centered on individuals in understanding, say, the

Bhopal chemical accident in 1984 would have to hold that if only the people who occupied key decision making positions had been different then the disaster would not have happened. Such an argument can be made plausibly in a courtroom, perhaps, but the kind of truth sought in a lawsuit is not the kind of truth we're concerned with here.

Organizations not only harm us, but are alone capable of salvation when things go awry. This dependence on organizations is appropriate, even helpful, most of the time. Complex, formal organizations, on balance, are better at solving big problems—including responding to disasters—than individuals, small groups, or nations. Most of the time at least. The reason this is so is that organizations, again most of the time, are better planners than individuals, small groups, etc. The reason organizations are better planners is partly because they have unique and often extended access to many types of resources. No large collection of unconnected individuals can move quickly and decisively at the drop of a hat, or a control rod.

Organizations, especially large organizations, have more money, person-power, and coordinative capability to accomplish tasks. Organizations also have a property that individuals (at least healthy individuals) don't have—they can differentiate, or splinter and divide themselves into ever finer units. Physicists speak of the "fractal" properties of nature, by which they mean that the units that comprise a larger structure tend to look like that larger structure. It's called self-similarity. Organizations, too, tend to be self-similar: break one in half and the units of each half usually look a lot alike.

That organizations are fractal means they can overcome the cognitive limitations of individuals when faced with a problem. When organizations form committees to study difficult problems, for instance how to expand the marketing department or what to do about cheating in the classroom, they are splintering themselves so that smaller bits of the problem can be farmed out to smaller bits of the organization. If it is a big enough committee, and a big enough problem, chances are good that subcommittees will form as well. Of course, splintering organizations and splintering problems don't guarantee that a *good* set of solutions will arise. Still, a broader set of solutions is more likely to emerge from such a process than if a single individual were handed the problem. In other words, when the problems get big, organization is the proper response.[5]

Another reason organizations are typically better planners than other units of social organization is that they have greater capacity for collective memory. History is embedded in the routines and files of complex organizations. This history takes the form of stories, memos, official histories, and institutionalized patterns of behavior. What's important, in this context, is that organizations can benefit from the experience of the vast number of individual members, storing information, and developing explanations about what works and what doesn't so that others can use it. In this way they make knowledge transitive across individuals. Again, of course, there's no guarantee that an organization will learn the *right* things about how to respond, say, to a major oil spill. Still, in principle, organizations have a greater capacity for such learning than do other units of social action.

Functional Planning

Functional planning is when actors have meaningful history to draw on and some reasonable, estimable probability that their plans can actually accomplish their goals. The history and conceptual scheme necessary to make good sense of that history allow actors to have some confidence that their predictions are likely to work out according to expectations. There are two views of functional planning, one from common sense and one from scholarship on organizations.

The most obvious reasons that organizations plan are to get something done and to tell themselves what to do. This is the reason given by common sense, and management consultant books. In this view, planning is a strategic thing, a course of action chosen to maximize utilities, profits, or interests. If a university is going to educate thirty thousand undergraduates, some curriculum planning is necessary. If a hospital is going to stay healthy, presumably in order to provide health to patients, it's going to have to plan which market segments to serve and which to ignore. Such planning is designed to accomplish a task, its function to accomplish an organizational goal.

Imagine a history department in a university responding to an administrative mandate to develop a five-year plan. This plan, according to the administration's wishes, should detail the department's existing strengths and weaknesses. It should specify what gaps exist in the department's ability to train graduate students, teach undergraduates, and provide the infrastructure for faculty to get their research and writing done. Next, the plan, if it is to be a good one, should specify as closely as possible which strategies the department will use to build on existing strengths and minimize existing weaknesses. Such a plan might declare that the department would hire an eighteenth-century Americanist, a contemporary Europeanist, and an Africanist. It might also state that there weren't enough black graduate students, and outline how the department would recruit more of them. The plan might also explain how a new network of computers would be purchased and installed, which would make it easier for scholars to write and also permit the department to get by with one less secretary.

Our history department is taking stock of its resources (both extant and future ones) and projecting them, along with its needs, into the future. By constructing and presenting this plan, the department will have created a blueprint that tells itself what it will do. If it is not an empty exercise, say a ploy by the administration to centralize power, the plan will create favorable conditions for the department to allocate resources within the department, for the dean to allocate resources among departments, and so on. Planning helps provide favorable conditions because if needs, wants, and gaps can be delineated then their costs (monetary and otherwise) can be calculated more easily, which can facilitate coordination and reduce waste. Finally, notice that *other departments and offices,* which form the primary audience for our history department, will recognize the plan as a sensible, even sagacious, thing to do. This is all highly functional planning, and prescriptions and descriptions of such planning (or of departures from it) routinely appear in management journals, popular business books, and the newspapers.

The second view of planning, drawn mostly from scholarship on organizations, can also see planning as strategic but concentrates more on how it reduces uncertainty for decision makers. By drawing on collective memory and allocating resources to planning, organizations make the troubles they face more predictable. Put differently, when organizations plan they construct a map of which contingencies are to be considered relevant. The very act of mapping gives some structure to the "data," ordering what could otherwise be a very chaotic world.

But what things are passably predictable and what is uncertain? Sociologist Arthur Stinchcombe, in *Information and Organizations,* says that organizations attend mainly to uncertainties about whatever constraints might impede organizational success, though he focuses chiefly on information, or the most important kinds of "news" for organizational functioning. "Uncertainty is reduced through news," he says, "then finally the residual uncertainty is transformed into risk, and people make their bets."[6] His main idea is that the key uncertainty, or uncertainties, faced by an organization at a given moment (they change over time) will prompt the organization to "grow" in that direction. This is so because formal organization is the predominately legitimate way of gathering valid information on a problem.

Stinchcombe is probably right that organizations pay the most attention to uncertainties that have some important bearing on effectiveness. The history department in the example above, for instance, won't hire a sociologist or recruit physics graduate students. These are not the kinds of uncertainties that are relevant—either to internal or external audiences—to a history department's mission. Yet notably, the pages of *Information and Organizations* are populated with examples of situations of low or moderate uncertainty. That is, they are the kinds of problems on which, in principle at least, enough information can be gathered so that outside evaluators, say banks, insurance companies, or government regulators, could agree on what constituted objective evidence in their efforts to solve the problems. They are the kinds of problems to which standards of formal rationality can be applied. And they are the kinds of problems for which it is possible for reasonable observers to agree on a common definition of "important."

Consider, briefly, the myriad problems that the AIDS epidemic created for a huge array of organizations. In *The AIDS Disaster* Charles Perrow and Mauro Guillen look at organizations and problems and see a different world than the one Stinchcombe sees. For them, "If an organization is challenged by a new problem, like AIDS, and that problem is sufficiently difficult or affects a number of internal or external groups, there is a good chance that the organization will fail to achieve its mandated goals."[7] This is a very different vision of failure compared to Stinchcombe's, which focuses on poor or inadequate information. That Perrow and Guillen disagree so sharply with Stinchcombe on this matter is probably because Stinchcombe's theory is functionalist while Perrow and Guillen's is more political-organizational. In any case, my concern for the moment is to downplay the political conflicts of interest in the organizational response to AIDS and to emphasize the uncertainties posed by it.

Perrow and Guillen "could not find a single convincing example of any *major* organization that took on AIDS . . . without question and without problems."[8] In their view, organizations could have looked to the histories of other epidemics, poverty, or nuclear weapons development for guidance. What Perrow and Guillen miss is that at the time that AIDS was being recognized as a tremendous social problem there were no categories available with which experts and organizations could fold problems into their existing mandates and organizational structures. No hospital can claim the eradication of poverty is within its purview. Few would disagree with Perrow and Guillen that the organizational response to AIDS was initially a massive failure. The point here is that the response improved only when hospitals constructed plans to deal with the rising number of patients, when social service agencies planned to provide some housing and counseling to people with AIDS, when political parties planned to work meaningful response to AIDS into their rhetorics about what constituted the public interest. Such plans were wrapped around already existing ways of talking about formal goals, decreasing the uncertainties that attended AIDS, making it somewhat more predictable, and enabling organizational action.

Since so much of this book's material is about disasters or near-disasters this may be a good place to say that functional planning happens all the time with disasters, especially natural disasters. Organizations and officials who do not plan for earthquakes in Los Angeles would be seen rightly as remiss in their duties. The same goes for hurricane planning on the east coast, especially the south and middle Atlantic states. I should also note that the connections between functional planning for disasters and successful response are far from obvious. I take up that issue in a later chapter.

Transforming Uncertainty into Risk

The classical argument from social science about planning and uncertainty is that they are inversely related: the more planning, the less uncertainty. This is so because more planning means decision makers have collected more information and made more benefit-cost deliberations than is the case when they do not plan. When investment houses diversify a portfolio they reduce the uncertainty of the market by spreading it around among different financial instruments. When the Nuclear Regulatory Commission specifies in fine detail the licensing process for a new plant it reduces the uncertainties of political conflict, lawsuits, and technical argument. When primary and secondary schools track students according to their presumed level of math or English ability they reduce the uncertainty of their raw material (students) by apportioning the variability to different organizational units.[9]

Put differently, what happens is that uncertainty is transformed into risk. It will help to explain briefly what these words mean. Explaining the usual conception of rationality in their classic book *Organizations,* James March and Herbert Simon said that *risk* is when there is "accurate knowledge of a probability distribution of the consequences that will follow on each alternative" and *uncertainty* is when "the consequences of each alternative belong to some subset of all possible consequences, but . . . the decision maker cannot assign definite probabilities to the occurrence of particular consequences."[10] More directly, risk is when you know the possible range of things that may happen following a choice; uncertainty is when you don't.

The economist Frank Knight similarly distinguished between risk and uncertainty. Knight's concerns were with economic theory but his conceptual dissection was incisive enough for us to borrow. Professor Knight held that risk and uncertainty were "categorically different," though they were often confused in common use and economic theory. When he said that "the power of one thing to suggest another is often quite mysterious, and might possibly not rest upon the possession of any common real qualities which will support a valid inference,"[11] Knight was noting the arbitrary character not only of thinking about the future but of thinking period. My claim is not so severe.

Risk in its general form is when it is possible, at least in principle, to estimate the likelihood that an event (or set of events) will occur; the specific forms of those estimates are the probabilities of adverse consequences. Uncertainty is when such estimations are not possible.[12] We can, for example, know the risk of divorce for first marriages, but whether any given couple will divorce is uncertain.

When organizations analyze problems, they try to transform *uncertainties* into *risks,* rationalizing problems previously outside the realm of systematic control. Such processes sometimes take the form of cost-benefit calculations, profit and loss algorithms, or any method that entails explicit estimation of future probabilities. For example, Ford Motor Company relied on a formal risk analysis when it declined to spend an extra eleven dollars for gas tanks that would not explode and burn after crashes at twenty-five miles per hour in 1970–77 Pintos. Ford's analysis clarified the tradeoff between revenue and safety, converting the uncertainties of Pinto failures into the risks of lawsuits and regulatory judgments.[13]

The organizational urge behind these transformations is part of the characteristic drive for rationalization in modern society. At one level, this urge reflects a societal-level expectation that organizations should be able to control the uncertain, and be able to respond effectively to the untoward. For their part, organizational leaders rarely admit that uncertainties may not be tamed by a rational calculus, unless they are trying to avoid responsibility for something. There are both pressures from without, and promises from within, that organizations subjugate time and chance—the two most difficult moments of uncertainty—to schemes of classification and command.

Yet time and chance conspire against organizational readiness. Effective uncertainty-to-risk transformations are inextricably bound to the past, because reliable predictions must be based on experience that is properly interpreted. A major fault of the infamous 1975 Reactor Safety Study by the Atomic Energy Commission (the Rasmussen Report) was a dire lack of experience on which to base predictions of reactor failures.[14] Organizations can thus be charged with the onerous task of effectively transforming uncertainty into risk *even without a sufficient experiential base or conceptual scheme appropriate for interpreting history.* This problem is especially critical for organizations whose failures may entail catastrophe.

If we arrayed problems faced by organizations along a continuum of clear to obscure, many would fall closer to the terminus of clarity. Those are the problems most amenable to rational planning, and indeed standard operating procedures institutionalize organizational norms for responding to them. Few indicators of rationality are more useful to organizations than written plans. Most previous work on organizational planning and decision making—two areas in which rationalization is highly advanced—has been concerned with clear to moderately obscure classes of problems.

This book explores the obscure domain: problems for which there are no solutions, and for which there will be no solutions in the foreseeable future. My main cases are evacuation plans for civilian nuclear power plants, nuclear war civil defense plans, and contingency plans for major oil spills. Note that just because some problems are wrapped in high uncertainty doesn't mean organizations don't plan for them. With those plans, however, operational utility is far less likely than symbolic utility.

Symbolic Planning

Operational, functional planning is what we usually think about when we bother to think about planning at all. Individuals and organizations expend considerable strategic energy in making functional plans that realize interests, utilities, or profits. But there are cases where the plan and the planning process *themselves* are the function. Sometimes organizations collect information but don't use it, or use their very collection efforts to signal that they are doing *something* about a problem.[15] Sometimes planning is more symbolically than operationally useful, the plans representing something other than a real capability to imagine the future and prepare for it.

Of course, all action can be infused with symbolic importance, so even the most mundane of plans can be imbued with surplus meaning. Anyone who has ever encountered an overzealous bureaucrat insisting on adherence to a trivial rule will quickly recognize the surfeit of symbolism in everyday documents. "It's not in your strategic plan, so you can't expand in that market," says the CEO, using the plan as a symbol of rational thought to justify a decision she has reached on other grounds. Still, it's useful to distinguish between functional and symbolic planning. Were there no such thing as truly functional planning nothing could ever get done.

Plans are a form of language, a way of expressing or communicating some thing. That "thing" can be anything from a claim about some mundane activity that will happen tomorrow (e.g. an appointment book) to a claim that super-knowledge allows experts to make decisions about a very vague future (e.g. the US Department of Energy's plans to bury high level radioactive waste safely). In any case, language, and hence a plan, is meaningful when it is shared. Language must be directed at someone else and that someone must share the meaning if what is being communicated is to be more than incoherent gibberish.

To make a plan is to claim expertise because planning, especially high-technology planning, requires that organizations and experts lay claim to mastery and thoughtfulness about some issue. Since claims to expertise are always claims that somebody should be left out of the decision loop, planning is deeply, unavoidably political. This little-noticed, almost invisible political character of planning is something that figures prominently in the pages to follow.[16]

So symbolic plans, which I call fantasy documents, are rhetorical instruments that have political utility in reducing uncertainty for organizations and experts. Earlier I asked, with Stinchcombe, "Uncertainty about what?" I can now answer the question more specifically: the key uncertainties that fantasy documents are trying to turn into risks have to do with how future events will evolve, and how future actors will respond to those events. Fantasy documents are thus based on an underlying sociological theory of events, meanings, and behaviors. Soon, I'll argue that the key mechanism through which such theories are expressed are "apparent affinities," claims that a catastrophic possibility is sufficiently like something we already know as to allow operational planning to proceed. Fantasy documents, generally, are *not* constructed to deliberately dupe various audiences (though they can have that effect) but are more prosaically rooted in organizational processes that are endemic to modern society.

Plans for recovery after general nuclear war are fantasy documents because the knowledge and experience necessary to know what would make for a realistic plan are unavailable. Those who propose the reality of nuclear war civil defense plans must assert their claims without knowing key details about how nuclear war would actually play out. The actual war plans are secret, though much is obvious too, about what would be hit. Still the knowledge is hardly precise. The same goes for blast yields, the number of bombs, whether the bombs explode in air or on ground, time of year and so on. All these uncertainties, and more, mean that projections of societal recovery are in large measure outright guesses.

Plans for evacuating after (or during) a total meltdown of the Shoreham nuclear power station on Long Island—the second of my three main cases—were fantasy documents for much the same reasons that civil defense plans are fantasies. While mass evacuations are indeed possible, it would be impossible to test the key parts of the Long Island Lighting Company's plan.

Plans for containing and cleaning up massive oil spills—my last main case—on the open seas are fantasy documents because such response is quite impossible. We haven't the requisite knowledge or technology to respond to such spills, and that's why there's never been a major oil spill success story.

The following chapters tell stories of how some plans are created, used, and fought over. Those stories in turn tell us some things about symbolism, rhetoric, and rationality in modern, beautiful, horrific, bureaucratized societies. The pattern, in general, is for officials and organizations to be confronted with opposition to their initial plans and goals. The result of that interaction is a cognitive transformation of an unknown or unmanageable thing into a known or manageable thing. Each of the three main cases has different lessons for how we think of planning, prediction, and persuasion. But they all share the property of involving planning processes with a very high ratio of symbolic to operational utility.

In the next chapter are the main fantasies I am concerned with, followed by a chapter on nonfantasy documents. After that, I show how organizations and self-appointed experts change conceptual terms of debate to make their plans look more reasonable, transforming incredible uncertainties into quite manageable risks. Then I delve into the histories of social conflict behind fantasy documents; these are the social histories without which the fantasies would not be constructed. In the last chapter, I talk about the meaning of the evidence for how we understand organizations and symbols, the construction of expertise, and the consequences of fantasy documents.

2

Fantasy Documents

Some plans are highly instrumental, but others are little more than vague hopes for remote futures and have virtually no known connection with human capacity or will. These are plans that are not functional in the sense of serving as blueprints for coordination and action but are functional in the sense of asserting to others that the uncontrollable can be controlled. Such plans are sometimes produced cynically by organizations and experts, and often have the effect of mollifying the public or other organizations. More often, I think, they are produced earnestly by organizations and experts who truly believe in their own constructions. Either way, the plans are fantasy documents, imaginative fictions about what people hope will happen after things go wrong. They are fantasies either because the promises they make can never be fulfilled (as is the case for oil spills) or because we can never know whether they will be fulfilled (as is the case for nuclear evacuations and nuclear civil defense) until major catastrophe befalls us.

Fantasy documents are rationality badges, symbols organizations use to signal they are in control of danger, whether they really are or not. These rationality badges originate in the everyday routines that organizations develop in response to problems, and in the social conflict engendered by organizations that produce them. Once produced, they are usually set in a rhetoric of technical competence, and often enough in one of national interest, providing a context that helps persuade (internal and external) audiences of their legitimacy. When audiences grant such legitimacy, fantasy documents work to set terms of political debate by shaping vocabularies within which discussion occurs. In this way fantasy documents justify and support systems that seem increasingly beyond our comprehension and control.

Fantasy documents read like scripts for plays or movies. They specify relevant actors and the story lines those actors are supposed to pursue: the high-level military officials are "tasked" to protect the national interest, the dispersant contractors will make most of the oil go away, the bus drivers will ferry people out of the way of a glowing, melted reactor core. Fantasy documents describe the scenery, necessarily neglecting much as they construct the organizational stage upon which the fantasy will presumably work itself out. Fantasy documents detail the timing of assault, of reaction, and of recovery: when the bombs will drop, when the "all clear" will be sounded, when it will be safe for wildlife to return to their home waters. Fantasy documents, like movie scripts, have a definite beginning, middle, and end, and the construction of these stories very much depends on who the audience is thought to be for them. In these ways, fantasy documents can be remarkably coherent, though the coherence is internal and thus uncomplicated by external forces and ambiguity: it is always clear who is firing the missiles, the requisite technology for oil spill response is at hand, people will evacuate during a radiological emergency without first collecting their children from school.

The coherence of organizational coordination and the simplicity of society that we find in fantasy documents are remarkable. There is, for instance, an entire book devoted to explicating a British nuclear war plan of the early 1980s. The book, *War Plan UK* by Duncan Campbell, a journalist, runs through an entire crisis-attack-recovery scenario. The plan has very detailed schedules of what would happen each step of the way: the Soviets foment the conflict by invading Europe, NATO responds reasonably and with most of its effort put on diplomacy, which then fails and leads to pockets of conventional warfare, which escalates to general nuclear war, after which the great industrial democracies rise from the radioactive ashes to approximate what they were before the six-hour attack:

1 Sept.: Start of the crisis

19 Sept.: NATO orders mobilization and reinforcement of Europe . . .

27 Sept.: War starts; Warsaw pact troops invade Europe, and conventional bombing starts on targets in Britain.

29 Sept.: Local authority war HQs and government bunkers are manned. Conventional bombing of British targets by Soviet bombers continues.

2–3 Oct.: Nuclear Strike during the night—six hours of nuclear bombardment anticipated.[1]

We may grant that the sequence of attack events is reasonable (if unimaginative) and still not quite fathom the terribly fantastic qualities about the plan. No important strategic targets are hit, and most major cities, though devastated, suffer no direct nuclear hits. Communications throughout the atomic trouble remain undisturbed and unclouded. Organizations, and society more generally, stay orderly. There is no sense of fundamental upset. Britain's fantasy document was a closed system and would only work by pretending there would be no outside disturbances.[2]

Note the surreal qualities, the sanitized, rational progression from conflict to mass death. Event sequences are clear, hostile signals are lucid, the end is definable. Yet at the very least we know that once nuclear weapons started to fall all sorts of communications would be thrown into utter disarray (because of electromagnetic pulses and the simple destruction of communication centers), creating all manner of uncertainty. Truly, this is a fantasy document.

Here's another example. There is a pile of dredged sand and silt that's partly in southern New Jersey and partly in northern Delaware. It is called, unceremoniously, Artificial Island though it's actually a peninsula, because over time it has grown into the mainland. Artificial Island has three nuclear reactors, and I'll say just a few words about Delaware's "Artificial Island 1991 Emergency Plan."[3] Delaware officials cleverly made their plan into a calendar that people could hang on their walls or refrigerators. Presumably, it would not there be forgotten. In the event of a big accident, people are to "listen for a 3 to 5-minute siren blast," "turn on your radio immediately" (call letters and dial locations are given), and "if ordered to take shelter" stay home and close the windows. "If ordered to evacuate," say the experts, "you will be given *Plenty of Time* (emphasis and capitals in original) to act in an emergency. *Do not hurry!*" "If children are in school . . . please don't go to schools to pick up children. They will be moved to a safe area and cared for until you arrive." Denizens are also given a map of a "ten-mile emergency planning zone," basically a ten-mile circle radiating (excuse the pun) from Artificial Island. The circle is transected like a pie into eight sections and people are told to "mark the compass direction of the section in which you live or work. . . . It is important to know your compass direction. In a real emergency, residents of some sections may need to take action. Others may not. For example, if there were an emergency, people in one section might be told to stay inside. Others may need to do nothing."

Now the Artificial Island plan is nothing if not sanguine. If we know anything at all about evacuations it is that people move as families.

They'll leave their children to the care of others, but only if they trust the temporary guardians *and* feel they have no choice. The condescending tone in the emphatic charge "Do not hurry!" belies the top-down approach that's typical of nuclear experts. Why on earth would people *not* hurry? They probably would, and should, just as they probably would not panic (that's another thing we know about evacuations—people don't panic). And Delaware planners apparently think people would really believe that radiation would move along the pie-shaped divisions of the local geography. The truth is that we can't know the things the Delaware planners claim they know so well. The real crux of the plan is that people should stay inside and close their windows.

There's not much detail in Delaware's plan though there was a lot in Britain's. In this, fantasy documents exhibit the same variation as other kinds of plans. Some plans are fine-grained, others are quite coarse. What the plans share is that they are entirely made up, fantasies that grow out of an managerial need to *do something* about potentially grave danger. As these organizations do their planning they transform uncertainty into risk, and the main tool they use in that transformation is a rhetorical one. For now I want to introduce the three main sets of fantasy documents I'll talk about: contingency plans for major oil spills, evacuation plans for civilian nuclear plants, and civil defense and post-nuclear war survival plans.

Oil Spill Fantasies

Regulators and corporate organizations in the oil industry claim they can contain and clean up massive oil spills on the open sea. Thus considerable intellectual and political attention has been accorded contingency plans for responding to such spills. These plans become lightning rods for political conflict—as we saw, for instance, in the huge spill when the *Exxon Valdez* ran aground in Alaska in 1989. After that spill we saw a great hue and cry because Alyeska, the consortium that owns and operates the Alaskan Pipeline, claimed in its contingency plan that it could control huge oil spills. When, quickly, it became apparent that such was not the case, many focused on the plan as a set of promises that Alyeska could have delivered on, if it had only devoted enough money, personnel, and devotion to the task. I detail Alyeska's plan later.

In the wake of the Exxon spill, the oil industry had to plan much

more extensively for large, open-sea oil spills. The Oil Spill Pollution
Act of 1990, in particular, caused the industry to consider more carefully worst-case scenarios. Part of the industry's response has been to
institute the Marine Spill Response Corporation (MSRC), consisting
chiefly of sixteen response vessels stationed around the country and,
of course, lots of plans.

Yet for all this effort, for all the money, for all the promises, the truth
of the matter is that even if those who responded to the Exxon spill
enjoyed best-case conditions they wouldn't have been able to control,
let alone retrieve, all the oil that came out of Exxon's boat (almost
eleven million gallons). And the truth is that MSRC and the vessel-
planning will be utterly useless when a big tanker breaks up off the
coast of Florida, California, or, again, Alaska. If we define success as
only 15 percent oil recovery and then look through the sordid history
of oil spills, we see that no major oil spill has ever been successfully
contained and there has never been a successful recovery operation.

I state this so strongly because the history of really big spills, especially from tankers, is recent history, with us only since the late 1960s
and especially the 1970s after the price of oil increased so dramatically.
Further, plenty of scientists have paid a lot of attention to every large
oil spill, so we actually know quite a lot about them.

Let's begin with the dramatic story of the *Torrey Canyon*, which in
1967 became the first huge oil spill from a tankship.[4] The *Torrey Canyon*
was 810 feet long (the *Exxon Valdez* was 987 feet) and grounded in the
English Channel with nearly thirty-seven million gallons of oil on
board. Between six and twelve million gallons of the *Torrey Canyon*'s
cargo leaked out within the first two days, soiling the Cornwall coast.
The British government feared the ship would founder and spill the
remaining oil. So on the fifth day of the crisis England went to war
with the *Torrey Canyon*. Eight bombers from the Royal Navy dropped
one-thousand-pound bombs on the crippled vessel in an attempt to
burn the oil. The *Torrey Canyon*'s stern caught fire but only briefly, so
fighter jets dropped five thousand gallons of aviation fuel on the wreck,
followed by eighteen tons of bombs. More than $500 million worth
of bombs were dropped on the *Torrey Canyon*, but even with enough
inflammable material to burn a small city the fire lasted but minutes.
The next day saw more bombs, with napalm added for good measure.
More fires started and again failed to burn the cargo. There is some
dispute over how much oil actually remained in the vessel at that point,
but on the tenth day after the grounding the *Torrey Canyon*'s back

broke, sending fifteen million gallons of oil south to Brittany, where the slick earned the epithet *La Marée Noire.*

After the breakup, the British and French dumped several million gallons of detergents or dispersants on the oil; thousands of troops and volunteers went to work on a cleanup operation similar to Exxon's in Alaska. That was the second disaster in the English Channel. As a National Academy of Sciences volume, *Oil in the Sea,* aptly noted, "Many of the impacts observed were due largely to the awesome cleanup efforts used and not to the spilled oil." We don't have trustworthy estimates of how much of the *Torrey Canyon*'s oil was recovered in the cleanup effort, but by all accounts it was paltry.

The *Torrey Canyon* is not alone in the category of "failure." In 1969 the Union Oil well explosion blew at least three million gallons in the ocean near Santa Barbara, little of which was recovered. In 1970 the *Arrow* spilled 2.5 million gallons near Nova Scotia, most of which was swept to sea. In 1976 the *Argo Merchant* delivered over seven million gallons to the Nantucket Shoals, much of which stayed on the surface, turned into petroleum pancakes, and floated into the Atlantic. In 1978 the *Amoco Cadiz* lost sixty-eight million gallons, contaminating three hundred kilometers of Brittany. In 1979 the *Ixtoc I* well blowout in the Gulf of Mexico dumped between 130 and 390 million gallons of oil over a nine-month period; optimistic estimates are that 10 percent was recovered. In June 1989, just a few months after the *Exxon Valdez* grounding, three large spills occurred within twelve hours: the *World Prodigy* leaked 420,000 gallons off Narragansett, Rhode Island; a barge in the Houston Ship Channel lost 250,000 gallons; and the *Presidente Rivera* spilled 800,000 gallons into the Delaware River. In 1990 the *American Trader* spilled 400,000 gallons near Huntington Beach, California.[5] In none of these cases were authorities able to control the oil nor were they able to clean it from the waters or the beaches. Any efforts to react to a major oil spill on the open sea are almost entirely futile.[6]

But, a skeptic might respond, perhaps my stories are ones of organizational and technological failure because conditions were simply too severe to permit any productive response: the seas were too high, the winds too violent, the catastrophe too sudden. What, we might ask, would happen if such conditions were a bit more forgiving? In 1987 the Canadian Coast Guard, Environment Canada, and the U.S. Minerals Management Service (from the U.S. Department of Interior) ran an experiment to evaluate "the containment and recovery capabilities of three state-of-the-art booms and skimmers."[7]

The researchers spent about a million dollars to deliberately dump about twenty thousand gallons of oil in the North Atlantic some twenty-five miles east of Newfoundland. The plan was to contain and collect what was possible to contain and collect, and to disperse the rest. The experimenters would string three separate rows of boom around the stern of the spilling vessel, and the skimmers and dispersants would try to make the spill disappear.

Conditions were favorable on the day of the experiment. The seas were two to four feet, the winds between ten and twenty knots. By 6:45 A.M. the vessels and helicopters were ready, and the first line of boom was strung. By 9 o'clock all the oil had been released into the first line of boom. Between 9 and 10 o'clock, when the media were allowed to watch, the experimenters tried to pull the second line of boom into place, but the boom constantly twisted in on itself. By 10:30, oil was escaping over and under the first boom.

The oil was then towed around in its boom for about an hour, the experimenters testing their ability to corral oil while heading into wind (they fared poorly, to no one's surprise). Then the winds picked up, which meant the oil was at risk of being lost entirely. The experimenters managed to get some of the previously twisted boom back in place and deployed the skimmers. "The first skimmer," says the report, "was deployed and no measurable recovery was observed." But that wasn't the only problem. Three types of skimmers were tested, two of which were "frequently submerged so that oil and water were washed into the sump of the skimmer." In other words, those two skimmers worked more as buckets than oil suckers. A third skimmer operated admirably during the test, recovering almost eighty-five gallons of oil per minute, though for some reason it was used only a short while before being brought back aboard. Rough seas and lack of sunlight finally ended the Newfoundland experiment.

Evaluations of the Newfoundland experiment conflict. The report itself claims that "the containment and recovery effort was one of the most successful on record," which may be literally true but not what most of us would recognize as successful. An official with the U.S. Minerals Management Service, one of the report's authors, told me he estimated recovery at between 15 and 20 percent. A month after the test, an official Canadian Coast Guard estimate claimed 33 to 40 percent of the oil evaporated, and that another 33 percent was lost to sheens, the rainbow-looking film that petroleum products leave on water's surface. The Canadian Guard also claimed that between 26 and 33 percent of the oil was recovered, a truly enormous amount for an open-sea spill.[8] Others in the Canadian Coast Guard and Environment Canada, however, rate overall recovery at closer to 10 percent and consider the experiment a "gigantic flop."

The Newfoundland experiment demonstrates convincingly that even under highly controlled conditions, with state-of-the-art equipment, state-of-the-art chemicals, a sufficient number of trained personnel, a well-coordinated set of organizations, and a completely predictable time of spill, substantial oil recovery is by any reasonable definition simply impossible.

Contingency plans for large oil spills on the open sea are fantasy documents. In later pages we will examine in some detail the fantasies revealed in Alaska when Exxon ran a large tanker up on a rock in 1989. The resulting controversy would involve major regulatory agencies as well as oil corporations. The "public," too, figured in the story of the production of contingency plans for major oil spills, though not in a highly active way. The Alaskan "public" was either too dependent on oil revenues or too powerless and disorganized (especially native communities) to have much role to play in the fantasy productions. In Alaska the drama was mainly played out by corporations and regulatory agencies.

The utility of contingency plans for major oil spills is more symbolic than instrumental. Their production gives the impression that organizations, especially corporations and regulatory agencies, can effectively manage the negative externalities of massive oil production. These plans, furthermore, organize political discussions about oil disaster, tanker safety, conservation, and offshore oil leasing. To the extent that they do so they shape the categories available with which to talk about corporate power, government neglect, and the consequences of huge oil spills from huge tankers on local environments. Oil spill fantasy documents contribute to the notion that "the problem" of major oil spills comes from insufficient money, lack of determination, and poor coordination. One consequence of framing the issue this way is that some questions—about conservation, about corporate power, and political risk—rarely get asked outside what is defined as the environmentalist fringe.

Radiation Fantasies[9]

On 3 June 1994 a barge took away the last shipment of uranium fuel from the Shoreham nuclear power station on Long Island.[10] It was the last of a series of thirty-three shipments, a process that took over nine months; 353 truckloads of more than five million pounds of other radioactive materials were also shipped away.[11] The plant cost $5.5 billion and never went online because a fifteen-year struggle killed it. "We've exorcised the Devil," said an opponent and member of the Long Island Power Authority, as the last shipment made its way out into Long Island Sound. Said another LIPA member, "It was a damn-fool idea to put a nuclear power plant on Long Island" in the first place.[12]

But it wasn't always such a damn-fool idea. In fact, it was not until the late 1970s that the notion arose that it might be dangerous to put a nuclear power station on Long Island. The "danger" people focused on, the conception of danger that animated people to oppose the plant, was not that of the risk of meltdown or radiation release. The key danger, that is to say the key definition of unacceptable risk, was the risk of not being able to evacuate a large part of Long Island.

The Long Island Lighting Company (owner of the plant until New York State bailed it out by buying Shoreham for $1) promised that it could evacuate a ten-mile radius around Shoreham (known as the EPZ, or emergency planning zone). Some uncalculated but substantial reason for the decline and fall of Shoreham was LILCO's failure to demonstrate to others that its promise could be kept. Shoreham's fate depended on the evacuation plan because part of the fallout from Three Mile Island was that utilities were (and are) required to have such a plan; that plan, furthermore, must be approved by the Federal Emergency Management Agency (FEMA), the Nuclear Regulatory Commission (NRC), and by local and state governments. These new requirements gave states and localities a warrant to insert themselves into decision processes that previously had been the exclusive province of federal agencies. It was this warrant that spurred the production of LILCO's fantasy documents. If LILCO could not present a highly credible case that its evacuation plan would actually work, then Shoreham, and possibly even LILCO itself, would be at risk.

The main argument from Shoreham's proponents was that there was nothing special about nuclear accidents. A good deal of research on non-nuclear disasters, largely by sociologists at disaster research centers, which LILCO cited, tells us that people do *not* panic in emergencies and that most of the time emergency workers at least try to fulfill their responsibilities. To illustrate the reasoning, listen to some testimony from LILCO consultants:

> The record is clear that emergency workers do their jobs when they understand that they have an emergency job to do, when they understand what that job requires of them, and when they have a sense of the importance of their job for overall community safety and to their work group. These understandings can be produced in different ways. For example, people who hold jobs that are in the routine of everyday life comparable to their emergency roles—for example, firemen—bring these understandings to the emergency setting.[13]

Were a nuclear catastrophe akin to a flash flood, an earthquake, or commuting—all allusions asserted by LILCO—it would mean that large-scale evacuation was merely a big project, not an insurmountable obstacle. More, it would mean that an organization could overcome the considerable uncertainties that would attend a very serious worst-case event.

For their part, Shoreham's opponents argued that the station was such an exceptional case that there were good reasons to think that officials and organizations would not be able to control an evacuation. They pointed out that denizens of Long Island evinced considerable distrust of LILCO and so wouldn't believe expert proclamations or follow official orders in an emergency. Worse, the same research that shows that most emergency workers in most disasters do what they are supposed to do also shows that when disaster comes what is highest on people's priority list is their families.

Not only would people fail to follow the plan in the event of a severe radiological emergency, Shoreham's opponents reasoned, but those asked to function as evacuation workers would likely try to protect their families first. If the whistle blew and people did not take their posts, massive unpredictability—not controlled evacuation—would ensue. Were that the case Shoreham would not pass a pivotal test for ensuring public safety. LILCO, in other words, needed people, and the courts and federal agencies, to believe their promises. The fantasy documents were crucial representations of those promises.

Of course, LILCO and the Department of Energy could not really test their evacuation plan, so LILCO conducted a series of real-time exercises. The sirens would not actually cry out and the public would not actually be moved. The radio and television stations would only pretend to announce disaster. The plant would not be SCRAMMED (an emergency shutdown), as it was not even online. One of the most significant parts of the plan that could not be tested concerned state and local governments. New York State, Nassau and Suffolk Counties, and most local governments (including the police, who were rather skeptical if not incredulous) refused to participate in any of the planning, declaring they were acting in accordance with the preferences of most Long Islanders (who, incidentally, were unaware the exercises were going on). That was a problem, because the federal licensing rules required just that sort of participation. LILCO's short-term solution to this problem was to convince federal regulators to act *as if* state and local governments participated.

Whatever these problems, I want to make two points here. First, what little we can learn from LILCO's exercise suggests the plan would have had a vanishingly small chance of success. Second, key parts of the plan were simply unknowable, even inestimable.

There were several LILCO exercises, but here I am focusing on one that took place on 13 February 1986. The exercise involved, among other things, sending evacuation workers on their missions, setting up media centers with pretend reporters, arranging command posts, telephone calling, and sending emergency vehicles to mock emergencies.[14] LILCO's main agent for organizing emergency planning was LERO, or Local Emergency Response Organization. LERO's plan used utility employees, contractors, private organizations, and the Department of Energy in both its plan and the exercises. Thirty-eight evaluators from federal agencies (e.g., FEMA, DOE, NRC) were on hand to judge seventeen key pieces of the plan, including emergency operations, emergency staging areas, medical drills, decontamination facilities, traffic control, bus evacuation routes, and radiological monitoring among others.

Federal regulators judged the exercise a success but it was anything but that. Many of the personnel at the staging areas were new and, without previous training, had to have their responsibilities explained *during the exercise*.[15] The start of the "emergency" was 8:19 A.M., yet none of the road crews—who were on official notice that they would be called—arrived at the three staging areas until after 10 o'clock in the morning. A few never reported at all. By 9:39 A.M., when a "General Emergency" had to be declared because all the plant's safety systems had failed, only 11 percent of the road crew—again, aware that they would be used—deemed essential by LILCO's plan were available.

Neither the Long Island Railroad nor the Federal Aviation Administration were notified of the emergency because no procedures were in place for it;[16] apparently no one thought of that. Note that the Long Island Railroad runs many trains through and around the EPZ and there is a large airport in the middle of Long Island (Islip); nearby is the site of the major traffic control center in the region, and planes bound for LaGuardia and Kennedy routinely fly over the area.

A large part of LILCO's evacuation plan depended on bus drivers. Those drivers would be especially important for people who needed extra help getting out of harm's way, chiefly children and the mentally and physically incapacitated. The children were perhaps the linchpin in the machine, for both symbolic and practical reasons. If the problem of evacuating the children could not be resolved the exercise would likely be seen as absurd. Symbolically, children are the pure, the pristine, the most innocent of victims. They could have had no say in whether Shoreham would be built, and it would be difficult for anyone to argue any fine points about risk/benefit tradeoffs in the face of cancer-ridden innocence. Practically, if the buses could not be counted on to evacuate the children, and if people did not *believe* the buses could be counted on to evacuate *their* children, the plan could never succeed. Instead of everyone moving toward the presumed safety of the Nassau County Coliseum, some non-negligible proportion of Long Island would be moving in the direction of nuclear danger to get their children. LILCO needed the buses to work.

Though the bus drivers, as one might expect, were drilled extensively before the exercises, the buses in large measure did *not* work. Bus drivers did not take time to read dosimeters[17] (some apparently did not know how to; it had been a problem on previous exercises and the same thing happened with some ambulance crews), a task required by the plan. One driver, asked by a FEMA evaluator to participate in the exercise, said that he did not "wish to drive as he had trouble reading signs. This driver even threatened to quit LERO."[18] Post-exercise assessments made clear that many bus drivers did not know the boundaries of the Emergency Planning Zone, which meant they did not know when they were or were not "safe."[19] Nearly one-third of the bus drivers failed to follow preassigned routes,[20] which means they either went their own way or they got lost; many did not contact the people they were supposed to contact. They were not alone, however, since some of LILCO's official "Traffic Guides" did not know the proper routes the buses were supposed to travel, nor did they know the organizational structure of LERO, or the plan's procedures.[21]

Another important part of the plan, and the exercise, concerned the procedures for communicating with the public. Since it was known well ahead of time just what the emergency would be, the announcements should have been carefully prepared, and we might reasonably have expected the responses to those messages, with minor variations perhaps, to be carefully crafted and accurate. This was, remember, a staged exercise. Such was not the case. Emergency Broadcast System messages were sometimes four single-spaced pages long,[22] which, read over television and radio, would surely have been too long for people to follow carefully, even if they had been constructed in a crystal clear fashion. In fact the EBS messages were crafted poorly. Sometimes there was conflicting information in the same message. One such message advised people outside the ten-mile EPZ that "no protective action was necessary," immediately followed by a paragraph advising that they take blankets, pillows, and medications as they "could be away for days."[23] Sometimes *new* information was presented at the end of the message, which would likely raise questions just at the time people would be expecting answers. As but one example, in a series of three Emergency Broadcast messages, the first two told people that children from a local school district would be taken to the Nassau Coliseum; in the last they were told the children were not in fact at the Coliseum but a different place (Hicksville) "for monitoring and decontamination."[24] Such a sequence of messages could have only produced anxiety for worried parents, parents likely to stop at nothing to ensure the safety of their loved ones.

This obvious anxiety was consistently downplayed by LILCO which had every confidence that its instructions would be obeyed. Yet even this conceit was not scripted. LILCO retained a world expert on radiation hazards from nearby Brookhaven National Laboratory—a government organization that took public positions supporting LILCO and its nuclear plant. He was to be the expert on hand in the Emergency Broadcast station, available to answer questions by FEMA workers posing as reporters. The reporters exhibited none of the ruthless questioning that might be expected under the circumstances, but one of them asked Dr. Brill, the expert, if he expected the population would evacuate the EPZ when they were asked to. Dr. Brill replied, remarkably, that they would but that he would not! He explained, certainly to everyone's surprise, that although he lived within two miles of the plant he would probably be one of the "diehards" who would not leave his home. This was at a time when LILCO had suggested the complete evacuation of the ten-mile EPZ and when the reactor core was two-thirds uncovered. Alarmed by this violation of the order, the FEMA workers asked "Why?" Dr. Brill's view was that the traffic jam would be so enormous that people evacuating would be exposed to more radiation in their autos than if they hid in their basements.

LILCO's expert would thus have made matters much worse. A key argument of those who opposed the plant and doubted LILCO's ability to evacuate Long Island in a few hours was that the traffic jam would be so enormous that only a minority would escape.[25]

Rumor response and press conferences evinced other failures. One prevalent failure in rumor response was a long lag between the time of a request and a response to the request. Examples included "people"— FEMA workers calling in pretending to be citizens—hearing fire trucks and calling the command center to ask about them. They usually received a very late response or no response at all. Others, preparing to evacuate, would call to ask what ought to be done with their pets; they also received delayed responses, or no response at all. Sometimes "residents" asking the experts for advice were told both to evacuate and to take shelter. A woman who had a pretend pregnancy of 4.5 months was allowed to drive through the EPZ without being reminded of the risk to her fetus. The simulated press conferences were full of evasive-sounding answers and dismissals of people's worries.

While FEMA judged the behavior of the traffic guides at the three staging areas, in Patchogue, Port Jefferson, and Riverhead, largely a success, in fact the earliest *any* traffic guides were dispatched was 10:25 and the latest completion was at 12:49,[26] which were, respectively 3.5 hours and 6 hours after local schools had been closed. Yet LILCO's plan held that emergency information would be disseminated to the public *every fifteen minutes* telling people that LILCO personnel would be guiding traffic. Thus the exercise would leave people with the impression that LILCO could not be counted on to help people evacuate should the need arise.

Much of this would be standard in a real worst case. Had Shoreham melted down we certainly would have seen—we invariably do—confusion in rumor control, conflicting advice, contradictory statements, and evasion or even dissembling at press conferences. But when we see these kinds of failures in an important exercise with prior planning and training, and plenty of warning, we must begin to wonder, "What are the possibilities and limits of organizational learning? Or, more specifically, what could make organizations fail so?" Truthfully, social science is at a loss to answer these fundamental questions.

LILCO's evacuation plan was a fantasy document. All such plans are tested against reality only rarely, since, for example, none of the following disasters were believed to be credible events by the organizations involved and therefore were never planned for: Three Mile Island, Chernobyl, Bhopal, the *Challenger*, and *Exxon Valdez*. In addition to being untested, the accident mitigation or evacuation plans are likely to draw from a quite unrealistic view or model of organizations. The fantasy is that most things will work right the first time, that most of the crucial contingencies are known and have been prepared for. Thus, LILCO designed an emergency organization, the Local Emergency Response Organization, LERO, that was even more complex and bureaucratic than its own organization, and expected it to work. The plans, buttressed by many experts, including the Federal Emergency Management Agency and the Department of Energy, allowed leaders to make bold promises that their organization could control a mass evacuation.

Of course, we would never judge exercises and planning as failures just because they were less than perfect. It's just not reasonable to equate success with zero errors. In the case of LILCO, though, I think we're looking at an exercise with great political significance, so that the planners and exercisers had a lot of incentive and time to get most of the key things right.

Nuclear War Fantasies

The 1976 plan for "nuclear civil protection" for El Paso County, Colorado, including Colorado Springs, is not special.[27] El Paso, at the time, had 236,000 people in it, "of which 217,707" lived in high risk areas. Though risky, nuclear war in El Paso would not have been devastating. "A nuclear attack on the United States," the report gravely begins, "would most likely be preceded by a period of international tension and crisis. Sufficient time would be available for protective actions to be taken, including the temporary relocation of residents of possible target areas to areas of lower risk." The next item in the document claims that "the Soviet Union has well-established plans to evacuate the residents of its major cities. . . . [Those] plans anticipate relocation of the urban population over a 3-day period." The plan details host areas, areas designated as having relatively lower risk. "All of the risk area population" will relocate and:

> relocation will be primarily in family groups using private vehicles over a period not to exceed three days. . . . The

minimum duration of the Relocation Period will be several days. The maximum duration of the relocation period is uncertain but could last several weeks. Return of the relocated population to their homes following crisis relocation will occur only at the direction of the Governor of Colorado.

There follows enumeration of civilian- and military-based populations and lists upon lists of organizations that will participate. In a nod to the pervasive presence of organizations, most of the people are listed by their place of work, so Don's Texaco would have evacuated with the El Paso County Coroner, which may have been convenient for Don.

If El Paso County could be saved, so could more diffuse targets. For example, the U.S. Post Office has a plan for delivering our mail after a thermonuclear holocaust.[28] Said a key postal planner in 1982: "We have developed postal preparedness plans which try to provide continuity of the postal organization and performance of essential functions under the diverse conditions of international tension, limited war, general war, or a nuclear attack on the United States."[29]

The plan exemplifies rationality, at least on its surface. There is a clear chain of command, there's forethought on who will succeed whom when someone dies, informational channels are detailed, there is resource allocation (e.g. trucks, buses, etc.). The division of labor described by the planners is highly functional and reasonably detailed. Most of the tasks the postal service promises to accomplish seem important. For instance the Post Office will assist Health and Human Services "to register a relocated population,"[30] so there's an elaborate plan to fill out emergency change of address cards.

So at first blush the plan looks carefully thought out, a fairly good contingency plan, at least given the enormous task confronting the planners. In the early 1980s a Congressional committee became interested in the postal plan, and I want to paraphrase some of the testimony.[31]

> *Congress member:* How do you respond to the charge that the Service has no clear conception of an attack?
> *Planner:* I don't know that I can respond to that.
> *Congress member:* What will you do if no one shows up for work, assuming anyone is left alive?
> *Planner:* I have no response to that, sir.
> *Congress member:* Can you tell us if this plan has ever been tested in any way?
> *Planner #2:* No, sir.[32]

Later, we learn from the planners that their "planning model doesn't deal in terms of casualties," only mail delivery. One of them says that "if Washington is completely obliterated," the Post Office command would move somewhere else. First to Memphis. If there's no Memphis, to San Bruno, and when a Senator asks if "San Bruno is less likely to be hit than Memphis," our erstwhile planner replies, "It's strictly opinion, Sir."[33] On a map of proposed nuclear targets, Washington, Memphis, and San Bruno (next to San Francisco) are black dots, and black dots indicate obliteration.

One of the senatorial inquisitors points out that the Federal Emergency Management Agency's own maps suggest "that the only place where mail could be deliverable would be the Everglades, Northern Minnesota, and portion of the Rocky Mountains area."[34] He presses the point:

> So what you are doing is establishing this very elaborate chain of command with the very great likelihood that most of the people who are in this chain of command will be killed in an all-out nuclear war, leaving very little likelihood that they will be able to operate any kind of national Postal Service at all except out of the most rural of postal offices. These would be the smallest of the small of all the facilities which you have right now, and somehow or other we are putting together plans that they are going to run a national mail service out of these remote rural areas; is that correct?

To which the planner replies, "In essence, that's correct, Sir."[35] At this point we start to wonder about the functions of the Post Office's plan. But there's more.

Another Senator inadvertently makes the point that the main purpose of the postal service is to serve capitalism, though without acknowledging that after the war there may be no capitalism left to serve:

> *Senator:* What percentage of first class mail is business mail?
> *Planner:* . . . about 35 percent.
> *Senator:* Would you believe 86 percent, 85 percent? Are you telling me that after a major nuclear war it will be one of your main priorities to deliver bills back and forth?

It's hard to know exactly what to think of the postal plan. Some people laugh when they hear of the postal service's determination to deliver radioactive Visa bills. Others moan. Whether levity or despair, the response is one of incredulity. I admit to a similar sentiment. But people don't laugh, or at least don't laugh as hard, when organizations and elites claim they can gather up 60 or 70 percent of a big oil spill. Yet we have seen that 25 percent would be an oil recovery rate that would qualify as an organizational and technological miracle.

Surely the Postal Plan is a fantasy document. But is it any more so than other civil defense plans? I doubt it. Minnesota has an emergency plan called the "Minnesota Population Protection Procedures." The plan focuses particularly, though not exclusively, on nuclear attack, and notes that even though the biggest nuclear threat died with the Soviet Union, as long as there are any nuclear weapons it will be "prudent to maintain . . . the planning base which would facilitate large-scale nuclear evacuations in Minnesota." The plan is not limited to nuclear attack, however:

> The purpose of this document is to facilitate the effective coordinated use of state, federal, and local government resources in a serious disaster which would require sheltering and evacuation. Should evacuation and sheltering of a community or communities be required, it is essential to have prepared plans available.[36]

We don't learn why it's so essential, but the plan lists, via the ever-present organizational chart, the key offices and the connections of authority between them, beginning with FEMA and the governor at the top and ending with local "political subdivisions" at the bottom. Such charts seem to indicate functional importance and expertise. Following the plan is a fairly detailed job description that should attach to each office, what law enforcement is supposed to do, what health services are supposed to do, and so on. There follow, as in all such plans, maps and lists, including a list of places likely to be "targeted" and a list of places it is safe to travel to. All these things are quite reasonable. But imagine "Hazard Area 5," which shows that Clay Boswell Nuclear Power Plant is "projected as a nuclear target."[37] The "reception area" for Hazard Area 5 is immediately adjacent to it, which is also quite reasonable, but only if the fallout and drifting nuclear release from Boswell obey the boundary lines.

As tempting as ridicule might be, we must count the Post Office's and Minnesota's plans as serious. They are also not singular. There have been numerous civil defense plans through the years, developed by a shifting network of organizations in the federal government. Those organizations have for some time planned to survive nuclear war, promising that with enough determination, money, and moral fortitude we could in fact prevail in a general nuclear war. A 1979 bulletin from the DCPA—Defense Civil Preparedness Agency—says that "if you could make the relocation work pretty well (though not perfectly), total survival could be 80 percent or better."[38]

In 1982 the Reagan Administration requested over four billion dollars for a program that the Federal Emergency Management Agency would soon claim could move to safety 150 million people from about four hundred cities. The program was called "crisis relocation planning."[39] FEMA created a map of "high risk areas," which are places where missiles, submarines, and soldiers live. Big cities, especially those with more then 250,000 people, are also high-risk areas. FEMA's map shows that every state has a fair number of such areas, though Idaho has but two. The entire northeast corridor, from Rhode Island to Washington, D.C., is blackened. The text accompanying the map says that "the population at risk can be protected (1) by providing high-performance blast shelters in cities; *or* (2) by relocating (evacuating) the people to low-risk 'host' areas outside the risk areas, over a period of several days during an acute crisis."[40] The "risk areas," note, include 250 metropolitan areas with more than fifty thousand people each. All together, FEMA says, "these risk areas cover only 2 to 3 percent of the land area of the United States, but in them are about two-thirds of our population and a somewhat higher percentage of our industry."[41]

To save 80 percent of the American population (some estimates were even higher) from radiating ruin would be an impressive feat. But how would that work?

Stanford Research Institute modeled evacuation of New York City and concluded that it could be done in a bit over three days. This could be accomplished by using 50 percent of all 747s in the country, 75 percent of America's DC-10s and Lockheed L-1011s, all freighters (which will be in Manhattan and unloaded) and automobile transport (all of which will have full tanks of gas and only 1 or 2 percent breakdown en route). All evacuees would go to Albany, New York.[42] In another report SRI concluded that 97 percent of targeted urban areas could be reentered within eight weeks.[43]

Many of us live in a different world than that of civil defenders. While most of us think of general or even limited nuclear war as nearly beyond imagination, the self-appointed experts are not so limited. For instance, during some 1982 hearings before the U.S. House of Representatives,[44] FEMA showed a movie which explained that nuclear attack would be "horrifying," but "it would not mean the end of the world, the end of our nation." We are urged to trust governments and to realize that we will "more likely" than not have "days, perhaps even weeks" to prepare. While,

> we are all inclined to think of our own hometown as target number one . . . Defense Department studies show that even under the heaviest possible attack, less than five percent of our entire land area would be affected by blast and heat from nuclear weapons. . . . The other ninety-five percent of our land would escape untouched, except possibly by radioactive fallout.[45]

There follows advice on how to survive a nuclear explosion: put out fires, don't look at the flash, don't clog phone lines because officials will need them, and so on. But what about the fallout: "With protection, you can wait it out."

Reading nuclear civil defense plans, and the words of the nuclear planners, makes two questions spring to mind. First, "Where did the idea that 80 percent of the population could be saved come from?" And second, "Well, what's wrong with what they say?"

Like Alyeska's claim that it could recover an astronomical, and unheard of, amount of oil in a disaster in Prince William Sound, the "80 percent" figure bears some close scrutiny. It was, after all, an important number. Experts and politicians would appeal to scientific authority with it: "Defense Department studies show . . ." FEMA used it to expand its activities. With it, FEMA began an education program, including providing camera-ready articles to the nation's newspapers, articles that described how evacuation should happen when the crisis comes. It provided medical and housing advice. And if the 80-percent target could in fact be reached then it would be possible, even, to win a nuclear war.

It seems to have become "hard fact" with President Carter, who in 1978 issued Presidential Directive 41. The goal of PD-41 was to improve nuclear deterrence by increasing the survivability of the American population, and by enhancing the continuity of government in case deterrence failed.[46] Time and again experts and politicians refer to PD-41 as the source of the 80-percent figure. "D Prime" was the civil defense component of PD-41 and was considered a way to implement meaningful crisis relocation.[47] Said a FEMA report:

> The D-Prime program is thus an accelerated effort to complete a civil defense system to implement the policies set

forth in PD-41 and in the September 1980 Title V amend-
ments to the Federal Civil Defense Act. When completed,
the D-Prime program has the potential for total survival of
some 80 percent of the U.S. population in a heavy mid-1980s
attack, compared to about 40 percent survival for the current
civil defense capability . . .

By 1982 we hear from a congressional member that "this scale is the
percentage of people who will survive an all-out nuclear attack."[48] But
no evidence is provided, nor are there examples or citations to literature that would allow one to assess the statement. A chart appears, but
it merely redescribes the claims, and provides no "source: xxxxx" at
the bottom.[49]

The next year, at similar hearings, a Missouri congressman claimed
that a study in Ohio had discovered that without civil defense 80 percent of people living in Ohio (nuclear explosions apparently obey state
lines) would die but with it 80 percent would survive. But there are
no citations to any studies.[50]

This mystical number became increasingly corporeal over time. One
1976 attack scenario, considered an allout war between the U.S. and
the U.S.S.R. but nonetheless of "medium" size; CRP-2B projected 85 to
125 million deaths and about 30 million injuries within the first moments of attack. "Medium" means about 1,444 detonated weapons to-
taling 6,559 megatons, or about a half million Hiroshima-sized explosions simultaneously.[51] CRP-2B sported a boring acronym (for crisis
relocation program), but was an important document because it served
as the basis of nuclear defense planning for a couple of decades. It did
so in several ways. It was itself the product of a computer program,
yet over time came to be referred to as a "study." Iterations of it were
given to contractors and simulators with orders to estimate, among
other things, survival rates and what people would need after the war
was over. The crucial aspect of it, for our purposes, was that it *assumed*
that 80 to 90 percent of the people would survive. Such then came to
be cited as *finding* that 80 to 90 percent of the people *could* survive.

Said Charles F. Estes Jr., director of strategic policy at in the Office of
the Undersecretary of Defense for Policy, about the 80-percent figure:

It was assumed at the outset that 80 percent of the population of hypothesized target areas would in fact have been
evacuated and would survive. . . . [T]his was an entering
assumption rather than one of the study's analytically derived findings. . . . It is important to note that the survivabil-

ity assumptions . . . of the computer model were derived from opinions of interested civil defense program managers, academics, and contractor personnel. These opinions were obtained through the use of accepted opinion survey techniques.[52]

Over the years, the 80-percent figure took on a life of its own. More precisely, the number was *given* life by agents who used it for their own purposes. By the early 1980s a high-level official could testify that "computer analyses have confirmed the *obvious*. Expected survival in large-scale attacks approximates 80 percent of the U.S. population, assuming good, but not perfect, evacuation of all U.S. risk areas prior to attack."[53] The nod toward imperfection would lend some credibility to the number—too much certainty about nuclear war looks strange, after all. But of course, computers no more analyze things than scarecrows shout at birds to scare them away. *People* do the analyzing, and if computer programs appear to do so it is only because people have programmed the computers in particular ways. The technical reports from consultants to FEMA and its successors show that a fairly small group of writers, self-referencing and sharing assumptions, elevated the 80-percent-survival figure from a pretend number to a hard conclusion. The promise to protect 80 percent of the American population is about as fantastic a number as we will see. The number is nothing like a scientific conclusion, but "an entering assumption, depending on the computer program used to model population evacuation."[54]

But let us set aside the false precision of the 80 percent prediction and look at the claim that *any* substantial proportion of the population could be protected. There are a number of assumptions in the fantasy documents produced by nuclear civil defenders. They assumed there would be adequate shelter, with food, water, waste removal, and radiation. They assumed the timing of attack would be long (in nuclear terms). Some plans assumed a week's warning before the bombs fell but the most common warning time is three days. Of course, the rest of the war-making system was premised on thirty minutes' warning, about the time it takes an intercontinental ballistic missile to traverse the northern part of the planet. If that were true, and certainly it's easy to know the speed of a missile—then there wouldn't be anyone left to evacuate. So if the timing assumption changed to thirty minutes then civil defense would be pointless. Another important assumption of all civil defense plans was (and is) that the buildup to nuclear war, as well as the war's progress, will be characterized by rationality, forethought, and accurate appraisal of what the other side is thinking. Should there be misreading of signals on anyone's part then a fragile deterrence might fail—breakdown of communications leads to instability in deterrence. Moreover, the civil defense fantasy documents assumed that the Soviet missiles would not be retargeted to the evacuating populations, even though such massive population movements would be seen by satellites and spies.[55]

Let's assume, for the moment, that civil defense in an age of first strike overkill and massive retaliation was a meaningful topic for conversation. All the major cities have been notified that atomic attack is imminent, the bombers have been scrambled, everybody's on full alert. Let's assume further that small, limited nuclear exchanges have been traded between the United States and the Soviet Union (or Russia or North Korea or China). Much of Manhattan and Washington, D.C., are gone but millions of people are still alive in those places and especially outlying areas. What should we expect? In one projection of official response, integrated local, state, and national evacuation plans go into effect, moving as many people as possible out of harm's way. As well, an array of expertly equipped emergency response organizations move quickly, limiting the spread of whatever damage will result. The response organizations control raging fires, collect the dead, gather body parts, and secure "continuity of government," as federal expert planners like to put it.

For such a projection to be realized as more than illusion requires the resolution of three fairly large problems. First, the enemy's retargeting capacity must be nonexistent or destroyed. If, staying with the U.S.-Soviet war scenario, the enemy were to detect preparations for mass evacuation then all that would be necessary to obliterate everyone would be to tell the computers to change the missile trajectories by a few degrees. Civil defense would be clearly pointless unless retargeting possibilities were assumed away.

Second, everyone must (more or less) share the same general conception of appropriate moral behavior and the same specific conception of the "national interest." "Everyone" includes the highest-level decision makers, middle-level bureaucrats, law enforcers, emergency management responders, gas station attendants, day care providers, and college professors. For if people have different notions of how to act and for what purposes, surely chaos would be the order of the day. Years of work from natural disaster researchers have shown that people don't break out into a raging panic just because all they know and love is suddenly upended. But it has also shown that when people have entirely different definitions of reality and entirely lose trust in the scope and existence of moral order, concerted, concentrated social action is impossible.[56] Unfortunately, I have not seen a single study or even a single serious treatment of this issue from proponents of civil defense. Their assumptions of social order and authoritative control in the middle of overwhelming social change are unknowable at best.

The third problem that would have to be resolved before our emergency responders could make their vision real is they would have to achieve tight coordination among social actors, chiefly key decision makers, organizations, and implementing agents. The plans assumed —could it be otherwise?—that all evacuations would be orderly and that everyone would follow the order (including those ordered to stay behind). "Coordination," I hasten to add, is a catch phrase of all planners, as well as people who write about planning, especially critics who evaluate what people and organizations did wrong before accidents and disasters. At its best, coordination means that two or more actors share knowledge and frames of reference so thoroughly that when those actors are called upon to perform some task they behave in ways that mesh without effort. For premises to be shared this widely and deeply, all negotiations over political jurisdiction, organizational responsibility, and personal authority must be worked out in advance. This is so because time spent on such issues results in delay and agents working at cross-purposes; time spent on such issues results in death and misery, given the topics under discussion.

Such coordination is not in evidence. In 1985 the General Accounting Office "reviewed the Department of Defense's policies and practices for coordinating emergency planning for nuclear weapon accidents with states and localities."[57] While the U.S. armed services certainly interact with states and localities on disaster planning, when it comes to the highest risk of all—the risk of accidental nuclear explosions or nuclear war—the Navy and the Army claim it is in the national interest not to coordinate disaster planning. The Air Force's official position is that since all of its bases must be able to accept nuclear-equipped aircraft, every base should have nuclear preparedness planning. The Air Force further holds:

> that strategic missile bases and bases with landing strips are nuclear-capable. As a result, Air Force bases coordinate unclassified nuclear weapon accident emergency planning, enter into joint written agreements, and share information in

bases' accident response plans with state and local government.[58]

But the Air Force's policy is to "neither confirm nor deny" whether nuclear weapons are on the base. This, along with the key phrase "unclassified nuclear weapon accident emergency planning," puts at least some key planning out of the reach of intensely interested parties.

The Navy had no coordinating efforts with local and state governments, since "Navy officials believe that entering a mutual support agreement would confirm the existence of such weapons."[59] Information, effort, and energy were also withheld by the Army. The coordination and shared definition of what people should do in disaster did not and do not exist in sufficient quantities to make civil defense meaningful. Thus a crucially important problem of organizational and cognitive coordination simply is not in place. The national interest, at least as the military defines it, does not include civilians.

As well, sociologist Guy Oakes is certainly right when he says that civil defense programs rested on a logical contradiction that made them "either impossible or redundant."[60] That is, for civil defense to work social order would have to already exist. Put differently, after the bombs fell there would probably be chaos and devastation, people would be stunned and possibly panicked; gauging the possibility of organized, directed, institutional behavior would itself be impossible. Yet civil defense measures (or at least massive, centralized ones) would need organized, directed, institutional behavior to work. Either the social order would not be destroyed, in which case civil defense was redundant, or social order could not get going again, in which case civil defense was impossible.

Planning to survive (and thus win) a nuclear war is fantasy planning. I do not claim to know what things would be like after a nuclear war. But I do think that the range of possibly relevant incidents has not been brought into especially official arguments about civil defense and post-Apocalypse reconstruction. One might argue, for instance (but also with considerable skepticism), that problems of so-called "nuclear winter" make the problem even worse.[61] Still, in the end the interesting thing about such fantasies is how they are made in the first place. An important part of the story I want to tell has to do with how people and organizations become so certain they know what the future will entail, and with the social relations behind rhetorics of safety, national interest, and technical competence.

Symbols and Uncertainty

Sometimes plans are based on history and meaningful expertise. And, as well, they are sometimes framed by a conceptual scheme that will make sense of that experience, which increases enormously the probability that they can work. These are the plans that we can make better by more attention to coordination, cooperation, and communication. These are the blueprints that organize so much of our lives.

Planning is an inherently interactive, social process. As books, speeches, and curses are directed at others, so are plans. Plans are, therefore, much more than blueprints for future action; they are also rhetorical devices designed to convince others of something. Symbolically, plans are public declarations that planners, or the planning organization, have thought carefully about some problem and have developed the necessary wisdom and power to establish dominion over it.

In Alaska, the main audiences for Alyeska's contingency plans were regulatory agencies who had to be persuaded that potential problems from oil spills were covered. With civil defense, the main audiences were local and state government agencies who had to be persuaded that investing their denizens' valuable resources was worthwhile. On Long Island, LILCO's main audiences were the courts who had to be persuaded that massive evacuation was possible, should its nuclear power plant get into serious trouble.

Symbolic plans are fantasy documents. Fantasies are whimsical speculations, flights of fancy in which scenarios are imagined with little regard to usual constraints of "reality." Fantasies, however incredible, are deliberate cognitive manipulations of the behaviors and meanings of everyday life. (Dreams, which are also obviously fantasies, are irrelevant here.)[62] Most fantasies are recognized as such by the fantasizers, and would be similarly recognized by others were they to hear the details of the fantasy. And as long as fantasies remain confined to the realm of the purely mental, few of us would be willing to judge them inappropriate or ill-conceived as guides for individual, or collective, behavior. What harm, or good, can a whimsical speculation do?

It seems that fantasy documents are more likely to be produced to defend very large systems, or systems that are newly scaled up. When they are proffered as accurate representations of organizational capabilities then the stage is set not only for organizational failure but for massive failure of the publics those organizations are supposed to serve. The fantasies can lead people working within high-risk organizations to be overconfident that their procedures are strong enough to prevent system breakdown; and they can lead people outside organizations to believe promises that their interests are protected.

Before talking about how and why fantasy documents are produced and defended, I want to address the question, "what are nonfantasy documents?"

3

Planning and the C-Shibboleths

I run the risk of implying two things that I don't want to imply. One is that fantasy planning is *failed* planning. The other is that normal, nonfantasy planning—more exactly, planning under low or moderate uncertainty—involves no symbolism. We can discharge the first implication fairly easily, but the second requires more effort.

Fantasy documents are often so outrageously unreal, at least to outsiders, that it's easy to concentrate on the likelihood that they won't work. Using *that* focus, it might be tempting to stop analyzing such planning once one came to the conclusion that any given fantasy document would indeed most likely not work.

Now, I think the odds are that fantasy documents *won't* work. The experts and officials who write them overpromise what they can do, and they overextend their own possibilities for garnering the resources necessary to make good on those promises. In addition, they tend to discount competing ideas and opinions concerning what is desirable and what is possible. The oil industry in Alaska is a good example. Environmentalists and those who would value the state's renewable resources, as opposed to or in addition to oil, did not fare well when they protested the Alaskan Pipeline. And it's clear enough that Alyeska's contingency plan failed to do what it promised. There is no way it *could* have accomplished those things. It was, indeed, quite the failure.

But in the cases of LILCO's evacuation plan and nuclear civil defense the matter is less clear. I doubt either set of plans would have done much good. In fact, I believe they would have failed miserably. But the point of fantasy documents is not that we know they will fail. More to the point, we don't judge a plan fantastic because of its likelihood of success or failure. This is so because failure and fantasy are different aspects and in principle at least they vary independently. Moreover, the distinctive characteristic of most fantasy documents is exactly that we *can't know* the probability that they will fail or succeed. Just because a plan fails doesn't make it fantastic; and just because a plan is a fantasy document doesn't mean that it could never work.

Nonfantasy Planning

The other implication that I want to avoid is that only fantasy documents involve symbolism. Life is full of symbolism. So probably all organizational plans serve symbolic purposes of one sort or another. One gets the sense from reading Robert Jackall's *Moral Mazes,* a book about the moral guidelines that managers use to get through their days, of the overwhelming, sometimes crushing weight of the organizational environment on planners and decision makers. He has one executive, for instance, saying that "there is no such thing as a marketing genius; there are only great markets." And yet life in business is always judged by results rather than by the intelligence that went into the planning. If managers really were completely controlled by things outside the organization, then all (corporate) planning would be merely symbolic because no one would think that strategy would do much good. Jackall's managers are surely overstating the case, or perhaps they are expressing their attitudes, rather than what really is and is not possible. Certainly, there is a difference between plans that serve several purposes, *some* of which may be symbolic, and plans that are *primarily* or *exclusively* symbolic. These latter plans are the ones I'm most concerned with in this book.

But there is obviously such a thing as nonfantasy planning. These are plans that have a meaningful chance of being a reasonable set of promises. Consider, for instance, a stock brokerage firm that develops an investment fund promising a conservative approach to investment. The organization can't guarantee a rate of return on an investment, but it can and will specify the percentage of the portfolio that will go into blue chip stocks, the percentage that will go into municipal bonds, the percentage that will go into federal certificates of deposit, and so on. While the brokerage firm can't absolutely claim fiscal survival for the U.S. government the likelihood of such a massive fiscal calamity is sufficiently outrageous that it warrants no credence. History, that is to say experience, in such cases is dependable enough that we would be unlikely to question the correspondence between the public claim and the actual fact: investing in blue-chip stocks and the federal government is, without argument, conservative.

Notice that in the examples above it would be ludicrous to accord credence to predictions of financial collapse because of both the high quality and the copious quantity of history on which we can base our judgments. What makes it high quality, of course, is that our lay and expert theories about how economies work, while far from perfect, are good enough to explain what is and is not highly risky. To really push the point, imagine giving a public lecture in which the main thesis is that the federal government is quite likely to self-destruct in the next five or ten years, and hence not be able to redeem certificates of deposit. The evidence that would be required to make such a case convincingly can be imagined, but only that. The prediction, and any plans based on the prediction, would be absurd.

Problems of prediction, risk, and uncertainty plague big social problems as well as daily life.[1] Consider the deeply contentious debate over "the greenhouse effect," which is the idea that the release of certain gases could lead to a warming of ambient temperature. The bad actor in the greenhouse drama is carbon dioxide, and the main source of carbon dioxide is burning fossil fuels. Since we are dearly dependent on fossil fuels, greenhouse possibilities, and especially proposed remedies, could have enormous impacts on industry, government, and individual lives.

Greenhouse modelers have to separate out natural warming effects from those that are human-made, a task made more difficult because the latter are small by comparison. There is, as would be expected, considerable risk involved just in making predictions of whether a human-induced greenhouse effect *has* happened, let alone what *will* happen in coming decades.

Sufficient data exist to allow scientists to conclude that over the past one hundred years the average temperature of the earth's atmosphere has increased (by .5 degree centigrade). The amount of greenhouse gases and especially carbon dioxide (which lets solar radiation in but blocks radiating heat from escaping) has also increased. But the lines of the increase don't move together: most of the temperature increase was between 1880 and 1940, and through the period of the greatest concentration of greenhouse gases, from the 1940s through the 1970s, there was no net increase in temperature. In any case, the basic procedure for greenhouse estimation is the same for all such exercises. In the words of some noted scholars in the field:

> The computations that attempt to achieve this precision are
> performed with a mathematical model of the earth and its

oceans and atmosphere. The model consists of equations
that imitate mathematically the forces controlling the earth's
climate. These equations are transcribed into a lengthy
computer program with tens of thousands of lines of
code.[2]

As noted, scientists can know many things about the greenhouse
phenomenon. They can know how much methane is in the atmosphere,
even how much CO_2 was in the atmosphere 20,000 or even 150,000
years ago (by digging into the ice caps to exhume trapped gases). But
to truly understand the greenhouse effect, researchers and modelers
must accurately model the oceans, the atmosphere, and the bio-
sphere—all that without even considering human behavior. It is not
an easy thing to do.

Part of the problem of knowing the reality of greenhouse is that
much of the earth—volcanoes are a good example—doesn't cooperate
in a predictable way, yet would need to be included in any really accurate greenhouse model. Another problem involves the sheer amount
of data required. Computing "the simulated climate for 100 years can
require as much as 10,000 trillion individual bits of arithmetic."[3] And
small changes in assumptions or model inputs can have dramatic
changes in model output. A valley on one side of a mountain, for instance, will have its own micro-climate that might be quite different
from the valley on the other side of the mountain and thus require its
own set of equations. Such problems mean the computing time for an
accurate model of the earth would be enormous. A mere doubling of
the detail treated in a model results in eight times as much computing
time.[4] Even clouds, which reflect sunlight back to space and infrared
light back to earth, can make a huge difference in the outcome of a
model. Modelers are left with no choice but to ignore many potentially
important variables. There are also massive *political* problems that
make prediction difficult.

Of course, even if all the data were available, the computing power
instantly abundant, and all the uncertainties settled it would still not
be possible to determine once and for all what to do about greenhouse
with a computer model. Such a decision would always be political, as
are decisions about whether nuclear evacuations should be under-
taken, or whether oil cleanup technologies should be developed. Even
were all the science clear, the politics would still engender considerable
uncertainty.

So there are a lot of problems with theorizing, modeling, and arguing about the greenhouse phenomenon. Many scientists agree that there has been some global warming and all but radical right-wingers agree that energy efficiency and lowering the amount of CO_2 in the atmosphere are good things. But so much is simply not known about the models that we can't conclude there is presently a strong anthropogenic greenhouse effect. Essentially what is involved is reliable weather prediction over hundreds of years, which is quite a daunting idea when you stop to think of weather prediction for next *month.*

In spite of all these complications, it would be a mistake to call the greenhouse models, and plans that might be based on them, fantastic. There is history. Soil, sea level, oceans, volcanoes, ice, mountains, rivers, dead animals, and the shape of the continents all have relevant stories to tell, because they all leave traces of what they did and how they did it. Because of all that history, and pretty good theories of the overall climate, greenhouse models and mitigation plans are not fantasies.

I should be more explicit about symbolism and instrumental utility. Just as it is obvious that plans *can* work, it is equally obvious that all plans have to a greater or lesser extent some symbolic significance. One's position on global warming and what to do about it become iconographic of a moral attitude toward the environment, and not merely a position one advances in a technical argument. When I present a syllabus to a room full of students I promise to follow the plan of topics I have written down. But the syllabus also allows me to claim that I have thought about the course in some detail, and through this claim—along with others about my right and obligation to evaluate the students—establish my rightful place as the course's leader. In this way the syllabus is not only a symbol of my power and authority, it also helps to establish my authority in the first place. We can say then that symbols are themselves useful. But to say that is not to say enough about how symbols work.

Although all plans, all organizational promises, can have some symbolic import, there are plans that have almost no instrumental applications. In this chapter, however, I talk about some instances where plans and planning had a higher ratio of instrumental to symbolic rationality than is true of fantasy documents. We will still draw some lessons about symbolism from these cases, but the lessons will be different than the lessons concerning fantasy documents. Interestingly, before we get to those lessons, we will have to revisit the issue of success and failure.

The Theory of Good Planning

It is not big news that organizations fail.[5] People are always complaining that their governments don't serve them, that the products they buy break down too soon, that the food at a favored restaurant has gone downhill. As well, it is hardly an earth-shattering revelation that disaster response, and evacuation in particular, often fails when the untoward comes to pass and there is no plan in place that could even *possibly* drive the response. One could even say that it only makes the best of sense that planning and response are causally connected. If you don't have an emergency response plan then emergency response is bound to fail.

TEXAS CITY EXPLOSIONS

The first set of tales are tales of woe. They are cases in which the expert and organizational responses to the calamity were failures. They are also instances where no contingency plan was available. These two master factors go hand in glove, or so it seems, and because of that correspondence the following stories ratify common sense and much scholarly judgment about the causal connections between planning and response.

Over the space of two April days (16 and 17 April 1947) in Texas City, Texas, two ships blew themselves apart. At the time, it was the worst industrial accident in history: six hundred people were killed and three to four thousand were injured.[6]

One ship, holding ammonium nitrate fertilizer, blew out every window in Texas City when it exploded on 16 April. The following day saw the second explosion, which wrought more property damage than the first but killed fewer people. The poor souls who lost their lives were coming to the area to help the first set of victims. Minor explosions—which were minor only in comparison with the mother blasts—continued for a third day and oil tanks burned for five more.

The first explosion was extraordinary. At least two thousand pounds of ammonium nitrate fertilizer were on the *Grandcamp* when a small fire began below decks. At the first sign of trouble the captain ordered the hatches closed and the ship's steam fire-smothering system turned on. That decision guaranteed disaster, apparently, because instead of smothering the fire, closing the hatches gave it safe haven. The fire burned for thirty or forty-five minutes, drawing a couple hundred of the merely curious as well as firefighters.

The blast was heard 150 miles away and sent a cloud of smoke and fire two thousand feet high. The ship disappeared. So did the onlookers. Most of the nearby houses collapsed. Secondary explosions and carnage were widespread.

Sixteen hours later the *High Flyer*, which was close to the *Grandcamp*, started its own little fire, soon to blossom into an explosion every bit as powerful as the *Grandcamp*'s. Only a few people were on shore to be killed, so the main damage was to remaining oil product tanks, which promptly exploded and burned like a pack of giant firecrackers. Fire, smoke, hot shrapnel, burning pieces of buildings incinerated people. It must have seemed like hell on earth.

People from miles around streamed to Texas City to help. But there were neither plans nor personnel available to coordinate the efforts. There were only haphazard instances of heroism, as there often are in catastrophes. Over the next couple of days some measure of coordination did emerge from the chaos: someone organized the would-be rescuers to put out the smaller fires, turn off gas lines, and look for the injured. But there was no coordinated response and no plan for one.[7]

The Texas City accident is clearly a case that ratifies the view that there is a causal connection between contingency planning and response. Had a plan been in place, and had it been executed, it seems likely that many lives could have been saved. A contingency plan would probably have specified that civilians wouldn't be allowed close to the docks, once fires were detected in a potentially explosive situation. We would also expect a plan to have its own arrangements for helping victims, using emergency workers rather than bystanders. Certainly we would expect a plan to call for moving other vessels away from ships that were on fire. Having no contingency plan in Texas, then, probably put many people at unnecessary risk.

CHERNOBYL CATASTROPHE

On 26 April 1986 Reactor No. 4 at the Chernobyl nuclear power station turned itself into a molten, radiating mass and retched most of its core to the atmosphere. It was the worse nuclear accident in history. Measured radioactivity didn't begin to decline until 6 May.[8] The official number of people who evacuated ranges from 116,000 to 135,000 but may have been as high as one half million.[9] It is possible to argue that the Chernobyl evacuations were a success. Scientists, managers, military officers, and party officials moved to the site quickly. Over a thousand buses and three hundred trucks were organized to take people out of Kiev, and perhaps thirty-five thousand people were moved within a four-hour span (though *not* within four hours of the accident).[10] That's a lot of people. Later, on 8 May, the winds shifted *toward* Kiev and by the middle of May nearly 250,000 children had evacuated from there.[11] The Chernobyl-as-success argument has some superficial merit. After all, had all those people not been spirited away the threat to human health would surely have been greater.

But I think officials and experts failed us at Chernobyl. The evacuation did not begin for thirty-six hours after the accident, and the general population was not told of the disaster before that evacuation began.[12] At that, the first to go were elite party members. Says David Marples, "The first health warning to the population of the 30-kilometer zone came only on May 5, 1986."[13] Children were not removed from the thirty-kilometer "danger zone" until the middle of May.[14] Party officials at first limited the evacuation to ten kilometers around the plant; it wasn't until 2 May, a week after the accident, that the evacuation was extended to the more extensive thirty kilometers. Luckily, Kiev lay to the south of the plant and the plume moved to the north and northwest. Marples reports that "the main body of evacuees, [at least] 23,000 citizens of Prypyat, were moved to Poliske, which appears to have been in the direct line of fallout."[15] The Chernobyl stories are among the few in the literature in which the word panic legitimately applies.[16] Thousands of people were put at unnecessary risk because of a failure to act quickly and in an organized way. That the Soviet Union was a highly organized society, at least at its official levels, makes the failure all the more glaring.

It does not appear that there was an evacuation plan in place at Chernobyl. If there *was* one, it is clear that it was not implemented, since the series of decisions concerning response to the burning reactor and to people at risk were incremental and somewhat less than orderly. People were unnecessarily exposed to Chernobyl's radiation, put at risk in ways that might well have been avoided.

Chernobyl and Texas City are two instances that support the idea that planning is causally connected to effective response to the untoward. Let us call this the *Theory of Good Planning*. Chernobyl and Texas City ratify this theory by showing that without plans in place, agents of rescue are likely to communicate poorly, if they communicate at all. Without communication between officials, experts, and the public, emergency response efforts won't be coordinated effectively.

Are there positive illustrations of the Theory of Good Planning? There are indeed, and I will analyze three of them. They show that planning can work well, smoothing communications and paving the way for emergency responders to coordinate their efforts in cooperative ways.

MIAMISBURG TRAIN WRECK

Near Miamisburg, Ohio, on 8 July 1986, fifteen freight cars jumped their tracks. Three of those cars contained phosphorous, molten sulfur, and tallow. When a concrete structure supporting the smoldering phosphorous tank car collapsed, "several hundred gallons of molten phosphorous inside the tank car escaped and ignited, resulting in an extensive cloud of phosphorous combustion effluents."[17] In other words, there was a big fire and a lot of dangerous fumes. Seven thousand were evacuated on the first day.

The initial response was somewhat chaotic. Some emergency documents said to "flood the area" with water, while others said not to. It was, even by the sterile and tidy descriptions in National Transportation Safety Board reports, an organizational mess:

> The firechief wanted to keep all personnel, including railroad personnel, out of the fire area until the fire was under control. . . . Because of limited access to the site and because water cannons with direct hose streams were the only available apparatus capable of reaching the burning cars, the firechief said that he had no choice at the time but to fight the fire at a distance using direct hose streams. The trainmaster challenged the authority of the city and the firechief to handle the emergency; he was escorted from the command post under threat of arrest.[18]

But after these initial troubles, local officials took tighter control of the situation and implemented a plan that took a lot of people away from a lot of danger. Again, the National Transportation Safety Board:

> The Miamisburg officials took early command of the emergency and implemented effective management procedures for [obtaining information]. The overall coordination among the many responding agencies was effectively managed during this 5-day emergency. Communications among the many area response agencies were well managed, and the high level of preparedness was reflected by the actions taken during this emergency. The high level of preparedness

greatly assisted local response agencies in effectively recog-
nizing and dealing with inconsistent information that was
provided following the derailment.[19]

The result of all that effort was the evacuation of thirty thousand
people, and while 589 people were treated for a variety of ailments,
and property damage exceeded $3.5 million, Miamisburg could have
been a much bigger disaster. There was a plan, and it seems to have
been implemented and made a good deal of difference.

WORLD TRADE CENTER BOMBING AND 1993 SNOW STORM

At the end of February and again in the middle of March in 1993 New
Jersey's emergency management system was tested. In February, ter-
rorists exploded a huge bomb under the World Trade Center in lower
Manhattan. In March, New Jersey sustained hurricane force winds and
a heavy snow storm. Both events required massive mobilization of resources, both were major challenges to organizations with responsibility for responding to such disasters. And in both cases, apparently,
New Jersey's response organizations responded well and according to
plan.

For both events, about a dozen officials met in a bombproof bunker
under the New Jersey State Police headquarters near Trenton, New
Jersey's capital.[20] They coordinated the response from there, responding to calls from municipalities and others for rescue workers,
trucks, and ambulances. The bunker was full of phones, fax machines,
radios, and telecommunications equipment. Merely having good communications technology, though, isn't enough. Tools are worthless
without a way to coordinate what they're used for. For that, officials
used New Jersey's Emergency Operations Management Plan, which
had its origins in civil defense. "In recent years, it has evolved into an
all-hazard type of plan," said Major Carl A. Williams, deputy director
of the Office of Emergency Management. ". . . And as it has grown, it
has become more of a challenge to execute."[21]

Emergency personnel were apparently up to the challenge. All organizations connected with the plan engaged in regular drills. When the
bomb exploded under the World Trade Center, the response team dispatched helicopters, emergency vehicles, and ambulances. They have
something called a "mass-casualty incident plan" which draws on resources from communities surrounding a disaster. "Every municipality
and each of the 21 counties has its own emergency management plan,"

all of which seem to have worked together during those stressful few weeks.[22] Overall, for the World Trade Center, "57 ambulances, 8 advanced life support units, 2 mass casualty rescue units and 4 support vehicles had participated in the rescue."[23] As one official said, "We've done this before, but each experience is a learning experience."[24] Reading accounts of the response to the two disasters, one is struck by the high degree of coherence of the organizations and the officials involved. It could easily have been otherwise, and probably would have been, for want of a plan.

LIVINGSTON TRAIN WRECK

One of the great stories in which contingency planning made a positive difference, and from which the Theory of Good Planning gets considerable support, is the story of Livingston, Louisiana. On 28 September 1982, before the sun came up in Livingston, forty-three cars of a 101-car Illinois Central Gulf Railroad train derailed. The entire town had to be evacuated because of the explosions and fires; "a virtual inferno" is how an authoritative report on the accident described it.[25] The explosions destroyed several homes, severely damaged seventeen others, and shattered many windows in town. In all, more than four million pounds of chemicals breached containment.[26] The great conflagration, it turns out, was a blessing, because it consumed a lot of the toxic chemicals. Still, much was not burned, and the local environment was significantly contaminated, perhaps indefinitely.[27]

The initial fire spread to other cars and the heat, along with smoke, at first prevented firefighters from getting to within one-half mile of the wreck. At three in the afternoon one of the cars containing a particularly noxious material (TEL, tetraethyl lead) exploded. To quote the Livingston Report:

> This event prompted the decision to increase the evacuation zone . . . to a 13 square mile area which included all of Livingston, and extended on an east-west axis . . . of approximately 3.5 miles.[28]

At 3 P.M. on 1 October the vinyl chloride car started to hiss and whistle in an ominous way, and the plume of escaping gas "changed from orange to white," which was not a good thing.[29] Twenty minutes later the car exploded, "shooting a fireball nearly 3,000 feet into the air, propelling the head end of the car southward, destroying a residence, and rocketing the tub end of the car several hundred feet northward through the forest, knocking down fence posts and a barn."[30] Lawns were burned and bark stripped from trees as far as a thousand feet away and a seven thousand foot plume of smoke rose over the site.[31] This explosion apparently convinced some denizens who were complaining about having to evacuate how grave the situation really was.

By 6:30 P.M. lubrication oil, leaking from a tankcar, burst into flames and increased the threat to the metallic sodium car, though officials weren't entirely sure where exactly that tankcar was. The strategy to that point was to keep people out of harm's way, rather than to try to deal with the harm directly. This strategy, developed locally, was subsequently ratified by specialists in hazardous materials. Note here that officials and organizations were operating under pressure that would not leave us surprised had big mistakes been committed. The fire spread to others cars, resulting in huge fireballs and black, toxic smoke.

By the end of the story, if indeed we can really say there was one, several millions of gallons of water had been treated onsite, hundreds of thousands of gallons of contaminated water had been removed from the area, thousands of water and soil samples had been analyzed, and 70,000 cubic yards of soil had been dug up and taken away from the site. The photographs in the available reports show huge holes that were dug in the ground, backfilled with clay and rock.

It could have been much worse. The train left its tracks about one-fourth of a mile from the main intersection of town. Massive devastation, toxic chemicals, conflagration—all the makings of chaos. Yet that was not the case. While the evacuation was going on state and federal agencies worked together, their officials engaging in a minimum of buck-passing and backbiting, at least compared to similar accidents. The Louisiana State Police followed its mandate, given by state law, to coordinate official efforts after a hazardous materials spill until other, more obviously appropriate organizations, could assume responsibility. Officials from the state's Office of Environmental Quality, responsible for managing hazardous wastes, and the Office of Health Services and Environmental Quality arrived quickly, and instead of proclaiming no risk to the general population, which is what we often see from officials, immediately assumed there might be some substantial risk. On that assumption, the agencies monitored people's health, adopted an aggressive stance for protecting the environment, and took responsibility for telling residents when they could move back into their homes. In taking on this last task, state agencies evinced a surprising willingness to take on the eight-hundred-pound gorilla of defining acceptable risk.

Two travelers reported a loud "boom" to the local sheriff's office within thirty seconds of the derailment. Within three minutes the fire department, higher officials in the sheriff's department, and the Louisiana State Police had been notified. Within fifteen minutes the local highway that runs parallel to the train tracks was shut down, and within twenty minutes the mayor, working out of a temporary command post (a car), had ordered evacuation.

Within thirty minutes of the accident the relevant specialists from the State Police, the state's Department of Natural Resources, the U.S. Coast Guard National Response Center, the federal Environmental Protection Agency and Department of Transportation had all been contacted. Within an hour all relevant agencies agreed that the entire town had to be evacuated. The Red Cross, local nurses, the state Office of Health Services and Environmental Quality, and the Louisiana Department of Health and Human Resources set up and managed evacuation centers. Control over access to the site was established quickly, as the State Police and a local judge issued the orders necessary to authorize officials to prevent anyone from entering the evacuation area. Note here the apparent lack of significant conflict over jurisdiction. Soon thereafter, at 11:30 in the morning, the governor made an official emergency declaration and authorized officials to forcibly remove anyone from the evacuation area.[32] Science too was on the move, with scientists taking samples, flying through smoke, running machines. The EPA soon arrived (from Dallas and Edison, New Jersey), as did the head of the Association of American Railroad's Bureau of Explosives; they cooperated with local officials.

Not only were organizations and their agents in effective coordination; so too were communications swift and effective.[33] Railroad personnel quickly contacted, and received assistance from, individual shippers concerning the materials that were on the train.

For all the anguish and conflict, for all the lawsuits and uncertainty, for all the chemicals and fires, the Livingston case was, for our purposes, a startling success. On its opening page, the Livingston Report said that:

> For the next fourteen days . . . eleven state agencies, six federal agencies, five non-governmental entities and the civic

resources of the two of Livingston and neighboring communities were focused on the mitigation of what has been described as the worst chemical transportation accident in the
history of the state.[34] There were no lives lost, no serious
injuries, and considering the magnitude of the accident, limited property damage.

The C-Shibboleths

The foregoing tales support our common sense about how to think
about and prepare for the untoward. We have learned something we
perhaps already knew, which is that planning and effective response
are causally connected. There are clearly times when contingency plans
help officials coordinate their responses. We also saw instances of response failure, and at least part of the reason for those failures was the
absence of a plan. We can regard this evidence as confirmation, even
proof, of the Theory of Good Planning.

The Theory of Good Planning, to be explicit, is that tight *coordination*
among organizations, clear *communication* among people who need information, and *cooperation* among individuals *and* organizations will
make disaster response more productive, saving lives and property.
These precepts, incidentally, would seem to apply to all sorts of planning, not just planning for accidents. If planning and response are indeed always and everywhere so tightly, causally coupled then coordination, communication, and cooperation should be related to each
other as follows.[35] Good communication leads to cooperation between
organizations which then enables coordination of efforts and thus successful response. Successful emergency response is usually attributed
to the planning and foresight of responsible organizations. In failures
it is typical to find people who are touched by the disaster and subsequent evacuation complaining about chaos and uncertainty, and placing responsibility for those unhappy conditions at the door of poor
planning.

Communication, cooperation, coordination: these are the *c-shibboleths*
we find in talk and writings on disaster response. We find them in accident reports from the National Transportation Safety Board and other
such agencies, in journalistic accounts of accidents and disasters, in
investigatory commissions, and in the courts. It would be imprudent
to venture an estimate of how often or in which combinations good
communication, high cooperation, and tight coordination go hand in
hand. Obviously they sometimes do.

Planning Sometimes Fails Us

But if we find, and to some extent ratify, the c-shibboleths in cases of success and failure, we also often find a measure of stilted imagination. Often enough, planning and success *do not* coincide but are loosely connected or even decoupled entirely. Sometimes there are huge failures to protect lives and property even though contingency plans *are* available. Those failures are interesting because they draw attention to the limits of our abilities to imagine and devise ways to respond to worst-case situations. And even more interesting are the cases in which successful evacuations occurred even though there were no plans at all. Such cases are interesting because they show that the world is much more variable than is captured by the Theory of Good Planning.

THE CASE OF THE WORST CASE

Plans and success sometimes coincide. The absence of plans and the lack of success also sometimes coincide. But sometimes neither condition is true. Even the best-laid plans sometimes come to naught. Confusion can reign even when contingencies are thought through carefully. Organizations can fail to follow their mandates even when those mandates are clear. Organizational masters and experts can dissemble or simply fail to understand that which confronts them.

Events can overwhelm all available resources. These are incidents where everything seems to go wrong at the same time. They are the kinds of things that elicit remarks like "That would never happen again in a million years," or "What a freak of nature!" These are the "worst cases."

Washington, D.C.'s Worst Case

Wednesday, the 13th of January 1982, was a difficult day for emergency responders in Washington, D.C. It was a day when planners didn't have to rely on simulations or models to guide their thinking. The snow, sleet, and freezing rain started at the end of the morning rush hour and before eleven in the morning the streets were thoroughly iced. There were so many traffic accidents that police departments simply ignored all but the most serious ones.

The worst was yet to come. The National Weather Service was predicting eight inches of snow; Virginia officials had already decided to close state offices at noon. The federal government's Personnel Management agency decided to dismiss all nonessential government employees three hours before their regular departure time. Even though decision makers had been informed by Washington's Metro subway system that the rush-hour schedule could not be moved up, because of the difficulty of recalling trains and operators, the decision seemed a wise one. Many people used their cars to commute into D.C. and the sooner they got on the road home, the better. Federal workers in Washington leave work on a staggered schedule anyway, so setting their dismissal at three hours before the regular time seemed as if it would provide a smooth commuting schedule. The announcement was sent to agencies at 1:40 in the afternoon, so people scheduled to get out of work at 4:30 were to leave immediately; those scheduled to leave at 5 would wait until 2 o'clock; those scheduled to leave at 5:30 would leave at 2:30.

All of this was according to plan. There are clear, written definitions of what "nonessential employee" means and there are written guidelines for early dismissal of government employees in the face of emergencies. There are documents describing the expected impact of early dismissal on government operations, and there are plans for making government work around the staggered dismissal schedule. There are also organization charts for communication flows between offices and between organizations, for distributions of authority, and for task allocation. There are, in other words, a raft of contingency plans for emptying Washington, D.C., of commuters in the event of emergency. So, the planners, for good reason, felt well prepared for bad weather days like 13 January.

But then the worst case started to unfold. A little before four in the afternoon Air Florida No. 90, a Boeing 737, left National Airport with ice or snow on its wings and crashed into the Fourteenth Street Bridge, which connects the District of Columbia with Virginia.[36] One minute later, the airport used the national Civil Defense 2200 (broadcast) Network to request help from all emergency facilities that had any connection with the airport. Ambulances, rescue squads, fire trucks, police officers, rescue boats, and fireboats were dispatched to the scene. "All departments responded," says the National Transportation Safety Board; "however, none were properly equipped to perform a rescue operation in the ice-covered river."[37] The official log from the District of Columbia's fire department says that at 4:11 the deputy fire chief responded; at 4:22 "Truck Co. No. 10 sighted bodies in the water."[38] Command posts were established and communications plans were put into effect. Helicopters rescued people, as did rescue workers and members of the general public. Seventy-eight people died, including four on the bridge; six airline passengers escaped the crash, though one drowned.

Descriptions of the accident and the response elicit feelings of horror, as is true of all plane crashes. Many people remember the television footage of the rescuers' inability to get people out of the waters. The ice in the Potomac River was so thick that rescue boats had trouble breaking through; a rescue airboat at the airport never did reach the survivors. I should point out that when I noted above the many plans that were available I did not even mention that National Airport and the Federal Aviation Administration have their own detailed plans for responding to everything from fuel spills on the runways to terrorist attacks to planes falling into the Potomac River. There are even separate plans for an accident on airport property and off.

But the conditions were so hostile that all that planning could scarcely have produced success. The traffic leaving town and the weather meant the fire department had to travel *south in the north-bound lane* to get to the scene of the accident. Worse, responders had to contend, in the middle of a traffic jam and bad weather, with a broken jetliner, crushed cars, freezing bodies, jet fuel, and huge chunks of ice. But those were not their only troubles.

At 4:30 in the afternoon, about twenty-five minutes after a jet smashed into a main evacuation route of Washington, D.C., a Washington Metropolitan Area Transit Authority train crashed deep in a tunnel near the Smithsonian station, killing three and injuring many more. Some of the rescue squads en route to the plane crash never arrived there because they were re-routed to the Metro crash. Fire department units were dispatched ten minutes later, command posts were set up, ambulances were sent to the scene (including four ambulances and one intensive care unit that were initially assigned to the plane crash). Special equipment to extricate people from the wreckage was sent. By 5:14 an onsite fire captain reported that people were being freed from the wreckage.

The National Transportation Safety Board notes, reasonably, that redirection of the rescue units sacrificed nothing to the Air Florida survivors: there just weren't enough of them to make a difference. It goes on, however, to say:

the occurrence of two major accidents within a 30-minute period in the Washington Metropolitan area during weather

conditions as they existed on January 13, 1982, placed a severe burden on the emergency response capability of those
jurisdictions required to respond to both accidents.

And then adds, flatly:

The concurrent emergencies, while unique, emphasized the
need for the District of Columbia fire department to review
its emergency response plans to assure that a residual rescue
response capability is available at all times.[39]

Who could have anticipated all those things going wrong at once!?
Too much snow, too much ice, too many cars, a plane crash, a train
crash. The subway platforms were completely full; the trains them-
selves were "crush-filled," as officials in public transportation call it.
So, too, were the roads. Listen to the director of D.C.'s Transportation
Department:

There was approximately 2 to 3 inches of snow on the
ground by 2 o'clock. Also by 2 o'clock we had . . . salted
and sanded all of the major arterials and collectors. [We
were then notified of an early out, so] we immediately set
about reversing the lanes of the major commuter bridges to
Virginia . . . and set about as well reconfiguring our traffic
signal system into a rush hour configuration. Both of those
steps take approximately an hour and a half, so that between
2:30 and 3 o'clock, I took a walking tour of the area on both
sides of the mall and in the downtown area. At that point,
at roughly 3 o'clock, most traffic in the downtown area had
come to a complete standstill. There was minimum movement on side streets, and hardly any on the streets like Constitution, Independence. . . . Most all traffic, including bus
traffic, had stopped at the point. I wanted to emphasize that
because it illustrates the difficulty that I think we had in
trying to get emergency personnel to the scene. . . . At
4 o'clock when the airplane hit the bridge, that meant the
closing down of the high occupancy vehicle lanes on the
14th Street Bridge, as well as the remainder of the 14th Street
Bridge. All three bridges were closed.[40]

But, really, there *were* plans in place, and they seemed to be fairly
good ones at that. As well, the Metro train system regularly ran drills
of train wrecks, including mass evacuations in tunnels. National Airport and the District of Columbia had run two Potomac River drills in
the past year, the last in October.

This case shows that outcomes and planning for catastrophe can be quite loosely connected. There is nothing about the presence of a plan, even a *set* of good plans, that guarantees success; as well, failure is not guaranteed just because planning is absent. Worst cases, like the Washington, D.C., case, could not be foreseen by anyone. They are the worst of times. And it really does seem impossible to plan for the worst of times. The plans in place for the airport, for the emptying of Washington, or for a subway accident were probably all very good plans and we have no reason to think that they would have failed if singly called upon. But they could not be expected to work if they had to be implemented at the same time! Plans can't guarantee safety even if they are the best plans in the world and are executed just as they're supposed to be.

ACCIDENTAL SUCCESS

Sometimes, people triumph in spite of themselves. More accurately, people triumph in spite of the bumbling of their organizations, the confusion of their officials, the ignorance of their experts. These are times when most people would expect massive failure but when instead they find accidental success. Worst cases are instances in which planning and response are not causally related because social or natural conditions are so overwhelming that little can be done. Accidental successes are instances in which planning and response are not causally related because either there is no plan for people to follow or people just ignore the existing plan. Let me give a few examples.

Ohio River Flood

The great Ohio River Flood of 1937 wiped out the entire Ohio River Valley over January and February of that year.[41] By 24 January, all prior flood records had been exceeded, and people started getting ready up and down the river, in Missouri, Arkansas, Tennessee, and the lower Mississippi Valley. Pittsburgh, Cincinnati, and Louisville are all on the banks of the Ohio.

In all, somewhere between one-quarter and more than one-third of the population of eleven cities along the Ohio left their homes.[42] Probably 1.5 million people evacuated, including some 50 to 70 percent of Louisville. Yet there were few or no plans in place, and though there was considerable effort from many organizations, including the Army, Coast Guard, Works Progress Administration among many others, those efforts apparently had little effect.

Duluth Train Wreck

On 30 June 1992 at about 2:15 in the morning a Burlington Northern
Railroad freight train left Superior, Wisconsin, with three locomotives
and fifty-seven cars, five of which were filled with hazardous materials, one with aromatic hydrocarbons (including benzene), one with liq-
uefied petroleum gas, one with butadiene, and two with molten sulfur. Thirty-five minutes later, says the National Transportation Safety
Board, the conductor and brakeman felt "a couple of unusual bumps
followed by an uncommanded emergency brake application."[43] Following the bumps, and with part of the train on a river trestle, fourteen
cars derailed, including three containing toxic materials.

Over twenty thousand gallons of toxic chemicals were swept down
the Nemadji River. The tankcar with the highly volatile aromatic hydrocarbons fell upside down in the river, either end on a river bank,
and ruptured. The car's effluents evaporated, creating a vapor cloud
that was twenty miles long and five miles wide. The wreck was close
to Duluth, Minnesota, so quite a number of people were at risk.[44] Before
the crisis was over, seventy-three people in Minnesota and neighboring
Wisconsin were in the hospital and the National Guard had been called
out. Some thirty to forty thousand people from Superior, Duluth, and
surrounding areas evacuated.

A disaster plan existed in Duluth but, as the National Transportation
Safety Board report dryly reported: "The . . . disaster plan was not
activated during the emergency response to the Superior accident."[45]
Yet the appropriate officials were notified, including CHEMTREC (an
emergency response service provided by the chemical industry), local
911s, the National Response Center, the Wisconsin Department of
Emergency Management, the police and fire departments, and Burlington officials. Local officials worked reasonably well together. More
important is that nearly one-half of the population at risk learned of
the danger and moved out of harm's way.

At least eight evacuation centers were set up, ranging from local high
schools to the Duluth International Airport. It took about five hours to
evacuate Duluth.[46] Local reports say the evacuation was both massive
and smoothly conducted. The downtown area, where one of the several
clouds migrated to, was cleared in a matter of minutes. "It was amaz-
ingly calm," said Duluth's police chief. "Everybody can take credit for
that."[47]

In the Duluth case it didn't seem to matter that officials didn't use their plans. They seemed to be able to respond appropriately even without formal mechanisms of coordination. Perhaps history mattered. In 1970 there had been a small (two hundred people) evacuation in response to a gas explosion nearby. In 1971 there was an airplane disaster at Toronto International Airport, which was within local jurisdiction. In 1975, a high school student went on a shooting rampage, prompting most of the area's officials to mobilize. The high school tragedy was soon followed by the explosion and fire at a nearby oil refinery that resulted in the evacuation of three thousand people, itself soon followed by yet another airline crash at Toronto International. Officials tried to fold their experience into the contingency plan, and from reports of the response to the accident they were remarkably successful in doing so. But in this case I think we are warranted in judging that the prior experience with response, which contributed to the evacuation's success, was embedded in *the people* themselves.

Three Mile Island

It is typical to judge the evacuation after the near meltdown of the nuclear plant at Three Mile Island in March 1979 a failure. But that judgment is too sweeping, and properly applies to the lack of organizational planning, coordination, and control. As evacuations go, it was in fact quite a success, even though there was also no plan in place to help the surrounding population. Before Three Mile Island, nuclear facilities were only required to have evacuation plans for the plant itself, and the very immediate surrounds of the facility. Two plans *had* been written but neither were approved by the Nuclear Regulatory Commission.[48] When the meltdown happened, there were no plans for evacuating all the people who would eventually evacuate.

Imagine the scene. The nation's heaviest nuclear hitters, including the Nuclear Regulatory Commission and the Federal Emergency Management Agency, and state emergency organizations were unable, or unwilling, to tell people much about a major atomic threat. Organizations would not be controlling players in the evacuations around Harrisburg. Federal and state authorities, as well as the utility, were highly distrusted and many people did not believe official statements.[49] An NRC study later concluded that "existing emergency plans at all levels of government" were strained and predictably blamed the problem on "inadequate communication networks."[50]

People at risk took matters into their own hands. Schools closed on their own and people closed their windows. Then they started to leave. A reliable count says that nearly 40 percent of the population within fifteen miles of the plant evacuated (145,000 people) in a massive, unplanned and undirected, fashion.[51] There was no panic, as the people left in their own cars in an orderly way. Very few visited the official evacuation center.[52] Meanwhile, officials deliberated. Here are the words of NRC Commissioner James Asselstine:

> There had been little planning by state and local governments responsible for dealing with the emergency, and the response was confused. There were no procedures for coordination among various governments; there were no clear lines of authority; there were no clear procedures for or means to disseminate information; there were no clear procedures for determining whether to take protective action or how to carry it out once it had been decided upon; and few if any of the other elements essential to an effective emergency response existed. Because of the disarray on the part of nearly everyone involved in the response to the TMI accident, people living in the area around the plant did not know what information was accurate and did not know whether it was safe to stay in the area or whether to leave. Most people simply did whatever they thought best.[53]

And it worked. At least it worked better than we might have expected. At a moment when most of us would be surprised at nothing more than total failure, that the evacuation went as well as it did might well be judged a minor miracle.

It appears that plans are not always necessary for there to be effective response to the untoward. More specifically, it appears that formal organizations, experts, officials, and bureaucrats are not always necessary for people to know what to do to protect themselves. Three Mile Island was like Duluth in the sense that the formal plan seems not to have been causally connected to accident response. TMI and Duluth were different, though, in that in Duluth officials *were* an integral part of the response, even though their actions were not plan-driven. Still, the interesting fact about both cases is the disconnection between officialdom and public safety. Apparently, the ties between the c-shibboleths are not as clear as the Theory of Good Planning says they are.

Planning, Experience, and Symbolism

My handful of cases in this chapter are hardly systematic. So I have no evidence on how often it happens that planning and response are causally connected, or disconnected. But numbers aren't everything and there are some lessons we can draw.

There obviously *are* important success stories; just as obviously there are important failures. Those cases usually support the Theory of Good Planning, which asserts a causal connection between planning for the untoward and effective response to it. But there are also instances in which the mere existence of the plan doesn't seem to matter much, because people don't follow the plan or abandon it as their crisis develops. In still other instances—the cases of accidental success—there is effective response but there isn't even a plan available.

It's common to find in social science and common sense bold assertions of direct, causal connections between planning, on one hand, and successful organizational and individual response, on the other. This is so whether we are talking about the so-called warning phase of catastrophe, the event phase, or the recovery phase. It just ought to make sense that contingency plans, good ones at least, cause (or at least make more likely) organizational coordination, which in turn causes successful evacuations.[54]

Consider, for instance, an article by two experienced disaster researchers that draws strong conclusions on how officials, organizations, and networks of organizations ought to behave in response to impending doom or catastrophe.[55] The article claims we know that when organizations are flexible, have good information, clearly defined positions for responding to disaster, and good communication they will respond to warnings more effectively. Further, "organizations must be able to see emergency response as their job, and have clearly defined roles to play. Emergency experience or planning can help fulfill this need." Coordination, one of the shibboleths that appears in all normative articles, "is enhanced through preparedness . . ." especially if authority relations within and between organizations are clear and uncontested. I mention this article not because it is exceptional but because it is not.

Or consider the newsletter called *Natural Hazards Observer*, which is published by the Natural Hazards Center at the University of Colorado. In it one can find, especially after the latest disaster, copious discussion of lack of communication, or the breakdown of coordination.[56] Sometimes there are comments even from high-level officials in FEMA, but more often the key articles are from academics. In any case, here's an example from an analysis of the official response to Hurricane Andrew—one of the worst hurricanes ever to hit the United States—in

August of 1992: "An inability to rapidly capture and transmit information from the disaster area affected estimates of the severity of the disaster and the deployment of resources."[57] Other communications problems are also listed. The point here is not whether the statement was accurate—I'm sure it was—but the implication embedded in the analysis that successful response to the disaster would have been possible if only communications had been better.

Some measure of success in responding to calamity *is* attributable to high degrees of coordination, communication, and cooperation. It was just such planning that coordinated the work of so many kinds of organizations in Livingston, Louisiana, and Duluth, Minnesota, allowing people to evacuate and minimizing what could have been horrendous damage. Evacuation *per se* is certainly not doomed to failure. Perhaps upward of tens of millions of people have been touched by evacuation this century.

And, though I've not spent time on oil spills in this chapter, there are instances of contingency planning that have enabled containment of contamination, even if only 10 or 20 percent, roughly, of the oil was contained.

In our success stories, and some of the failures too, contingency plans sometimes had considerable utility. Standard operating procedures were in place, leaders knew who they were supposed to call, people knew who was in control. Such planning and institutionalization of response were possible because experienced-based knowledge helped organizations and experts impose order on what might otherwise have become chaotic. Those cases exemplify operational rationality, which is when routines and standard operating procedures permit successful or effective uncertainty-to-risk transformations.

Operational rationality is when actors transform uncertainty into risk in such a way that they can control the key aspects of the problem. Manufacturers of airliners design their planes (most of them) so that all the fuel can be dumped in flight, thus giving pilots some meaningful degree of control over the likelihood of conflagration in a crash. Large oil tankers are designed with their cargo holds as self-contained cells, so that when they run up on the rocks they are less likely to disgorge all their contents. When a bomb exploded under the World Trade Center, organizations in New Jersey and New York followed the plans that permitted effective organizational coordination. Perhaps part of the reason the evacuation was a success in Livingston is that many people in the town and surrounding area worked in chemical plans and oil refineries, and thus were substantially aware of the risks.

Operational rationality is based on well-interpreted experience. When an official laboring at the site of the World Trade Center bombing said that "We've done this before," he didn't mean they had responded to a bombing at the Center, but that they had responded to burning buildings and other instances in which large numbers of people needed medical treatment. The same can be said of oil spills on *enclosed waters*. There are plenty of stories of successful response to such spills because there exists a stock of considerable experience on which to draw, so that experience then gets embedded in the plan. Transformations of uncertainty to risk result in operational rationality when in-kind experience is available for organizations to learn from.

There was considerable operational rationality evident—though of course unevenly distributed—in the response to Hurricane Andrew. In Louisiana, where several thousand people evacuated from New Orleans, which lies low, people had several days to prepare for something they had seen before. Similar stories are available for floods, fires, trucks that overturn while full of toxic chemicals, gas pipeline breaks, or chemical plants blowing up.[58] Planning for such things isn't easy. Communities along the Gulf Coast, from Florida to Texas, had a hard time preparing for Andrew. In one community in Texas there was a line of cars fifty miles long, prompted by an official recommendation to evacuate, especially important for the originating terminus of the line, since it was filled with petrochemical plants and oil refineries, prime candidates for massive environmental assaults.[59] Nearly a million people from three Texas counties evacuated successfully. And the Air Force evacuated its base in Homestead, Florida, which was a good idea since the base didn't exist after the storm went through it. But terrible as it was, people knew it was coming. Operational rationality was possible in the case of Hurricane Andrew partly because of the (semi to be sure) predictability of the event but also because of the effects of its force. There was little uncertainty about what the thing would do.

Yet the stories in this chapter also show that the correspondence between plans and successful response is often illusory.[60] That correspondence is often more something we'd *like* to believe is there than something real. For to admit the obverse—that planning may have little to do with successful evacuation—is unnerving at best and at worst undermines the main supporting beam of Western rationalism: control based on expert knowledge. That's one reason why social science writings on disaster and recovery abound with admonitions that poor communication leads organizations not to understand each other, or that conflict among local officials robs the *important* event (i.e., the disaster) of key official attention.

In fact, it clearly happens that sometimes planning makes no difference for responding to system failures. This is probably so because of *how* planning is done: experts centralize knowledge, elites centralize decision-making power, organizations centralize communications. We just don't know enough about the circumstances under which planning can work and when it cannot.

More research into those circumstances would help us know more about how to construct good plans, but also how to analyze the degree of symbolism in all plans. It is common in some quarters of scholarship to insist on the symbolic nature of nearly everything. I think that approach to symbols is misguided because it seems to deny that there is functionality, intent, motive, or any purpose other than communicative ones in social action. Yet I don't think it helpful to approach the matter in binary terms. So I think fantasy documents have relatively higher *degrees* of symbolism in them, even as I think that nonfantasy documents can also be symbols. The function of the success stories is to illustrate some of the variation in functional and symbolic utility.

I am resolutely *not saying* that we shouldn't plan for catastrophes in particular or the untoward in general. It should also be clear that in-kind experience doesn't guarantee effective planning or response. The lessons I wish to draw here are quite different. If planning and response for planning and recovery can be loosely connected then it becomes much less clear how to assign responsibility for system breakdowns (response should be thought of as part of the system) and thus less clear how to characterize well-functioning social systems. We must start to wonder about the functions of experts if what they claim to know doesn't match well with how the world actually works. These experts are, after all, presumably knowledgeable in how social systems operate and in predicting and prescribing what will happen when those systems go awry. If that knowledge is more variable than is usually thought to be the case, it seems our theories of how expertise works ought to take account of that.

Fantasy documents make claims to audiences that the event being planned for is understood and controlled. We don't usually see plans that say, "This is way beyond our competence. There is so much uncertainty about this issue—we can't predict people's behavior, we can't know if we'll be able to coordinate the organizational response, we don't really understand the technology—that we think it best not to pretend we can do much about it. We can't control the uncontrollable." Instead we end up with appeals to the C-shibboleths, which are useful enough as homilies, but the fact is that we just don't have enough of the kind of research that would be necessary to specify the conditions under which communication, cooperation, and coordination matter in which particular ways.

In a little while I'll say why I don't think organizations, experts, and officials will admit, or even know, the limits of their knowledge and ability to control. First, I need to show *how* organizations *can* make the claim that they can control the uncontrollable. The chief mechanism that enables such claims is, like much about fantasy documents, rhetorical. That's the topic of the next chapter.

4

Apparent Affinities:
Normalizing Danger through Simile

Organizations and experts can not, in the case of large oil spills, control what they claim they can control.[1] Organizations and experts can not, in the cases of civilian nuclear evacuation and nuclear war recovery, know the extent to which their claims are valid. The problem is not that they assert an ability to predict the future. Nor is the problem that their predictions and forecasts entail theories of social organization and technology. Predicting the future is something that organizations credibly do all the time; and we know quite a lot about how social and technical systems work, although organizations frequently don't fold that knowledge into their operations.

The problem is that they assert an ability to know futures or control events that *no one else* can know or control. The problem is that the theories they build into their plans have so little valid support that they are more ideology than knowledge. There's nothing inherently wrong with ideology; we need ideology to maintain a meaningful social life. But when ideology is represented as if it were science or knowledge it obscures the constructed, artificial nature of expertise, prediction, and discovery. When fantasy documents are presented to audiences as if they were anything other than flights of fancy, and when organizations and audiences start to act as if such fantasies actually reflect organizational capabilities, we then see deception, obfuscation, or worse.

We can hardly envy the positions in which planners find themselves. Their social, political, and organizational environments have created for them extremely high expectations, demanding from them levels of competence usually attributed to psychics or deities. What answers are possible when high-level decision makers demand a plan to rebuild America after massive nuclear confrontation with an evil empire? It's difficult—very nearly impossible—to say, "Ms. Decision Maker, your charge is unreasonable, undoable. At best, we have no way of knowing if it can be done." What can planners do when the Congress, the Coast Guard, and the CEO of Exxon mandate, as they have, a plan to contain and collect twenty million gallons of oil off the coast of New Jersey? It's barely conceivable that anyone replies, "It can't be done. We've never been able to respond effectively to such a spill, and any claim that we can is either disingenuous or self-deception." What can a contingency planner say to high-level corporate officials and federal regulators when told to devise a scheme to evacuate everyone in a ten-mile radius off Long Island in short order? Should she, could he, tell powerbrokers, "Sorry, we simply haven't the technical and social expertise to know if we can do such a thing"? Probably not. So act they must.

But act on what? We know that organizations take big problems and break them up into manageable pieces and that indeed they are better at that than individuals are.[2] But since actual, operational control can not be established over big spills, civilian evacuation, and post-Armageddon reconstruction, it is far from obvious exactly what problem they're supposed to solve. How, in other words, can organizations identify the problem that needs breaking up?

Apparent Affinities

When problems are unclear, organizations create, sometimes amid conflict, always amid negotiation, *apparent affinities* between categories. By apparent affinities I mean that symbolic links are created with extant bodies of knowledge, expertise, and experience and that these links make recognizable that which is unknown or unknowable.[3] To create an apparent affinity between phenomena is to claim that things are alike in essential ways, and that one knows what those essences are. To put phenomena or events in the same category makes a claim that if we know something about event number one we also know *the same thing* about event number two. So apparent affinities are important tools that organizations can use to solve problems—especially thorny *political* problems like convincing audiences to accept their definitions of acceptable risk.

Now, to this point I've emphasized the importance of experience in formulating functional plans and I've said that *lack* of experience is a key factor behind the production of fantasy documents. But of course experience is not the same thing as *good knowledge*. Experience can lead us astray. For instance, for several years after the Alaskan Pipeline was opened each tanker was escorted out of Prince William Sound with a tugboat. Since no serious accident happened during that time, industry officials decided that their experience proved the oil transport system would be safe without such escorts. Experience, indeed, can lead us to believe that we're safer—or more at risk—than we really are.

Furthermore, we *do* have ways to learn that seem to go beyond direct experience. Aircraft manufacturers are apparently relying more and more on computer simulations, rather than building test models, before going to production. Similarly, NASA trains astronauts in various simulators on earth before rocketing them into outer space. Companies that want to insure offshore oil platforms use similar mechanisms to project past direct experience.

So experience doesn't speak for itself but instead requires the proper frame of reference. Those frames can turn experience into knowledge, or noise. Consider the following examples. In Bhopal, India, where perhaps ten thousand people died after a Union Carbide plant leaked a deadly gas, "the need for [evacuation] plans was not identified, either by the local management or by the experts from headquarters who conducted the periodic operational safety surveys."[4] At Love Canal local, state, and federal officials neglected signs of toxic chemicals. And at Chernobyl officials long ignored a dangerous reactor design. In each of those cases there were good reasons, and even experience, to suggest that there was greater danger than officials believed was present. But because officials had a stake in keeping those systems running, they turned a blind eye to that experience. Put differently, they constructed their frames of reference so that the danger-indicating experience was noise rather than knowledge.

In another, harrowing, example Diane Vaughan writes that there was plenty of experience to show that the O-rings used in the solid rocket boosters on space shuttles were highly likely to fail. "We never perceived," said one engineer, "that we had to make a radical design change to the joint based on the observations that we were making from the return hardware."[5] Unless they had it in their perceptual tool kit to interpret the data as indicating danger, the engineers wouldn't see anything fatally wrong with their propulsion systems.

Yet while history doesn't have to repeat itself exactly before we can say we have meaningful experience, there does seem to be some threshold of experience, history, or data above which we enter the fantastic realm. With the space shuttle program, for instance, it is really only with 20-20 hindsight that we can see that there was sufficient experience in the system to suggest that it was unacceptably risky. Vaughan points out that the engineers had "no ability to test the vehicle under

full environmental forces." Too, the data they had from in-flight performance "had no predictable pattern."[6] Why stop the flights if the evidence showed no pattern? Or, consider the first atomic explosion at
Trinity, some fifty-five years ago. There was an event whose prediction
was based almost completely on *theory*. There *was* experience with the
sun, of course, and some laboratory evidence that led those nuclear
pioneers to think their theory was right. But they didn't really *know*
they were right, and some of the Manhattan District's scientists were
not sure, at that first explosion, that they weren't going to ignite earth's
atmosphere.[7]

I don't have a rock-solid answer to the question of what makes experience meaningful. Experience (data) never speaks for itself; yet some
measure of it is usually (not always—that's the point of the Trinity
example) necessary as a reality check on fantastic guessing. Perhaps
the best we can do is to treat experience as necessary but not sufficient
in functionally solving problems.

The idea of "solving problems" is actually about two phenomena. It
is resolving some difficult dilemma so that people can get on with
whatever they're doing. We can't trade stocks today until we get somebody to fix these darned phones. But solving problems is also *convincing* others that deliberate thought and careful consideration are routinely brought to bear on the trouble at hand. Of course we'll figure
out the phone problem, because that's the kind of professionals we
are. "Rationality" thus has both instrumental and symbolic functions:
organizations use it to fix problems and they use it to persuade others
that they *can* fix problems.

When organizations are able to convince others to accept their apparent affinities, that is to say when organizations legitimate their symbolic constructions, they create what philosopher Kenneth Burke called
a God-term, a term whose basic assumptions go unquestioned. Burke's
term, itself a rhetorical device, is overly dramatic, since most of what
it refers to is the routinization of behavior and the institutionalization
of ideas: over time much of behavior and thought becomes routine and
thus taken for granted. These are important phenomena, and Burke
was right to point to their rhetorical significance, but they are not heav-
enly. Still, Burke's idea does suggest more than just routinization and
institutionalization. It also refers to a strongly normative or ideological
attachment to an idea. In this chapter I show how apparent affinities
can be created and how organizations try to turn them into God-terms.

In the case of civil defense and post–nuclear war survival the key apparent affinity has been asserted through the concept of "dual- or all-hazards planning." The claim is that planning is generically similar across hazards so that to plan for the one is to plan for the many. Specifically, all hazards planning says that natural calamities are the same as technological, and especially nuclear, calamities. If that's true, then we would know quite a lot about postwar possibilities because we know quite a lot about social and physical reconstruction after hurricanes, earthquakes, and so forth.

For Shoreham and the evacuation of Long Island after a nuclear catastrophe, organizations relied on an affinity between evacuation and commuting. Long Island, said the experts intense with credulity, evacuates five times a week. If so, then we would have plenty of very good knowledge about nuclear evacuation because throngs of people do indeed leave Long Island every weekday. Presumably, were Shoreham to melt down such commuting would be quite effective since the National Guard, etc., would be in control.

For large oil spills organizations rely on an apparent affinity between big spills and small spills. Planners point to their numerous successes containing and cleaning up spills on lakes, rivers, and bays. On those success stories they plan for very large spills of say, over 100,000 gallons. The claim is that small spills on closed waters are the same as big spills on open waters.

Following their rationalist urges, and demands from their environments, organizations sometimes try to control the uncontrollable. Since organizations are paralyzed when confronted with huge uncertainties they transform such problems into smaller, more manageable entities. Such transformations change uncertainties into risks; they also normalize danger. An apparent affinity allows those transformations to happen in the first place. Let us look in more detail at three apparent affinities.

Oil Spills and an Ecological Fallacy

Oil is very slippery, and that is one of its most valuable properties. But that property also makes it enormously difficult to control once it gets out of whatever contains it. That is one reason why organizations can't control oil spills on the seas. Another reason is that oil on the seas tends to be moved from oil fields to refineries in very large boats. And when big oil boats break open they make big messes.

Most of the time oil spills on water are not caused by big ships breaking open but by pipeline ruptures or small barges running aground or shoreside containers leaking. That small containers make for smaller spills does not mean the problem is trivial. Far from it. America is so addicted to oil that there are really a lot of small spills every year and they add up. We need not bother with the precise numbers. We can simply recognize that oil officials, on the defensive after the *Exxon Valdez* ran aground in Alaska, were not wrong when they protested that the risk of small oil spills far exceeded that of big oil spills.[8]

So small spills are important. They are important because they are the source of most oil spill contamination but they are also important because, unlike oil spills on the open sea, it *is* possible for organizations to respond effectively to relatively small oil spills on enclosed waters.[9] The sordid, and often quite technical, literature on oil spills and responses to them, has plenty of cases in which organizations successfully contained or cleaned up oil in lakes, rivers, streams, and inlets.

Oil spill contingency plans are attempts to model resources and trouble. They formalize for organizations the kinds of materials, technology, and personnel that might be necessary to respond to problems. Contingency plans also put forth an organization's goals; they often include elaborate justifications for those goals as well. By spelling out all these things, or at least trying to spell them out, contingency plans help to reduce the main uncertainties that organizations most worry about. When the plans are fairly close to the actual competencies that organizations command they make oil spills more tractable to remedial action. Contingency plans reflect risk assessments, although they are less formal than the mathematical and statistical models usually used to express probabilities, risks, and benefits. Perhaps the most important (manifest) function of contingency plans is to serve as blueprints for interagency coordination of responsibility, authority, and information flows.

Let's now consider some key aspects of the contingency plans in place at the time of the *Exxon Valdez* catastrophe. I want to illustrate how organizations made the connections between a smaller spill and a larger one, how they created an apparent affinity between two fundamentally different phenomena. That connection, in turn, became the foundation of the publicly proffered fantasy that a huge oil spill in Alaskan waters could be controlled. One effect of the fantasy document was to facilitate a measure of complacency about danger.

When the *Exxon Valdez* ran up on Bligh Reef, the oil industry and regulators had at least five contingency plans that they could point to as evidence that they could control the danger they were creating. Each plan promised, in one way or another, to soften the blow of the horrors that oil spills can bring. The plans included:

- The National Oil and Hazardous Substances Pollution Contingency Plan,

- The Alaska Regional Oil and Hazardous Substances Pollution Contingency Plan,

- The State of Alaska's Oil and Hazardous Substances Pollution Contingency Plan,

- The Coast Guard's Captain of the Port Prince William Sound Pollution Action Plan, and,

- The Alyeska Pipeline Service Company's Oil Spill Contingency Plan for Prince William Sound.[10]

Each plan delineated different functions and procedures to be performed by myriad organizations in the event of a minor, moderate, or major oil spill. Each plan told what organizations ought to do, whom they should contact, what they were responsible for. I focus on one contingency plan, Alyeska's *Contingency Plan for Prince William Sound*,[11] because it was the one that addressed most explicitly the risk of oil spills in Prince William Sound. It also clearly stated Alyeska's responsibility for immediate response to a spill in the sound. That it made such clear and enormous claims was probably a main reason that it became a lightning rod for political attention after the spill.[12]

The contingency plans in Alaska were developed over a number of years, some dating back to the beginning of the trans-Alaska pipeline in the early 1970s. Some of the plans contained explicit scenarios of major groundings and founderings of large tankers. Alyeska wrote the main plan, and it was approved by state and federal government agencies. Although precise on promises, technically Alyeska's contingency plan was a somewhat vague, general document of roughly 250 pages, perhaps two-thirds of which were maps and lists of equipment. Maps and lists are necessary for spill response, and indeed they are what constitute most oil spill contingency plans. Still, the plan was a bit sparse on details. As someone I interviewed in Alaska put it, the plan "doesn't really get down to specifics, and it's usually those details that'll kill you."

But there was plenty of content in Alyeska's *Contingency Plan for*

Prince William Sound, and especially revealing were the oil spill scenarios, one for a 4,000-barrel spill, the other for a 200,000-barrel spill (see table below). Note that the larger spill scenario was for practical purposes equivalent to the *Exxon Valdez* spill of 260,000 barrels (1 barrel = 42 gallons). These scenarios represented the outcome of considerable, sometimes conflicted, negotiations between oil companies and regulators regarding hazard mitigation.

Two Oil Spill Scenarios for Prince William Sound, Alaska

4,000-Barrel Spill	200,000-Barrel Spill
• seas less than 5 feet	• seas less than 5 feet
• currents less than 1.6 knots	• currents less than 1.6 knots
• waves less than 2 feet	• waves less than 2 feet
• at least 2 miles visibility	• at least 2 miles visibility
• weather conducive to cleanup	• weather conducive to cleanup
• winds at 8 knots	• winds at 5 knots
• ship, shore boomed within 3 hours	• ship boomed within 5 hours, shore "immediately"
• dispersants on site in 9 to 17 hours	• dispersant arrival not estimated, presumably 9 to 17 hours
• communications flawless	• communications flawless
• all agencies coordinated	• all agencies coordinated
• 100 barrels unrecoverable	• 10,000 barrels unrecoverable

Sources: Alyeska Pipeline Service Company, Oil Spill Contingency Plan; Clarke, "The disqualification heuristic."

The first scenario assumed a spill of 4,000 barrels (168,000 gallons) at 6 in the morning, the "sea state is less than five feet," "currents are less than 1.6 knots," "waves are less than two feet," with at least two miles visibility. It is "sunny to overcast with some light rain," and there are eight-knot winds. "The ship and shoreline, which is heavily oiled, will be boomed [within three hours of the accident] and skimming operations will begin."[13] Alyeska's "dispersant applicator contractor," in Arizona, will be on-scene and working within nine to seventeen hours.[14] Communications among officials and organizations are flawless; interpretations of those communications are unclouded.

Soon after the grounding, all the appropriate organizations were to be notified. Once notified, those organizations would share a common vision of what constitutes appropriate response, so an efficient and effective division of labor among organizations would be instituted almost immediately. Fully understanding their respective roles, the agencies would implement those parts of the plan for which they were

responsible and best suited. The actions necessary for effective response would be executed as needed by other agencies, who would
proceed in like manner.

The cleanup would last two months and be highly effective.[15] Of the
4,000 barrels 400 (10 percent) would be lost to "weathering and evapo-
ration," skimmers would collect 1,000 barrels (25 percent), another
1,000 barrels "will be dispersed," and 1,500 of the assumed 1,600 barrels
to make it to shore would be "recovered" (a shoreline recovery rate of
94 percent). Only 2.5 percent, 100 barrels, "would not be recovered and
will be naturally dispersed."[16]

I'll return to this scenario in a moment. What was most important
in Alaska, naturally, was the 200,000-barrel spill (8,400,000 gallons).
The size of the spill was so close to that of the *Exxon Valdez* that many
Alaskans saw Alyeska's scenario as evidence that they had really considered a spill of that magnitude, and were ready to respond to it. It
is worth noting that Alyeska objected strongly to including the larger
scenario in the contingency plan. It appeared there only because state
regulators insisted on it. The scenario's second sentence reflected Alyeska's reluctance: "[Alyeska] believes it is highly unlikely a spill of
this magnitude would occur," adding that safety was ensured because
"the majority of tankers calling in Port Valdez are of American registry
and all of these are piloted by licensed masters or pilots."[17]

The 200,000-barrel scenario assumed the sea state, currents, waves,
visibility, and weather would all be like those of the 4,000-barrel spill;
there would be five knot winds (compared with eight for the smaller
spill). The scenario prescribes that booms and skimmers would be onsite within two and a half to five hours, although it does not explicitly
claim booming will be placed around the vessel or the spilled oil by
that time. The scenario further supposes that several other important
actions will "be simultaneously initiated."[18] Within twelve hours private commercial vessels and local aircraft from the town of Valdez
would be enlisted to help, backup personnel and equipment mobilized,
and another barge or ship would have arrived to lighter the grounded
vessel.[19] "All oil spill contractors in the state of Alaska would be asked
to mobilize and move to the site."[20]

Myriad other organizations would also be activated, many of them
moved to the small town of Valdez (which provided half the name for
Exxon's tanker), which would be a base of operations. As with the
smaller spill, communications would be uninterrupted and unambigu-
ous, and interagency coordination unproblematic. The scenario esti-

mates 50 percent (100,000 barrels) of the oil "will be recovered at sea, either directly after the spill or at a later time by being washed off of the rocks, contained and skimmed off of the water."[21] Fifteen percent (30,000 barrels) would evaporate before hitting the shoreline, another 15 percent be "recovered from the shore," 15 percent would "naturally disperse and approximately five percent [10,000 barrels] will remain in the environment."[22]

Both scenarios rely on nearly best-case conditions. It is hard to imagine conditions more favorable for implementing a spill response, which contrasts somewhat with training and contingency planning in other industries that can wreak catastrophic harm. Of course, an absolutely worst-case scenario in Prince William Sound (a foundering vessel in the middle of the night during severe winter storms far into the Sound) would mean complete immobilization. An Alaska Department of Environmental Conservation (ADEC) official said that "you couldn't even come close . . . you couldn't burn, you couldn't deploy dispersant, you couldn't recover, all you could do is watch. That's all you could do. You couldn't do a goddamn thing about it."

Still, there is substantial room for planning between best- and worst-case conditions, so one might reasonably expect explicit consideration of some untoward conditions.

That Alyeska neglected conditions that might hinder response to a major spill in Prince William Sound is instructive. Chief among those conditions was that if a ship broke apart in the first place it would likely (not always, though—the *Exxon Valdez* ran aground in clear weather) be in weather quite unconducive to cleanup. Alyeska's contingency plan reflected organizational perceptions regarding future untoward events, making claims that the risks of oil spills had been thoroughly considered. Of course, the promise was not just that the risks had been considered but that they were *covered*, thus lending the impression that those risks had been eliminated. In this way, the contingency plan was a rhetorical tool, useful in convincing audiences—chiefly ADEC and the public in Alaska—that an effective risk management system had been instituted.

In March of 1982 ADEC reviewed Alyeska's 1980 contingency plan, and initially issued only a "conditional approval" of it. ADEC took exception to Alyeska's "maximum probable spill" of seventy-four thousand barrels, noting that some vessels carried over twenty-five times as much oil. Alyeska's response was to "question" whether ADEC had jurisdiction over Prince William Sound contingency plans, complaining that regulations "do not require submission of any plan respecting areas outside the Terminal's area of operation."[23] Alyeska was not denying the importance of contingency planning beyond the Terminal, since it was already developing such plans. Rather Alyeska was denying that ADEC had any legitimate claim to oversee what it was planning. By June 1982 Alyeska claimed it could recover 100,000 barrels (more than four million gallons) within forty-eight hours. Four years later ADEC required Alyeska to recertify its contingency plan, and asked that a 200,000-barrel-spill "scenario" be included in it. Alyeska produced one, reluctantly. As one Alyeska official complained:

> These scenarios are a real bear cat and boy we've learned this time. . . . We do a scenario because [people] want to know how you will respond to a given situation, but then they assume that is how you'll respond to anything in that range. Well, there are thousands of potential scenarios . . .

The larger scenario is wildly optimistic, and that would be an understatement. It is certainly true that the weather in Alaska is sometimes calm enough that the winds are soft and the seas low. And I'm sure, because I have seen it, that visibility on Prince William Sound can be much greater than two miles. Probably the currents can be as low as Alyeska projects. But this is all true only on a very good day. Prince William Sound and the Gulf of Alaska, into which the Sound feeds, are enormous bodies of water and all enormous bodies of water are subject to violent weather patterns. That too is an understatement. Alaska is the frontier. It is almost at the top of the world, and it is normal for the environment to be hostile. There, tranquility is not normal—the cold weather, the ocean currents, and the mountains mean that extremes are not at all out of the ordinary. Death-dealing temperatures, massive snow storms, gale force winds, and huge chunks of ice from receding glaciers are all commonplace in Alaska. In the town of Valdez fifteen-foot-high stakes are painted red on the top before being driven into the ground next to the fire hydrants so that fire fighters can know, in deep, deep snow, where to find water.

The assumptions about how the organizations will work are more fantastic than those concerning the natural environment. Even in the best of times organizations aren't so perfectly coordinated. Rarely do organizations, or collections of organizations, work like well-oiled machines.

But do *any* contingency plans project the lack of coordination, the confusion, the ambiguity that one usually finds in real-life crisis situations? Not really. After all, plans are inherently idealized; they *can't* anticipate all contingencies. They would become too cumbersome and in fact might even strike us as unreal in their overattention to detail. Yet successful planning in cases of earthquakes, volcanoes, train wrecks, and the like show that such idealized conditions *can* derive from concrete histories and thereby lose their fantastic character. The important point is that representations of such capabilities come to be believed by people who work in organizations and by people who those organizations are supposed to protect. Those representations, in the case of fantasy documents, are more rhetorical than accurate representations of what organizations can do.

I've already suggested that the claim that only ten thousand barrels of a 200,000-barrel spill are "unrecoverable" would be a miraculous recovery rate. No such rate has ever been approached in any large spill. Oil is too slippery and it moves too fast for humans to hem it in with the primitive tools presently available. Forgetting about response technology, the technology involved in creating huge oil spills guarantees continued cleanup and containment failure. That is, oil tankers are technological behemoths and they simply carry so much oil at once that tanker breakups, which are inevitable, will continue to overwhelm response attempts.

These gloomy conclusions only hold for large spills on open seas. But that's the point. It *is* possible to respond successfully to oil spills on closed waters. The containers, be they barges or pipelines or small tankers, can't possibly do as much damage as supertankers, they can't spew as much effluent, they can't so easily overwhelm the technology and the social organization brought to bear on them. And when oil breaks out in a river or on a lake, the landlines provide natural boundaries, assisting emergency response in a fundamental way. Organizations responding to such spills still aren't likely to be perfectly coordinated but neither do they have to be. Huge spills prompt organizations to commit huge amounts of resources and so conflicts and poor coordination have much bigger effects on disaster response.

The key point is that there is such a thing as successful response to small spills but there is no such thing as successful response to large spills. So before Alyeska could even write, or be forced by regulators to write, its contingency plan, it had to create an apparent affinity between the two genres of oil spills. Earlier I asked the question, "act on what?" in wondering what expert planners could do when asked to control the uncontrollable. In Alaska the answer was for planners to act on that which they knew well, that which they could indeed control. Listen to one of the state's contingency planners, a thoughtful fellow with responsibility for thousands of pages of plans:

> The earlier plan . . . I think it was just a continuation of what was done before. I don't think anyone made the decision that "no, we don't need the maps," so eliminate these. I think Alyeska just did somewhat of a repeat of the old plan and we commented on where we thought it needed to be updated and made current, and perhaps in a few places in the earlier plan where it was not complete enough or where there were mistakes to correct those. So I don't think there was a great deal of revision from the earlier plan on the new plan. If mistakes were made, I think it was unfortunately a continuation of the earlier plan that nobody felt had the power by himself to say "no, we don't need this, let's delete this."

With time key decision makers committed the organization to fantastic promises by the rhetorical device of equating one thing with another when in fact the two were quite different things. Had they not made that equation the fantasy would have been impossible and organizations would have had to admit to their audiences that they were creating risks of very severe danger, danger in which others, not they, would bear the greatest costs when things went wrong.

Civilian Nuclear Evacuation and the Suburban Condition

The death of a nuclear power plant is not a pretty sight, and the killing of the Shoreham station on Long Island was downright gruesome. The killers used every arrow in their political and legal quivers to fell the monster. That they were successful at all was Herculean because such a thing had never happened before. Shoreham's death was unprecedented in that local and state governments prevailed over federal bureaucracies in forcing the closure of a *finished* nuclear plant. I'll explain later how that struggle shaped risk-rhetoric, and specifically uncertainty-to-risk transformations. For now, simply note that Shoreham's opponents tried an array of tactics to make Shoreham fall but the gambit that finally worked was the one that convinced courts, officials, and the public that a substantial part of Long Island could not be evacuated in the event of catastrophe.

That the "evacuation problem" would be huge seems obvious now, but it wasn't in Shoreham's early days. The nuclear industry, and its highly supportive regulatory agencies, had never lost a reactor battle on grounds of evacuation problems, and indeèd a considerable part of the industry's future rested on the outcome of the Shoreham argument. The conflict over Shoreham was in fact iconographic of several seething and emerging conflicts: over existing distrust of the Long Island Lighting Company, over assumptions of who should and could control nuclear development, and of course over definitions of acceptable risk. To deal Shoreham its death blow thus became a goal whose symbolic significance extended far beyond an electricity generator on the north shore of Long Island.

Shoreham's killers could not succeed in their quest by sheer power. For one thing, there was no way for them to garner enough money and political support for the job. I say this even though Shoreham's opponents had plenty of both. Rich and poor alike on Long Island were opposed to the plant (and to Long Island Lighting Company [LILCO] more generally), and they were supported and led by county government *and* state government. So while the Shoreham conflict would eventually be more a battle of the Titans than a David and Goliath saga, the opponents *were* up against LILCO, the utility industry, Wall Street, and the federal government. Were Shoreham a matter of a mere slugfest the plant would have opened long ago.

To succeed, Shoreham's would-be killers would have to develop and exploit *cultural* resources. Shoreham's opponents, though certainly locked into a conflict of material interests with the plant's proponents, could not realize their goals without winning a deeply rhetorical game. In particular they would have to change the reigning vocabulary of risk, shifting the terms of debate from one about jobs, electricity prices, national security, and *probabilities* of some remote incident, to one of *possibilities* that children and homes would be irreparably damaged.

Shoreham's future rested on the "evacuation problem," which itself consisted of two subproblems: establishing what would be considered legitimate expert knowledge and establishing the very definition of what was possible. For Shoreham's promoters the rhetorical task was to convince the public, politicians, and courts that evacuating a huge part of Long Island was within the Long Island Lighting Company's purview of expertise. The main mechanism LILCO used in that effort was to rhetorically transform a meltdown into an ice storm and a massive retreat into a daily commute. For Shoreham's opponents the rhetorical task was to argue convincingly that evacuation was impossible and further that it was *inherently* impossible because organizations are incapable of creating and maintaining the requisite levels of competence. That LILCO and its supporters in the federal government failed affords an interesting lesson in power-politics, one that underscores how important it is to control the language people use in their struggles with each other.

Meltdowns Are Ordinary

Let us visit some of the claims that LILCO made, especially some of the testimony by social scientists who supported LILCO.[24] I don't mean to judge the individuals who testified for or against the Shoreham plant. I know some of those people, on both sides, as friends and as scholars and they are intelligent, virtuous, and of general good sense. What I am interested in here are the ideas and their consonance with organizational needs, not individual personalities or competencies.

Much of LILCO's battle for Shoreham was fought in court. There it put forth a fascinating position: that public opinion on evacuation was irrelevant to the potential success of the contingency plan. The opposition used opinion polls that purported to show that people wouldn't necessarily follow LILCO's plan. But LILCO would hold that people's expressed values were irrelevant to what they would actually do. Now, everyone agreed that people *would* evacuate when the whistle blew. *How* people would evacuate, though, was another matter. LILCO, the federal Department of Energy, and the Federal Emergency Management Agency's view was that people would follow the contingency plan. Like third-graders filing out to the playground after hearing a fire alarm, all would go according to plan, all would be orderly. Authority would be unquestioned. Nobody would get hurt.

The view of LILCO's opponents, including the expert academics who played such important roles in defeating the plant, was quite different. As they saw it, people would indeed be influenced by official proclamations and orders but not in the way LILCO claimed. Instead of trusting LILCO, people would overinterpret what officials said to such a degree that the evacuation would not be controllable and would possibly even be chaotic. Moreover, not only would people fail to follow the plan, but those asked to function as evacuation workers would behave according to their own decisions and needs rather than those of the organization. If the whistle blew and people didn't take their posts, massive unpredictability—not controlled commuting—would ensue. The public safety, in that event, could not be assured.

In surveys people would often say that they felt their first responsibilities were with their families. While hardly earth-shattering, if this were true it would mean people might not follow the orderly, official evacuation plans. A bus driver, for instance, on whom LILCO would depend to ferry people out of harm's way, might forsake his official duties to ensure that his small children were protected first. One survey reported that 75 percent of the bus drivers might forego their duties to help their families.[25] LILCO might not be able to control the evacuation, after all; nothing in the plan even mentioned the need for evacuation when workers were on strike.

This was a problem. LILCO claimed it could control and protect the public. But what if the public didn't cooperate? LILCO drew on expert opinion to excise the problem. LILCO's behavioral scientists first said that opinion polls on the issue were meaningless. "Asking a person to make a cold judgment," to quote from some official testimony, "about how one might hypothetically react in a complex future situation, and giving him a few seconds to answer, is not a good predictor of future behavior."[26] The experts, by that logic, knew what people would do if disaster struck, so it didn't matter what those people said they would do. "[T]he factors that influence human response to emergencies," they said with little qualification, "are relatively well-known and accepted as valid by most scientists in this area."[27] Thus it logically followed that "these factors can be addressed in an emergency plan to help achieve good response when the plan is put into operation."

LILCO's experts argued not only that public opinion was irrelevant to evacuation planning but that the public *per se* was irrelevant. "[A] plan is primarily composed of the actions of *organizations*," they claimed, "not individual persons. The plan does not depend on 'public' opinion, or an individual's opinion; it depends on an organization functioning to do the work and give public information." *People* disappeared in this part of LILCO's argument. Finally, and crucially important, they claimed that "the substantial evidence of how emergency workers have dealt in previous natural and so-called 'technological' disasters" shows that "most emergency workers can be relied upon to do their jobs promptly and effectively when duty calls, and that role 'conflict' does not hinder overall group performance." This statement, by the way, also contradicted what people were saying in surveys.

So LILCO's position was that the public would do what they were told, but if you didn't believe *that* then its position was that the public was irrelevant. The contingency plan wasn't about the public at all but about organizations, so there was no reason to consider the public when trying to decide if the plan would work. Furthermore, the emergency workers could be fully counted on to do their jobs—they presumably were *not* part of the general public—because from studies of *other* disasters we know that emergency workers do indeed try to fulfill their designated functions more often than not.

There was a certain logic to the idea that plans are only about organizations, though it does seem a bit odd to neglect that the plans were to protect the public. In any case, I want to spend a few words on the issue of the emergency workers. LILCO, as we just saw, said the workers could be fully counted on. LILCO's opponents held otherwise. A couple of the opponents' experts said that "[T]hey will attend first to the welfare of their families and will be reluctant to report for emergency duty until such time as they have been assured of the safety of their loved ones or have seen to the safety of their loved ones themselves."[28]

LILCO's plan did accept as truth something that could be demonstrated only in the breech. The plan assumed that once an emergency was declared, over 1,300 people would rush to their positions, many within the ten-mile Emergency Planning Zone without first ensuring the safety of their families, many also within the EPZ.

LILCO's defenders were absolutely right about one thing: the plan would be executed by *organizations*. Since there would be no way to really test how well the organizations would, or would not, respond if catastrophe struck, the *argument* over the plan would depend in large measure on the underlying theory each side held about how organizations behave.

But the devil is in the details and sometimes the best-laid plans can falter for want of one or few apparently minor details. For Shoreham's contingency plan, one of the key details concerned school bus drivers. That is, the force of the argument that evacuation workers would first want to protect their families concentrated on worry about children. LILCO's idea was that, upon an emergency declaration, schools would be let out early, with children boarding school buses that would deliver children not to their parents but to the Nassau County Coliseum, in neighboring Nassau County, some fifty to sixty miles away. The parents, for their part, would follow LILCO's evacuation directives. So the entire plan rested on the willingness of school bus drivers to forget *their own* families, drive into a hot zone, and deliver other people's children on roads that would be packed with evacuating vehicles.

It was an implausible idea, and the anti-Shoreham experts focused on the notion of "role conflict" to make their case. Someone experiences role conflict when they face mutually exclusive demands. Now, I should say that LILCO's experts were correct that most of the time emergency workers will indeed stay and take care of the problem at hand. Even at Chernobyl some workers more or less willingly gave their lives to put out the blaze. But *this* part of the plan—and it was an important part—rested not on trained, full-time emergency workers but *school bus drivers*. LILCO's opponents argued that evacuation workers—and especially school bus drivers—would be more likely to resolve the conflict in favor of their own families than someone else's.

This made sense, since people *do* tend to evacuate in familial units, and plenty of disaster research, which the opponents pointed to, confirms this. Emblematic, perhaps, is that hospitals around Three Mile Island had trouble because many hospital workers were evacuating with their families.[29]

The workers were a problem, but one that seemed rather minor in the larger scheme of things. Workers might do this, or they might do that. The whole problem might be sidestepped in another way: to put nuclear catastrophe into the category of the nonspecial. In other words, the rhetorical stratagem was to transform nuclear meltdowns, about which we have very little information, into something we do in fact know a lot about: natural disasters and commuting.

This was a transformation of some significance, because we have extensive knowledge of and history with natural disasters and, of course, commuting. If nuclear meltdown is mundane, there should be no massive uncertainties but only calculable risks. If there are only calculable risks, organizations can control what is otherwise uncontrollable. By LILCO's lights, the problem was one of risk rather than uncertainty because, in the first place, the argument that nuclear events are unique "is contradicted by the empirical evidence."[30] In the second place, "the determinants of human behavior," said LILCO's experts, "in emergencies in contemporary America are . . . transferable across emergency types."[31] This was so, they said, for two reasons. The idea that nuclear events are unique "argues against the basic premise on which the social sciences rests: that there are knowable reasons and patterns in human behavior that are discoverable through systematic scientific inquiry." LILCO was saying that to argue that anything is singular is to deny social science; since social science was undeniably real, claims to singularity didn't make sense. Of course Shoreham's opponents were not arguing this point at all. They were, rather, arguing the point that radiological threats are *interpreted* in ways that differ from those of natural disasters. They were not saying there are no patterns in social life but that the patterns LILCO believed were there were, instead, fantasies.

LILCO's claim that its opponents' position was not supported by evidence was a claim of a different kind. It said that the opponents were depending more on ideology (where pure belief is paramount) than on science (where evidence is paramount) to support their case. This was a tricky argument to make given that LILCO also had no evidence for its position. The solution to the dilemma was to create an apparent affinity. Thus:

> [N]uclear reactor accidents are something like a flash flood that occurs on a sunny day. ... Put simply, the "what," "how," "when," "where" and "why" of emergency preparedness are known, and planners can take into account variation in the "quantity" of each determinant across different types of emergencies to draft sound plans for response in nuclear power plant emergencies.[32]

Of course there was no evidence whatever on which to base these claims, but in an important sense that didn't matter. The transformation was a rhetorical one and such changes are not mainly about evidence. To effect the transformation was to create a set of images that LILCO's employees, the media, politicians, and the (once irrelevant) public might believe. Cognitively, even the wildest of hurricanes is less threatening than a nuclear emergency. People on Long Island have lived through hurricanes. They are frightening but they don't contaminate you and your home forever. They knock down trees but trees grow back. Organizationally, too, an ice storm or even a very large fire are things we *have* responded to with great effectiveness.

With the apparent affinity in place, there would be no need at all to worry about workers responding to their calling. "[I]t is a fact," they said with the authority of a physicist explaining the speed of light, "that in an emergency *some few* would almost certainly step forward to volunteer for such duty." The point is worth quoting at length:

> The record is clear that emergency workers do their jobs when they understand that they have an emergency job to do, when they understand what that job requires of them, and when they have a sense of the importance of their job for overall community safety and to their work group. These

understandings can be produced in different ways. For example, people who hold jobs that are in the routine of everyday life comparable to their emergency roles—for example, firemen—bring these understandings to the emergency setting.[33]

These experts knew full well of course that fires and radiation aren't the same thing. But this did not mean, for them, that emergency workers would "come to believe that it would result in their own death, and flee their posts to protect themselves. The reason is that emergency workers can be trained and equipped to accurately assess the risk." How this "accurate" assessment of the risk was supposed to happen was never made clear.

Yet, as I say, there was a consistent sort of logic in LILCO's position, if you first accepted its apparent affinity. One would simply tell workers the facts, train them in proper procedure as if they were police officers or school teachers. The tasks that might be asked of LILCO workers would thus not be outside the realm of human experience. LILCO officials said that "the company is required to perform extraordinary service in times of storm-induced power outages." On this logic, sending line crews to Pennsylvania, as had once happened, to help another company was evidence that LILCO could be counted on. Another example was a huge ice storm, in January of 1978 on Long Island, which interrupted service to 300,000 people. LILCO held that its response during that storm should inspire people's confidence:

> The ensuing restoration took 138 hours and involved 606 LILCO crews, assisted by 408 crews from 17 outside utilities and contractors. During snowstorms, [they continued,] when most companies are closing and advising their employees to stay home, the vast majority of LILCO employees come to work as expected.

If nuclear meltdowns are the same as ice storms, and mass, nuclear-inspired evacuations are the same as the daily commute to New York City, then it makes little sense to say they're uncontrollable. If knowledge about natural disasters transfers to radiological ones, then we know quite a bit about how people will respond when things go awry. Were the public to accept LILCO's apparent affinity as real, then the evacuation problem was surmountable, given enough communication, coordination, and cooperation. LILCO and its supporters couldn't draw on real precedent or history to make the case that they could control massive evacuation. Gone was the day when they might have made the claim that because they were the experts people should trust them. So arose the transformation of the uncertainties of evacuation into risks through the rhetorical device of an apparent affinity.

Civil Defense and Dual-Hazards Planning

The pictures of nuclear horror from Hiroshima and Nagasaki naturally elicited ideas that Americans should try to protect themselves from total destruction. The federal government provided evidence that this was possible in the early reports from the Strategic Bombing Survey, right after World War II, which detailed how people survived massive bombing raids and fire storms. It seemed logical, to some, that the lessons from the Bombing Survey would apply to nuclear civil defense. There followed a series of programs, pronouncements, and laws directed toward creating that defense.

By the 1960s the federal government was claiming that it could save perhaps *80 percent* of Americans in the event of nuclear war. Such claims apotheosize assertions of controlling the uncontrollable. Even Armageddon could be avoided! Successfully managing nuclear holocaust would be a considerable accomplishment, stretching organizational capacities to plan and execute plans to magnificent heights. Far more important, to *survive* a nuclear war would be to *win* a nuclear war. As in a demolition derby, to have any person left standing after a nuclear exchange has been the definition of "victory" since the advent of thermonuclear weapons. Effective nuclear civil defense would thus mean ultimate victory.

Indeed, one reason it is important to know about how organizations and elites have shaped the meaning of civil defense concerns the radical disjuncture between official talk and actual war-planning behavior. In the world of nuclear politics and nuclear diplomacy there exists the idea of "declaratory policy," which is a fancy term that means, "what leaders say in public." Declaratory policy contrasts with what organizations and leaders really *do*, often enough, and quite dramatically in the case of nuclear war planning.

The historian David Alan Rosenberg has pioneered the analysis of America's actual war plans, working from recently declassified documents and a knowledge of the nuclear establishment that is rarely evident in the writings of officials. Rosenberg shows that the war-planning reality has not been the same reality depicted in declaratory policy. The war planners have always had very strong incentives to plan to fight and win nuclear war.

The 1940s saw the early development of war planning. "Lt. General Curtis LeMay, named commanding general of the Strategic Air Command (SAC) in October 1948," with "full support from top Air Force policymakers" wanted to "ensure that the Strategic Air command was capable of delivering the atomic stockpile on the Soviet Union 'in one fell swoop telescoping mass and time.' "[34] The basic plan—to strike first, massively—never changed through the years and once intercontinental ballistic missiles were born, in an important sense it could never change. For once you can strike within fifteen or thirty minutes with huge numbers of warheads, the only decisive way to fight a nuclear war is to strike first.[35] Yet while the actual plan has been first strike, much official talk has been about "no first use" of nuclear weapons, "no cities," and other such misleading catchphrases.

Just as talk of nuclear weapons as defensive devices was always mostly disingenuous, so proclamations about civil defense were out of proportion to actual official commitment. There were some big statements in favor of it. Kennedy justified spending on civil defense, as have many others, as something of a patriotic duty, or at least of a presidential responsibility. Listen to a bit of a speech, some of which concerned accidental nuclear war, to Congress on 25 May 1961:

> [Civil defense] cannot be obtained cheaply. . . . [Once the possibility of accidental nuclear war] is recognized, there is no point in delaying the initiation of a nationwide long-range program of identifying present fallout shelter capacity and providing shelter in new and existing structures. Such a program would protect millions of people against the hazards of radioactive fallout in the event of a large-scale nuclear attack. Effective performance of the entire program not only requires new legislative authority and more funds, but also, sound organizational arrangements.[36]

A couple of months later, on 26 July 1961 Kennedy said on national television, "In the event of an attack, the lives of those families which are not hit in a nuclear blast and fire can still be saved if they can be warned to take shelter and if that shelter is available. We owe that kind of insurance to our families and to our country. . . . The time to start is now."[37] But no meaningful effort followed. An article in the popular magazine *Smithsonian*, in the only estimate I've seen, claims "200,000 families, wanting only to outlast Armageddon, planted such hollow seeds of hope"—in the form of underground shelters—in the early 1950s, though no evidence is cited for this conclusion.[38] There were calls and reports—from Rockefeller Foundation, RAND, the National Academy of Sciences, among others—for a shelter program. Indeed congressional hearings and the like were commonplace through the 1950s and 1960s, usually with officials using the opportunity to decry the offensive nature of communists while affirming in the strongest possible ways their support for the lives and property of God-fearing Americans. Civil defense was reorganized several times during that period, with offices combining and new organizations arising, proposing the same kinds of programs that their predecessors had proposed. Yet through the 1960s congressional appropriations for civil defense, especially in the form of blast shelters, declined.[39]

If civil defense were really an important part of overall American nuclear strategy, we would expect much tighter coupling between the strategic elements. Such was never the case. There was some talk through the late 1940s and early 1950s of developing huge programs of both blast and fallout shelters that people could hide in while atomic warheads devastated their homes and homeland.[40] But neither Congress nor taxpayers would pay for it. Any serious, that is to say massive, program of fallout and blast shelters would always fail to garner public or congressional support. Senator Richard Lugar noted in a 1979 congressional hearing on civil defense that "there was a time back in the early 1960s when we were supporting the idea of a much, much more compressive civil defense program, and we finally concluded that this was a waste of time and a waste of money."[41]

By default, then, the U.S. nuclear civil defense program developed into an *evacuation* program. As a 1979 FEMA report puts it, "Frustrated in its efforts to improve protection against blast and fire in large cities, civil defense turned to evacuation of cities as a low-cost survival alternative."[42] FEMA reports, ruefully, that "since a replacement program of blast and fallout shelter was not available, the concept of evacuation persisted in planning and training for many years."[43]

Of course, evacuation would have many of the same logical and strategic problems that blast and fallout shelters had. One problem was that of short warning time. To provide any protection at all from blasts or fallout would require that people actually make it to the bunkers. Getting people into shelters would take time. Up until the Soviets put a dog in space it was reasonable to think there *would* be time to get people underground. After all, London had done it during Germany's bombing raids. But that little dog, war planners knew, could have been a warhead, which meant that an attack could happen in a few minutes rather than the few hours required if the weapons were delivered by airplanes or submarines. As well, any mass movement of people, whether to underground shelters or to rural areas, would be readily detected by enemy satellites, which would allow the enemy to retarget missiles. If those missiles *were* retargeted, there would be no way to evacuate the evacuation centers. And the biggest question of all would never be addressed in any writings, reports, or speeches from the defenders of civil defense: "Would there be anything to return to?"[44] By their own logic, the answer would be "No." If that were so, however, and if the overall society had been leveled in nuclear warfare, what, finally, would be the point of trying to defend against nuclear attack?

Such questions were never addressed. To admit them openly would have been to admit the very strong possibility that nuclear civil defense wouldn't work. As important, to admit them openly would have said that the "experts" had no idea of whether their plans would in fact work. That would be like saying, "Let us spend millions, even billions, of your dollars on something whose effectiveness we can't even fathom."

To mount an effective case that it makes sense to talk about defending against thermonuclear bombs and restoring to normalcy a society devastated by nuclear destruction demands that the singularity of nuclear war be dispensed with. While it is not necessary to argue that nuclear war is some sort of everyday affair,[45] it *is* necessary to argue that it is sufficiently like something that we know as to lend itself to operational rationality. The reason this is so is that if the event is singularly, ultimately, overwhelmingly destructive, then how could it be reliably known? To simply say, "I don't know," would be almost impossible for these organizations: their environments demanded it of them, and they demanded it of themselves. They would, capable or not, control nuclear war.

Instead of confronting the problems of nuclear civil defense head-on, officials deflected them by creating an apparent affinity. In the early 1970s arose the conceptual turn, the rhetorical twist that at least had the potential to transform the rarefied world of nuclear war planning into something more mundane and hence more rational. Listen to Secretary of Defense Melvin Laird in 1972:

> [T]he Defense Civil Preparedness Agency can make a significant contribution to total civil disaster preparedness. Civil defense preparedness planning and natural disaster planning are often similar if not identical. This new Agency

will stress the dual capability and utility of civil defense preparedness and natural disaster preparedness at local government level . . .[46]

In the turn of a phrase, officials could claim that the organizational,
technological, and psychological demands of nuclear war were about
the same as similar demands from other disasters. Nuclear war was
now not much different than a hurricane. This idea became institutionalized with the notion of "dual- or all-hazards planning." After 14 July
1972, the day the Defense Civil Preparedness Agency came into existence, says an official history of United States civil defense efforts, com-
missioned by FEMA:

Virtually all DCPA programs . . . came to reflect this emphasis on dual-use of emergency systems: the States and localities would be helped to develop their capabilities to prepare
for, and cope with, peacetime disasters as well as the effects
of nuclear attack.[47]

President Ford would soon (on 18 March 1975) recite the litany:

I am particularly pleased that civil defense planning today
emphasizes the dual use of resources. Through development of the capability to support and assist our citizens in
time of war, we are also improving our ability to respond
to humanitarian needs during national disasters . . .[48]

The more general term for the phenomenon was "full spectrum preparedness." Says a FEMA report:

[At the Federal level] the dual-use approach was seen as
making sense on grounds of economy and effectiveness—
basically because the concerns of State and local governments for peacetime disasters preparedness helped moti-
vate them to take actions which were also essential for attack
readiness.[49]

The idea had the blessing of major officials, including Defense Secretary James Schlesinger:

Civil defense readiness generates, as a bonus, an improved
capability on the part of a State or local government to conduct coordinated operations in the event of peacetime emergencies. If State and local governments are prepared to deal
with the worst of all possible situations—a nuclear emergency—it is a reasonable assumption that these govern-

ments can handle lesser emergencies . . . effectively and efficiently. But should a State or local government turn a blind eye to the nuclear attack aspect of civil preparedness, its ability to respond to a lesser disaster becomes questionable.[50]

There ensued several efforts and programs, some of which I consider more carefully in the next chapter, designed to make such an emphasis palatable to states and local governments. The years 1974 through 1976 also saw the development of the last major element of full-spectrum preparedness—contingency planning to relocate (evacuate) people from U.S. metropolitan areas and other risk areas during a period of several international crises.[51]

Of course, we do know a lot about evacuating populations in front of natural catastrophes. So this apparent affinity meant there would be only technical problems, not major obstacles, to instituting mass nuclear evacuation. Said FEMA in 1981 appropriation hearings:[52] "Emergency Management organizations and plans are definitely tested and exercised by disaster events. So too are systems such as warning, communications, mutual aid."

Scientists make a big deal out of "testing." It is through testing—evaluating ideas about how the world works in the light of evidence—that scientists claim superiority for their ways of knowing. It is testing, ultimately, that allows us to decide whether some idea or theory is right or wrong. And testing is really based on experience that is interpreted with the appropriate conceptual apparatus. So when nuclear war was transformed into just another disaster, ideas about how it would work were given an imprimatur of science and expert knowledge. As *that* happened a class of people was created who had jurisdiction over nuclear thinking. This is FEMA in 1982:

> It is a difficult and complex problem requiring much planning, but it is possible. After all, we relocate millions of workers from our big cities every evening rush hour. We have moved hundreds of thousands to safety in time of hurricane or flood. And in a case like this, it could save as many as 100 million lives. It would be an orderly, controlled evacuation. Your own local authorities would give detailed instructions through radio, television and the press, telling you what necessities to take along, what arrangements have been made for transportation—by bus, train, or private car—where you will find safety in a small town or rural host area and what routes to follow to get there.[53]

If all that were true, it would make perfect sense for Louis Giuffrida, director of FEMA in 1982, to pronounce confidently that [t]he utility of civil defense plans and systems "has been demonstrated repeatedly. . . . Crisis relocation plans have been used when hurricane threats required evacuation of coastal areas."[54] And another high level FEMA official, also in 1982, could say:

> There are obviously more uncertainties associated with crisis relocation than with a blast shelter system. Nevertheless, we believe, based upon extensive research and on experience with many peacetime disasters requiring evacuation, that crisis relocation is a feasible, moderate-cost option . . .[55]

This apparent affinity made it so that organizations moving people away from bombs was merely another, nearly routine, task. Representative Mitchell put it all very well in some 1981 congressional hearings:

> The purpose of [a civil defense program he introduced] is to move Americans out of the most likely target areas before the missiles are launched. The option I introduced, called D Prime, would save 85 percent of our people and cost $1.7 billion more than we spend now on civil defense. The blast shelter option would protect 95 percent of our people and cost nearly $100 billion. Our experts tell us in an all out nuclear exchange less than 5 percent of the land area of the United States would be hit by nuclear warheads.[56]

Folding natural disasters and nuclear attack into the same category normalizes nuclear war. The "experts" could now say that evacuating ahead of the falling missiles was like any other evacuation, and that nuclear disaster was *essentially* like any other disaster. As horrible as hurricanes and tornadoes can be, they do not bring the end of millions of lives. There *is* recovery from even the worst of earthquakes. There *is* a place to go to even in the biggest of fires—because you could go to another city until yours is rebuilt. The all-clear *will* eventually be sounded. There *will* be life after the catastrophe. With the apparent affinity between civil defense and preparations for natural disaster, we suddenly know quite a bit about nuclear war and its aftermath. People will cooperate with officials, there will be people around to do the cooperating, there will be places to return to, and if not, there will be people and materials available to create new places to return to.

By the time the equivalence is complete, by the time the apparent affinity becomes institutionalized, planning for the end of the world is little different than any other sort of planning. Including nuclear evacuation and nuclear war in generic prescriptions for disaster response makes the problems of nuclear war generically like automobile accidents, race riots, and earthquakes. Effecting such a transformation is no trivial thing. Race riots are qualitatively different from a nuclear war. The words "nuclear war" conjure images of mass destruction, a leveling of urban terrain, as in Hiroshima, conflagrations that consume everything so that by the time the dust has settled there is little evidence that humans ever inhabited the now desolate space. Even the worst race riots, by contrast, destroy only relatively small sections of a city, usually that part of a city inhabited by the people who riot. The devastation is bad, but a walk through the rose garden compared to atomic attack.

To rationally plan for mass nuclear war is an attempt to claim that after the usual routines of everyday life are gone they can still be had. The very existence of such planning constitutes a claim that adequate thought and hard work can allow adequate control over highly uncertain, unpredictable events. More broadly, it is a rhetorical claim that a meaningful knowledge base can be constructed: that the information can be gathered, that it will be valid and reliable, that it can be drawn upon.

Risk Similes and the Normalization of Danger

When apparent affinities actually work—meaning if people actually *accept* them—they accomplish the job of convincing people that they should play the risk game as defined by powerful organizations. This is similar to the idea that if employers can just get workers to consent to bargain with them, they have in effect secured from workers legitimacy for a game that's set up for employers to win.[57] If you can get people to focus on the fairly trivial possibilities—ice storms, low-level pollution, commuting—then you might be able to distract them from the bigger issues. In any case, you end up getting people to consent to the rules by getting them involved in playing the game.

Those who claim to know how nuclear war would be fought, and recovered from, assert their claims ignorant of key details about how nuclear war would actually play out. Although the actual war plans are secret, many targets are clear. Even knowledge of the latter is hardly precise. The same goes for blast yields, the number of bombs, whether the bombs explode in air or on ground, time of year and so on. All these uncertainties mean that projections of nuclear war, as well as refutations of the probability, are in large measure speculative and even outright guesses. And there is nothing our risk estimators can do to lessen their decisional burden.

Those who claimed to know the sequence of events should Shoreham melt down, and the response of organizations and of the public to such a catastrophe, had to make projections without sufficiently certain knowledge of those things. Near meltdowns had happened, certainly, and Chernobyl would give real data in April and May 1986 of such events. But here is an instance in which it is not a trivial truism to say that all events are unique. For the combination of events leading to destruction of a nuclear plant would be enormously important for how people and organizations would respond. More crucial for the Shoreham controversy, and for our purposes, is that to assert knowledge of how evacuation would proceed could not be based on meaningful history.

Those who claimed to control, in Alaska, precisely how organizations and technology would respond to a huge oil spill could not base those claims on any available success stories. Here the problem is a bit different than with the nuclear cases, as we actually do have considerable knowledge of how oil spreads on open waters. That knowledge tells us, and should have told the organizations claiming they could control a large spill, that there is very little anyone can do to effectively respond once large amounts of oil get away from a boat in large open spaces.

Fundamentally, our organizations and experts faced tremendous problems of prediction. Without sufficient history or technical capability to draw on, they created apparent affinities between phenomena. Those affinities then allowed prediction, and transformed mammoth uncertainties into manageable risks.

Once an affinity is created, successes in one area are automatically evidence of success in another. So if civil defense in natural disasters is like civil defense in nuclear war, then evidence that we have successfully managed peacetime natural disasters is counted as evidence that we can manage civil defense in a nuclear war. Evidence from one domain is transferred wholesale, so that any natural disaster is really a drill, testing the machinery that will protect us all at what might otherwise be the end of the world.

It isn't necessary to construct apparent affinities for more routine system failures, if you'll excuse the term, such as earthquakes, floods, and hurricanes. Such events, though tragic, are known things; we can soften the blow from them, we know that recovery from the damage is possible and even a reasonable thing to expect. We know, too, that as bad as an earthquake might be it is not likely to entail wholesale destruction of a society as does nuclear war.

But when functional, operational control is outside their reach, organizations and experts must try to establish symbolic control of the problem. They create a set of symbols that signify that they do in fact command expert knowledge and organizational competence. These symbols then become tools that organizations can use to satisfy environmental demands, legitimate their actions, and fend off intrusive political pressures. Organizations and experts control the uncontrollable by creating apparent affinities, which are then folded into fantasy documents. Those documents, when wielded successfully as rhetorical devices, allow organizations to continue functioning without high levels of outside oversight. Another way to think of this is that risks are defined, effective risk managers are created, and risk acceptability is established. All of this is very much a social construction, and organizations are the main constructors.

The production of fantasy documents requires first that The Problem be identified. But not just *any* problem; rather a problem that will yield to reasonable effort. To identify a solvable problem the identifiers—those claiming special knowledge about that which is identified—must establish that they are the *rightful* knowers of the requisite special knowledge, and their particular identification, their particular construction of reality, must be transmitted to relevant audiences.

Organizational problems, or any kind of problems, are created as actors (organizations, groups, etc.) negotiate the meaning of some trouble as large enough to warrant big attention. Note that thinking of problems in this way is not advised by usual treatments in the social sciences or public policy. There, the existence of problems is usually taken as *given*, as things that confront decision makers in a more or less clear way. In the main cases of this book, however, the very definition of "the problem" is a product of social agreement. Put differently, before the organizations could do their planning they first had to define the problems as tractable. Out of the barrage of information and belief available to them, organizations created something recognizable as a problem they *could* solve. The organizations socially constructed the very thing their plans were intended to address. Those construction processes—fundamentally processes of simile—were ones of risk selection. Risk selection under conditions of high uncertainty, then, involves creating apparent affinities between disparate categories.

The general process behind the creation of apparent affinities has not gone unremarked by philosophers and social theorists. This general process has to do with how from the weltering mass of ideas people create categories (that is, things and potential things) and place in them objects and ideas said to be similar.[58] Here I am less concerned with statements of how such categories are created generally. I am more concerned with showing how the specific process of creating apparent affinities happens in organizations. Those constructions emerge from social conflict, the topic of the next chapter.

5

Authority and Audience in Accepting Risk

Risk becomes normalized through simile, which means uncertainty-to-risk transformations are fundamentally rhetorical transformations. This is not to say, not even to whisper, that the transformations are mere talk games. Behind the rhetoric are experts, organizations, and the elites who try to control organizations. There are also unevenly organized publics who must bear the brunt of decisions made in their name. So it is important not to forget that uncertainty-to-risk transformations have histories of social relations, themselves embedded in clashes of vision and conflicts of interest.

It's helpful to know about those histories of social conflict because they tell us how and why transformations happen in particular ways. We might call this a political constructionist view, one that emphasizes how power operates in creating what people regard as real. To see how uncertainty-to-risk transformations happen is to see how organizations and power work in creating rhetoric, and in making important choices about the dangers we face.

From another angle, we can say that to transform uncertainties into risks is also to define, or at least contribute to defining, the very "acceptability" of risk. This is so in the sense that such transformations contribute to the creation of the very menu of choices from which we pick our poisons. When we speak of risk acceptability we are *always* talking about issues of political value and moral choice. How could it be otherwise? For the issue of acceptability always entails the question "acceptable to whom"?, a question that is meaningful only from a particular point of view. There are no neutral, completely objective standards that could help us decide which risks are acceptable and which are not. In political arguments over danger, some will claim that *their* standard should be used to judge what is normal while their opponents will claim the opposite. Acceptability can be judged only against some*one's* standard.

If risk acceptability is a matter of political negotiation rather than objective fact, a number of things follow. First, acceptability turns on being able to create or establish authority over an arena or domain of knowledge. To successfully make the claim that one's standard *should be* the guiding standard is to succeed in establishing one's self as expert. So part of the uncertainty-to-risk transformation involves the creation of expertise. Second, establishing authority, as opposed to exerting power, is a matter of persuading one or more audiences of the rightness, perhaps even the moral propriety, of a particular position. So another part of the transformation is to convince others that they should share your framing of what's right and wrong, what's good and bad.

Experts, Organizations, and Social Conflict

Experts are a key mechanism through which organizations use rhetoric to define social realities. They digest raw materials and produce studies, research, and scientific conclusions that are then put to use justifying decisions made by others. They are, increasingly, the boundary spanners of organizations concerned with technical information, which means that experts increasingly talk to constituencies outside organizations. It is they who increasingly fashion political rhetorics in the guise of technical, value-free language to persuade others of the rightness of a particular position. Importantly, when experts enter the realm of "rightness" and "wrongness" of a particular position, they leave their realm of expertise proper for the more conflicted realm of moral vision and political value. They become salespeople, public relations artists, or flak-catchers.

Experts are nothing without legitimation. A good measure of legitimation can come just from organizational affiliation. Experts and organizations are often ineluctably connected in that experts rarely have any claim to authority without occupying an organizational position.[1] Organizational position seems especially important for experts who would contribute to huge issues with ambiguous parameters, which is certainly the case with civil defense and power plant evacuations, and arguably the case with oil spills. That experts are connected to organizations in this way means that organizational interests and forces can shape what an expert is, how an expert acts, and the rhetoric an expert uses.

This doesn't mean that experts are merely puppets or mouthpieces for those with real power, although that happens often enough. And it doesn't mean that experts deliberately conspire with powerful decision makers to dupe the public. Yet in any particular controversy, especially a technological controversy, one can usually discern an association between organizational interests and expert knowledge. In the cases that occupy the bulk of this book think tanks, political organizations, regulators, and corporations have been the main organizational actors, and their allied experts have created and espoused the political and technical positions that justify the knowledge claims made by those organizations. Think tanks and political organizations create "missile gaps," "bomber gaps" and other such prominent themes in nuclear weapons politics since Eisenhower. They create oil skimmers and chemicals to dump on oil spills. They create evacuation exercises. They create rhetorics of national interest that equate the social good with corporate profit and military definitions of reality. And, of course, they create fantasy documents that foster the belief that organizations can control the uncontrollable.

But experts and organizations don't create such images in a vacuum. Rather they create images and make claims in particular social contexts, contexts usually characterized by contested interests and symbolic battles over moral positions. To account for how fantasy documents are created we need to borrow several ideas:

- From scholarship on organizations and experts we borrow the idea that organizations are the key players in creating dangers and pushing to have others accept those dangers as reasonable. Analyses of risk and danger that neglect the pressure and force of formal organizations miss the target.[2]

- From sociology we borrow the idea that social life is replete with, even defined by, negotiation and social conflict between actors. The basic idea is that meaning and patterns of behavior emerge from social interaction. The utility of the idea here is that we understand symbols, including fantasy documents, as the result of social conflict.

- From scholarship on rhetoric we borrow the idea that "audience" crucially affects the form and content of the symbols and language used to persuade. This notion tells us that how speakers (read organizations, experts) conceive of the audience for what they have to say will shape what they end up saying.[3] In this way the rhetor constructs the publics, the audiences, to which fantasy documents are directed.

Borrowing all these ideas leads to the proposition that organizations use rhetoric in power struggles with other actors, and that by taking into account the needs and demands of those others, fashion their rhetoric according to environmental influences. More concretely, fantasy documents become what they are out of conflicted interaction. The usual way of looking at planning would have us understand the problem that the plans are intended to solve. My argument is that to understand the character of fantasy documents requires understanding who the plans are intended to persuade.

Experts figure prominently in the following stories, but they are *always* experts in alliance with organizations. So arguments between experts, and claims made by experts to audiences they try to persuade, are meaningless unless explicit account is made of institutional context. Attending to those contexts illuminates the institutional bases of transformations of uncertainty to risk. Thus as we follow the history of social conflict that stands back of fantasy we trace the shifting audiences, and their political constructions of reality, toward whom fantasy documents are directed.

Power in Alaska

There are two main ways that power and social struggles forged the character of the oil industry's contingency plans for oil spills in Alaska. One is quite general and has to do with the political economy of oil. The other is more specific and has to do with how organizations negotiated jurisdiction over safety and profits.

INSTITUTIONAL CONTEXT OF FANTASY

The spill from the *Exxon Valdez*, and the fantasy documents claiming mastery over such spills, never would have happened were it not for the Alaskan Pipeline, through which flows the source of 85 percent of state revenues and 25 percent of U.S. oil production. In the heady days of the late 1960s and early 1970s, after huge oil deposits were discovered but before the pipeline was constructed, there wasn't much discussion about whether the oil would be produced. State officials, federal agencies, Alaskan residents, native groups, and of course the oil industry all shared that goal. There were some rumblings, however, over whether a pipeline-tanker system was the best available transport system. Some environmental groups such as the Sierra Club argued that the mere presence of a trans-Alaskan pipeline would spoil much of Alaska's great beauty. They pointed out that most of the pipeline route would rest within twenty-five miles of recorded epicenters of major earthquakes, and each mile of the eight-hundred-mile pipeline would carry about 476,000 gallons of oil at any one time.

Environmentalists had good reason to sound alarms, and indeed there is some sense in thinking of Prince William Sound (and much of Alaska) as a long earthquake, punctuated by periods of calm. On 27 March 1964, almost exactly twenty-five years before the *Exxon Valdez* wreck, the worst recorded North American earthquake struck Prince William Sound. Registering an estimated 8.3 on the Richter scale[4] (the San Francisco quake of 1906 was 7.7), the "Good Friday Earthquake" caused substantial ground displacement and sent forty-foot waves onto shore. Rushing water snapped spruce trees 100 feet above the low-water mark. One hundred and thirty-one people died in the disaster. The earthquake wrought so much damage that Valdez had to be moved to safer ground, three and a half miles away. Today, all that physically remains of Old Valdez is the former post office's concrete slab, decorated with a placard commemorating the dead and the forty children orphaned by the quake. The town of Valdez now has annual earthquake drills (and plans for nuclear attack, though none for oil spills), but across its harbor are eighteen storage tanks capable of holding 378 million gallons of oil. A major earthquake in the area could rupture the tanks, resulting in a spill thirty-four times larger than the one from the *Exxon Valdez*.

The alternative to a trans-Alaskan pipeline system was a Canadian pipeline, terminating somewhere in the Midwest United States, probably near Chicago. Such a route had much to recommend it. The segment of Canada that the pipeline would run through was significantly less seismically active, Canada had already agreed to the project and had begun to facilitate construction, and indeed some of the system (including rights-of-way) was already in place. Some economists even concluded that a trans-Canadian pipeline would be cheaper than an Alaskan one. And, as environmentalists pointed out, a Canadian pipeline completely eliminated the risk of tanker spills.

Yet the Canadian alternative was never really a serious contender. The oil industry was squarely behind an Alaskan system, partly because it left oil transport completely under American corporate control, partly because oil companies wanted the option of selling to Japan (difficult to do with a Midwest terminus), and partly because then Prime Minister Pierre Elliot Trudeau was making nationalization noises in the energy sector. The Interior Department's 1971 draft Environmental Impact Statement barely considered Canadian possibilities, and the final report did not discuss Canadian routes in detail, though it did note "the magnitude and frequency of future seismic events [in Prince William Sound] are qualitatively predicted to be high."

Later, in 1973, the Senate considered a bill, with encouragement from President Richard Nixon, that effectively bypassed the National Environmental Policy Act's requirement for considering environmental impacts and a viable Canadian route. The Senate vote, with two Senators absent, was 49 to 49. Vice-President Spiro Agnew cast the deciding vote, and the House passed it soon thereafter. Any possibility of seriously debating whether the pipeline should have been built in the first place died with Agnew's vote. Construction of the pipeline began in the summer of 1974. The supertankers were already on order.

Outnumbered and outspent, opponents of the pipeline were disposed of as quickly as a dry oil well. There was simply too much money at stake for the project not to come to fruition; there was too much ringing rhetoric of superpatriotism and national security for reasoned and reasonable discussion.

Despite their failure, however, protestors of the pipeline-tanker system could claim the success of forcing a more careful assessment of the environmental effects of the pipeline than would have otherwise been the case. The oil companies, for instance, initially claimed they could bury nearly all the pipeline, thus lending an impression of an undisturbed ecology. It was only after environmentalists pointed out that the hot oil (180 degrees Fahrenheit when it comes out of the ground) passing through the pipeline would melt the tundra, thereby weakening the pipeline's base, that the massive burial plan was dropped. Similarly, the entire Oil Spill Contingency Plan constructed by Alyeska consists of fifteen volumes, twelve of which are devoted to specifying precisely what would happen should a section of the eight-hundred-mile pipeline fail. Although huge sections of the pipeline could be destroyed if a large quake hits, on average the pipeline is a safer mode of transporting oil than are tankers. And although pipeline failures in other places have been the source of major spills, those spills have usually been land-based, making cleanup easier than is the case with oil in the sea. For this reason contingency plans for the Alaskan pipeline are less fantastic than plans for tanker spills.

The main point is that the large-scale political and economic context of oil production shaped oil spill contingency plans in Alaska. That context didn't *cause* a fantasy document, certainly, but constituted an institutional framework in which a fantasy had to be constructed. Had important political and economic forces aligned themselves in slightly different ways, a contingency plan of the Sound and the Gulf would never have been written. Once the trans-Alaskan pipeline and tanker system was in place, however, the dangers of a massive oil spill would need to be handled in some way. That meant, primarily, spending a little more money on spill response equipment and the construction of some certificate of competence that would verify organizations' claims that there was no meaningful danger. Alyeska's fantasy document would serve that purpose well.

MICRO-STRUGGLES

There is another way that power struggles contributed to the creation of Alyeska's contingency plan. Elsewhere I've used the term "disqualification heuristic" to refer to a tendency among experts to neglect ideas and evidence that don't fit their preconceived views about the safety of a sociotechnical system.[5] This mechanism disqualifies bad news and emphasizes good news. The disqualification heuristic in Alaska came from a history of organizational conflict that constricted honest discussion about the danger of oil transport. When government and industry planners started writing the early contingency plans, in the early 1970s, they were supposed to design a system that would work for spills in the small Port of Valdez. That was reasonable enough because the pipeline would terminate there, so oil spills could be expected when vessels were taking on their precious cargo. Such spills, planners assumed, also reasonably, would be fairly frequent but also fairly small. Although it was (and is) certainly possible to have a truly major spill in the Port of Valdez, Alyeska's contingency plan ended up predicting, again reasonably, that "the most likely spill volume for vessels underway in trade with the Valdez Marine Terminal during the expected 30-year operating lifetime of the Marine Terminal is 1,000 barrels."[6]

However, when changes in spill size had to be considered, the old, small-spill assumptions were extrapolated to large ones, even though, as I've explained, qualitative differences exist between small and very large spills. This apparent affinity meant that organizations were planning to use a solution that was appropriate in a particular context, but only superficially relevant to the new problem—large oil spills. The transfer of assumptions—the creation of the apparent affinity—was rooted in the history of conflicts between the Alaska Department of Environmental Conservation (ADEC) and Alyeska.

The history of relations between ADEC and the Coast Guard is one of constrained regulation. Through the 1970s and 1980s, ADEC concentrated on decreasing levels of water pollution in Valdez harbor from the vessels parked there and from Alyeska's ballast water treatment plant. Those were serious enough problems for the town of Valdez, and at times the conflict was intense. "They've spent years trying to get rid of our [lower level] environmental people," said Dan Lawn, once ADEC's district office supervisor in Valdez, of Alyeska. Alyeska's director of public affairs claimed the oil industry was "beleaguered," over-regulated, and that ADEC was a "renegade" agency with vindictive and unreasonable demands.

One area of disagreement between ADEC and Alyeska was over practice drills for oil spills. There was a time when ADEC pushed vigorously for such exercises, even, after a fashion, surprise drills. The last one was described to me in this way by an ecologist with ADEC:

> I think it was '86. We can't really legally throw oil in the water and say come out and clean up the oil. We used oranges. They float and they're visible, and they're biodegradable. Oranges just don't react like oil, but [Alyeska] went through the exercise, basically the motions. . . . But that's the last one we had. They had exercises since, probably one a year, but they weren't what I call surprise exercises. The Coast Guard will hold some, but they are paper exercises. They say there is a 500,000 spill out there, Alyeska, so what are you going to do. But it's all paper. They call up, it's on the phone type of thing. You get in the board room and they plan everything, but no one leaves. It's all done on paper.

That ADEC could wring any concessions at all from the oil industry was probably significant. The power of oil is extremely strong in Alaska. But the focus on paper drills and local pollution precluded attention from being directed at issues such as large spills and major tanker accidents.

The biggest regulatory conflict in Alaska was how much legitimate oversight the Alaska Department of Environmental Conservation could have over the Alyeska Pipeline Service Company, and the oil industry more generally. The industry in fact enjoyed more control than ADEC over the safety of oil transport, narrowing actual regulatory efforts to pollution of Valdez harbor, small spills, and practice drills. While those efforts were important, the structure of the situation was such that major oil spills were neglected by default.

The Alaska Department of Environmental Conservation, Coast Guard, EPA, and other government regulators *could* have required more realistic contingency plans. I think an important reason they did not do so is that the categories of argument between regulators and regulated—especially at the state level—were narrowed so that major oil spills fell outside the legitimate purview of government regulation. The oil industry gained control of the issue of planning for oil dangers. The rules of argument, or conflict, between regulators and regulated were thus organized so that tanker catastrophes were outside the realm of legitimate discussion.

The apparent affinity between small and huge oil spills became a natural way to reason about the dangers of oil. Once oil companies established themselves as the controlling experts of oil dangers, the small-to-huge affinity became the appropriate way to transform unimaginable uncertainty into a more controllable risk.

Federalism on Long Island

Before Three Mile Island the nuclear industry mostly ignored needs for evacuation. The Atomic Energy Commission and the Nuclear Regulatory Commission, its successor, mainly *promoted* rather than regulated nuclear power. Since evacuation plans are a highly visible admission that the chance of catastrophe might indeed be something worth worrying about, it's understandable that they were ignored. This is not to say there weren't plans—there were—but they weren't considered a terribly important part of the regulatory process. Emergency plans prior to Three Mile Island, for instance, weren't reviewed before the issuance of a construction permit but at the issuance of the operating license—a process obviously premised on granting the license and structurally disallowing the possibility that a nuclear plant would fail to make it as a going concern just because people couldn't be evacuated if things went wrong.

After Three Mile Island a utility applying for an operating license had to produce an evacuation plan that would cover ten miles around the plant, an area that became known as the Emergency Planning Zone (EPZ).[7] After Three Mile Island, too, federal regulations said that local and state governments could devise their own plans. But authority for approving an evacuation plan would still rest squarely with the Nuclear Regulatory Commission and not the people who would be directly affected by an accident.

After Three Mile Island, evacuation plans had to classify accidents into four categories, and certain protections were tied to those categories. An Emergency Planning Zone had to be established and a mechanism developed to notify local officials. A plan had to be developed that would allow people to understand the accident and to map the dispersion of any released radiation. These maps would then suggest evacuation strategies. Time estimates for evacuation had to be developed, and there had to be an overarching contingency plan that would drive the evacuation.

Federal agencies, working with industry, would have the final say-so. Still, the effectiveness of the plans rested on the cooperation on local and state governments. They were the ones closest to real people, knowing local cultures and terrains; they were the ones who would have in place, to some degree at least, a social system designed to mobilize people in particular ways. The idea, the hope, was that that social systems could be redesigned to evacuate huge numbers of people, should the worst case come to pass. Besides, propinquity alone would mean that local agencies would respond more quickly if things went bad. And when things go bad with nuclear reactors they can go bad very quickly.

There were many forms of micro-dissent that Shoreham's opponents used. Working within extant institutional systems, local governments availed themselves of a handful of oppositional mechanisms. They couldn't possibly compete with money; with sufficient dollars they could have simply bought Shoreham and closed it down. Instead, they had to work with the hand that the legal-risk system had dealt them. One strategy involved Nassau County, the county adjacent to Suffolk, closer to New York City. LILCO's plan called for using the Nassau Coliseum as an emergency reception center, but Nassau County's board of supervisors refused to allow it. Another example is that some Long Island towns ruled that decontamination trailers, a key part of the plan, would violate local zoning laws. School districts across Long Island also refused to allow their facilities to be designated official reception areas, and the radio station that had previously agreed to serve as an emergency broadcaster pulled out of the deal. There were, thus, myriad small ways that people expressed their grievances.

The really powerful tool available to Shoreham's opponents—thanks to Three Mile Island—revolved around the legal presumption of local participation in emergency planning. They could refuse to participate in the planning process, refuse to ratify a utility's plan, and thereby effectively veto the federal government. This strategy would ultimately work.

It was an unprecedented strategy. Unlike natural disaster response, nuclear power had always been a federal program. If the federal government was behind it, there was little reason to think that any particular nuclear power plant project would fail. LILCO didn't even apply for a building permit until 60 percent of the reactor vessel was built, and $70 million had been spent.[8] In prior cases, such as Indian Point in New York and Diablo Canyon in California, county governments fought utilities, claiming the right to produce their own evacuation plans. In both cases, state governments stepped in to preempt the counties and work directly with federal organizations.

The seeds of dissent over evacuation were planted early on Long Island. In 1970 a local protest group made the claim that population centers would not be protected in the event of a major accident.[9] Still, Suffolk County actually cooperated with LILCO in the construction of a plan until 1981. But popular opposition grew all the while, and was based on concerns about safety, cost, and the competence of the utility. By the summer of 1982 the safety issue would be paramount. At that time Suffolk County financed a survey that showed 25 to 50 percent of people on Long Island would evacuate even if directed not to. Shaken by the image of millions of people not playing follow the leader, the county then developed its own evacuation plan covering a radius of over twenty miles. Local hearings were held and local groups were mobilized, and soon (early 1983) the County Executive was proclaiming the impossibility of evacuating Long Island because of the massive traffic problems involved. "It is impossible to establish emergency preparedness in Suffolk County," he said, "that can protect the public health, safety, and welfare in the event of a serious nuclear accident at Shoreham."[10] Soon thereafter, Governor Cuomo ordered the state not to approve any evacuation plans. By then LILCO had spent three billion dollars.

The money was important because the cost of the plant would eventually be shifted to taxpayers. But there were more subtle issues that were just as important, and highly contentious. One of those issues was the question of who had the authority to say what "major radiation release" meant. McCaffrey reports that "LILCO's consultants estimated that five rems of radiation would be exceeded at ten miles once in 400,000 years. Suffolk County's consultants estimated that five rems would be exceeded at ten miles once in 6,000 years."[11] Obviously such proclamations were not based on empirically based science. The database just isn't there on which to make a study. In the throes of such ambiguity everyone has the potential to become an expert. LILCO was basically saying that a serious radiation release could not happen. Suffolk County, by comparison at least, was nearly projecting catastrophe. The county's worst-case scenario had the plant melt completely and had the winds blowing toward New York City. So the radiation would be headed toward one of the most densely populated areas of the world and would also be blowing over the evacuating people. In the worst of cases, they said, seven thousand people *outside* the EPZ would die.

So there were some fairly serious differences of opinion. And with little respected expertise available that could qualify as an authoritative voice, social conflict was likely to intensify. One place to see clearly how that conflict unfolded is in a series of planning exercises held by LILCO and the federal government.

It is not unusual for emergency plans to be "tested" in pretend ways—fire drills at elementary schools are exactly that. But what, exactly, could testing *mean* for a nuclear power station on Long Island? You can't tell millions of people to leave. You might just hold a tabletop exercise. But Shoreham's supporters needed something more substantial than that. In June 1985 the NRC told FEMA to conduct "as full an exercise . . . as is feasible to test off-site preparedness capabilities" at the Shoreham plant.[12]

The first and most important test, which I described in chapter 2, was conducted in February of 1986. It began at about 7 o'clock in the morning with a small leak, proceeded through a series of other failures to a probable full-core melt, with attendant major radiation release at about 9:30 in the morning. A "general emergency" was declared at 9:40 (after rush hour) and continued through the morning. The 140,000 or so people were evacuated to the Nassau Coliseum, in neighboring Nassau County. LILCO soon announced nearly complete success. Federal officials, mostly from FEMA, were on hand to "evaluate" how well the evacuators did their jobs. It was all in earnest, from one point of view, but all in theater from another.

One important reason for the latter sentiment was that local, county, and state agencies refused to participate. Legal precedent and prevailing political judgment held that evacuation, and even planning for evacuation, was meaningless without local participation. Yet the locals weren't participating. FEMA's official position was that local participation didn't matter, proclaiming in November 1985 that it could, and would, "test" the plan even without local participation.

There were some voices of dissent from within FEMA, as when its regional director said in his final assessment of the exercise that "since the LERO [Local Emergency Response Organization] plan cannot be implemented without State and local participation, FEMA cannot give reasonable assurance under [federal regulation] NUREG-0654 that the public health and safety can be protected."[13]

That regional director was then forced from his job, FEMA's director claiming that it was inappropriate for FEMA to render judgment on "off-site preparedness." Four days after the regional director's "resignation" FEMA judged LERO as capable of responding "effectively to most scenario events."[14]

On 17 April 1986 FEMA issued a very detailed "Post Exercise Assessment."[15] It would give new definition to the word arcane to delve deeply into FEMA's report. In the last chapter I talked about some of the problems of communication, coordination, and foresight in the exercise. Here I want to spend a few pages on one particular issue, because a few issues particularly became the symbolic center of the Shoreham controversy. More to the point, those were discussed in the context of the apparent affinity between commuting and mass, nuclear-inspired evacuation.

I realize that the phrase "discussed in the context of" is terribly vague. But there's a reason for that. I can't specifically tie the apparent affinity in the Shoreham case to particular social interactions. In Alaska, it's clear that the conflict between oil corporations and regulators (and environmental groups to some degree) was behind the equation of small and large spills. With civil defense, I'll show in the next section, conflict between federal agencies and local and state governments gave rise to the equation of natural disasters and nuclear war. But it just wouldn't be accurate to say that the battles between LILCO and the NRC (and others), on one hand, and state and county governments (and others), on the other, specifically led to the creation of an apparent affinity. In part, the idea that mass nuclear evacuation is a known thing was brought into the Shoreham controversy already formulated by the very organizations that pushed nuclear civil defense for so many years (especially the Atomic Energy Commission, forerunner to the Nuclear Regulatory Commission and the Department of Energy, and FEMA). Alas, the world does not always fully obey the categories we use to analyze it.

Still, there is some sense in talking about Shoreham's apparent affinity in the same breath as the conflicts I detail. As I've noted, a huge amount of the Shoreham war was conducted on the courtroom battlefield. Reading even a small part of the testimony used there quickly reveals that the very basis of LILCO's argument was the assertion of a similarity between something that we know about and something that we know almost nothing about. For instance, in some testimony that was prepared to defend LILCO's failures in its February 1986 exercise, two disaster researchers promise that "emergency response organizations are like most other organizations. On both theoretical and applied grounds, organizational behavior in relation to emergencies reflects the findings of research on complex organizations in general."[16]

Similarly, the mainstay of LILCO's rebuttal to charges of impossibility or of vanishingly small probability of effective response (e.g., that LERO was overly complex, that controlling millions of cars was impossible) was always that the experts in natural disasters and in organizational behavior had determined that evacuating Long Island was manageable through studying the things they knew. So it was almost invariably the case that arguments about whether the exercise was a success, or whether LILCO could be trusted, or whether bus drivers would follow the plan, or whether citizens would do as officials advised were simultaneously arguments about whether it was possible to evaluate those things in light of previous experience with natural disasters, commuting, and so on.

A key issue in the controversy over the "test" was the absence of state and local governments. This was an important "limitation" to the exercise because it would have been surreal enough *with* the actors who would surely be key players in the event of an accident. FEMA and LILCO solved the problem in two ways. First, they solved it by acting *as if* they were assisting state and local officials. They appointed FEMA "simulators," pretending they were working with state and local officials. Second, they created the "realism doctrine."

Opponents argued that the exercise and thus the plan were too unrealistic to be meaningful. LILCO, FEMA, and the NRC by contrast argued that it was meaningful by default, asserting that LILCO personnel did everything *they could* to make the exercise realistic and so it was, because of that effort, realistic. In court documents, LILCO lawyers, relying on testimony from NRC staff, emphasized that "there's no NRC requirement" for all elements of a plan to be exercised to qualify for the definition "full participation."[17] Listen to LILCO officials, quoting FEMA documents:

> [FEMA] made every attempt to ensure that preparation for and evaluation of the February 13, 1986 exercise of the LILCO Transition Plan for Shoreham was consistent with the parameters and process established for other full-scale Radiological Emergency Preparedness exercises evaluated by FEMA Region II.[18]

By the logic evident in this statement, that which it was possible to do was sufficient to establish all that should be done. LILCO claimed it had "reasonably achieved" sufficient testing of the emergency plan because where any particular element was not demonstrated, it was due to one of the following reasons:

(1) Mandatory participation by members of the public or non-LERO organizations would have been required.

(2) FEMA had identified the element as being non-essential for this exercise and was not going to instruct their personnel to observe the element.

(3) The political/legal situation on Long Island made the demonstration of an item inadvisable.[19]

The meaning of realism thus became sufficiently narrow that nearly anything LILCO did and nearly anything LILCO ignored was the right and safe thing to do.

Nuclear power has never had much to do with democracy, and federal agencies tried to find other ways to undercut its opposition. In March of 1987 the Nuclear Regulatory Commission argued, bluntly:

> [S]ignificant policy questions of equity and fairness are presented where a utility has substantially completed construction and committed substantial resources to a nuclear plant and then, after it is far too late realistically for the utility to reverse course, the state or local government opposes the plant by non-cooperation in off-site emergency planning. A forced abandonment of a completed nuclear plant for which billions [of] dollars have been invested also poses obvious serious financial consequences to the utility, ratepayers, and taxpayers. Finally, at least in situations where non-cooperation in off-site emergency planning is motivated by safety issues, vesting State or local governments with de

facto veto authority over full-power operation is inconsistent with the fundamental thrust of the Atomic Energy Act
whereby the commission is given exclusive de jure authority
to license nuclear power plants and to impose radiological
safety requirements for their construction and operation.[20]

In other words, especially when it comes to safety, local populations
and groups ought to have only a confirmatory role to play in defining
acceptable risk. They can rubber-stamp, but not, as they say, just say
no.

What to do? The most effective way to win a power struggle is not
to beat your opponents over the head with a stick but to convince them
that their wisest action is to do what you want. An intermediate strategy is to structure the available opportunities for action so that your
opponent has little choice but to act as if they wanted to do what you
want. So the NRC tried to enact what it called "the realism doctrine."
The idea was that in an *actual* emergency state and local governments
would not turn their backs on the tasks that would be necessary to
protect their denizens. The NRC said that "the Commission believes
that State and local governments which have not cooperated in planning will carry out their traditional public health and safety roles and
would therefore respond to an accident. It is reasonable to expect that
this response would follow a comprehensive utility plan."[21]

The Nuclear Regulatory Commission's position was a difficult one.
For one thing, it was claiming that nonfederal definitions of acceptable
risk were strictly politically motivated, while those of federal organizations and experts were value-free and objective reflections of the actual
possibilities of danger. For another thing, it seemed a bit odd to assert
knowledge of realism in such a fantastic situation. Basically, it was
impossible to tell, on grounds of evidence at least, whether *any* position
was theater or reality.

Something more interesting was going on as well. The NRC was
saying that present local behavior could not be used to predict future
local behavior, or more exactly that there was a radical disjuncture, a
nonrelationship if you will, between how local organizations and officials act in a nonemergency compared to how they would act in an
actual one. Yet the NRC and LILCO's *own* case for safety depended
precisely on the same assertion: that it could reliably guess how organizations would respond to unknown untoward future events on the
basis of how they responded, and said they responded, to known un-

toward past events. It was a contradiction that went unexploited by Shoreham's legal and expert opposition, as far as I know.

In any case, the fight on Long Island was obviously over whether or not millions of people could be effectively evacuated by an organization that few trusted. The opportunity to kill Shoreham came from Three Mile Island, which gave entrée to local intervention in what had hitherto been reserved for federal agencies. The case could scarcely be made that sufficiently certain knowledge on how to evacuate was available. But a strong case could be made that organizations knew a lot about getting away from the damage of natural disasters. A strong case could be made that Long Island evacuated five days per week. A strong case could be made that the Long Island Lighting Company had responded to severe naturally caused emergencies. If a nuclear plant meltdown was the same as natural disasters or commuting, then the question of whether Long Islanders could be protected was answered before it was asked.

Local Wisdom and Civil Defense

Responding to natural disasters has for most of American history been a local affair. Mobilizing and paying for disaster response has been left to states, counties, and towns, who in turn have often depended on nonprofit relief organizations. In the 1950s federal agencies started paying more attention, but it was sporadic, prompted by specific incidents rather than based in a continuously running complex of organizations and policies designed for disaster response.[22] In 1979 a slew of civil defense and disaster response agencies were folded into the Federal Emergency Management Agency, centralizing purpose and budget, and signaling the dawn of a new day for disaster planning, and not coincidentally, for civil defense too. Yet the federalist legacy of disaster assistance would remain, one aspect of which was the generally low prestige of state-level disaster programs.[23] Even with the dual-use designation through which Congress authorized funds, FEMA would continue to put civil defense measures at the top of the list of hazards.

Through the years there has been some scholarship and a great deal more official proclamation that the American public has thought nuclear civil defense a wise thing to do. Such statements usually begin with the earnest and high visibility efforts of civil defense organizations. For example, the Federal Civil Defense Agency implemented

Alert America in the summer of 1951. Sociologist Guy Oakes says that "its specific objectives were twofold: to provide to the entire population comprehensive information on civil defense as self-protection, and to persuade some 15 million people to volunteer for training in one of the specialized civil defense services."[24]

Alert America tapped the array of mass media devices, including the production of comics, radio and television programs, and newspaper inserts. In 1952, thirty large trucks "toured the country for nine months. Visiting armories and civic centers in some seventy cities, it was seen by 1.1 million people."[25] And in the mid to late 1950s the civil defense establishment engaged in a series of exercises, part table-top and part actual practice, designed to demonstrate to people that mass mobilization in the cause of evacuation could be reality and to drum up support for the cause. In more recent times the Federal Emergency Management Agency has summarized official thinking on public attitudes and civil defense—saying that "public surveys over a period of twenty years show a very consistent level of public support for civil defense, all kinds of civil defense programs fallout shelters, blast shelters, and evacuation."[26] Indeed, FEMA finds so much support that:

> the public just does not perceive opposition to civil defense.
> . . . If there ever was a question in the minds of the public
> about whether we should have a civil defense program, it
> was resolved in favor of the program during the Berlin crisis
> and has now reached a sort of "ceiling" at which support
> cannot significantly increase. It is not likely that we will ex-
> perience greater support or opposition in the future.[27]

Yet with the exception of two or three short periods in American history, few local or state governments ever really accepted the idea that their communities could be protected in the event of nuclear war. Public rejection of civil defense is quite important for explaining how the apparent affinity between natural and nuclear disasters was created. I'll return to this point.

Inside nuclear circles, two principles of conventional warfare were carried over the nuclear threshold:[28] (1) that nuclear war does not necessarily entail total devastation, because (2) the damage can be limited through civil defense measures and sufficient military strength.[29] During the first roughly fifteen years after Hiroshima, these two notions were well-reflected in declaratory policy.[30] They were, however, mainly ignored by those in charge of nuclear weapons. *Their* working policy was that upon detecting threatening atomic moves by the enemy (chiefly the Soviet Union), the U.S. would strike first in a massive, obliterating attack. In the mid-1950s military planners aimed "for 90 percent probability of inflicting *severe* damage to at least 50 percent of industrial floor space in the urban-industrial targets."[31] Here's a planner explaining what "severe" means:

> Severe damage is the highest category—higher than moderate and light. You could look at it this way: Light means rubble, moderate means gravel, and severe means dust.[32]

Starting with Robert McNamara's influence over nuclear war planning *and* nuclear war diplomacy, and becoming more refined through the 1970s, a shift in declaratory policy brought with it a shift in civil defense planning. The single, massive, preemptive strike was seriously challenged from *within* the nuclear establishment; that challenge then suggested important changes in civil defense. The idea was "flexible response"—there was no reason, it was said, that war fighters *had to assume* that they would have to release the entire arsenal at once.

The key time period, for purposes of understanding the origins of the apparent affinity we're interested in here, was during the 1970s. The National Security Decision Memorandum (NSDM) 242 was signed by President Richard Nixon in 1974 and generated considerable debate within and without political and planning circles. NSDM 242 enhanced nuclear guidance, or doctrine as experts call it, to broaden the range of Soviet targets, and authorized something known as NUWEP (Nuclear Weapons Employment Policy), which Secretary of Defense James Schlesinger signed in April 1974. The NUWEP set targeting objectives and attack options and specified that under all conditions U.S. forces must be able to destroy 70 percent of the Soviet industry necessary for postwar recovery.[33] The new planning increased warhead targets from twenty-five thousand to forty thousand, which naturally meant an upward ratcheting of nuclear weapons.[34]

NSDM 242 also prescribed the notion of "escalation control." The idea was to present National Command Authorities[35] with more options than simply to end hundreds of millions of lives in a wild spasm of radiating annihilation. Rather than overwhelming, immediate retaliation, those with their fingers on the nuclear buttons could be presented a menu of response choices so they could execute their options in a more thoughtful way. Thus did the 1970s see greater rationality infused into plans for Armageddon. Listen to Schlesinger's description:

> In the past, we have had massive preplanned nuclear strikes in which one would be dumping *literally thousands of weapons on the Soviet Union.* . . . With massive strikes of that sort, it would be impossible to ascertain whether the purpose of a strategic strike was limited or not. *It was virtually indistinguishable from an attack on cities.* One would not have had blast damage in the cities, but one would have considerable fallout and the rest of it. So what the change in targeting does is give the President of the United States, whoever he may be, the option of limiting strikes down *to a few weapons.*[36]

Flexible response was lent credibility by increasingly accurate warhead delivery systems. The ability to deliver two warheads to a target (the second would be necessary in case the first was a dud) within roughly one hundred *yards* suggested the idea that once all the important targets were destroyed then the bombing could stop. If the bombing could stop before complete destruction, someone could, after all, win a nuclear war. But to win would still entail having some *people* left to govern. That's where civil defense came in.

The problem was that the public didn't believe the experts. Research for the Survey Research Center at the University of Michigan, from the National Opinion Research Center (NORC), and from the Sociology Department at Oklahoma all showed little support for civil defense, even before the 1970s. In 1951 NORC reported that "general admonitions to the public regarding the course of action to be taken in the event of an explosion, fire, etc., do not appear to be effective in guiding the behavior of persons who are suddenly exposed to the threat of bodily danger." A 1953 Stanford Research Institute summary of a Survey Research Center study echoed that "a recent survey of public reactions to civil defense in the United States has indicated, among other findings, that since 1951 there has been a decrease in public willingness to take part in civil defense activity."[37]

Not only the American public, but local and state governments never really shared the views of federal civil defenders. Local and state governments have never had the political commitment or the fiscal resources to become extensions of federal civil defense efforts. Insofar as local and state governments represent the preferences of their voting constituencies, one might say that the people have not seen their civil defense interests as coterminous with how federal organizations have seen them. Local reluctance has always frustrated federal planners and legislators, who over the years designed many devices to convince lower governmental units to defend themselves civilly.

In a comprehensive review of attitude surveys and other research on the matter, Spencer Weart, historian and physicist, shows that while there have been ups and downs in popular support of civil defense, by and large Americans have never much believed federal proclamations. The 1950s saw an upsurge of interest in popular interest in civil defense, as well as state and local support, after the Federal Civil Defense Administration issued shocking reports, produced movies and traveling slide shows, and planted stories in the national media about the horrors of nuclear attack.[38] They even exploded an atomic bomb in 1953 with the press attending. Later, reporters were allowed to photograph the pieces of mannequins, faux Americans torn asunder by the surrogate Soviet forces. In 1955 federal civil defense officials blew an air raid siren over Oakland, California, for almost ten minutes. The "raid" was completely unannounced. The Survey Research Center at the University of Michigan ran a follow-up survey in the area to get people's reactions.[39] In the Research Center's sample, only 15 percent even had a "first thought" that the raid might be real; only 2 percent did anything at all to "protect self" or "protect others." It is true that schools across the nation had some civil defense training ("duck and cover"). And it is true that especially in the early 1960s, following the Berlin blockade and then the Cuban Missile Crisis, that there was a flurry of activity around civil defense, with calls from various officials and agencies for better planning and more money. But cities, counties, and states did not support it to any significant degree. Weart makes the point that "most had made up their minds to do nothing. . . . Even the RAND strategists and local civil defense officials who worked professionally on fallout shelters usually did not build one for their own families."[40]

The halcyon days for civil defenders were 1962 and 1963. In 1962 Congress at first gave the Kennedy Administration about $87 million of its requested $105 million, then supplemented that amount in the same year with a whopping $207 million; in 1963, the corresponding figures were $113 million (though Kennedy requested $695 million) and $15 million. But most years civil defense appropriations ranged from about $50 million to $70 million, with Congress regularly reducing the amount requested by 40 percent or more.[41] As Gary Kreps— longtime author on disasters—puts it "[Civil defense] and other war-related emergency management programs had static or declining budgets over most of the 30-year period prior to the establishment of FEMA."[42] As Garrett notes:

> [T]he Federal Civil Defense Administration . . . proposed ambitious programs including surveys to identify structures that would provide blast shelter, and proposals for upgrading existing structures on a matching funds basis. These proposals failed to gain Congressional support. Frustrated in its efforts to improve protection against blast and fire in target cities, civil defense turned to evacuation of cities as a low-cost survival alternative.[43]

The interesting case of North Dakota gives life to these generalities. In 1982 the city council of Grand Forks, North Dakota, voted *not* to participate in the North Dakota Civil Defense Crisis Relocation Plan.[44] This was no symbolic protest from leftists, as we might expect from fellow progressives in neighboring Minnesota. At the time of the Council's vote (as now) North Dakota had two air bases and a huge number of nuclear missile silos, and these facilities were not installed over the intense objections of the good people of North Dakota. Those people, especially because of the silos, would be among the first targets to be hit. The city council reasoned that since warheads could rain on Grand Forks in thirty minutes, and since there were so many missile silos, and since even the most militant civil defenders realized that those silos were the *first* thing an enemy targeter would want to hit, that poor Grand Forks stood no chance if the big ‚one came. A city council document explained that "[Our] map indicates the approximate location of the 150 silos just in eastern North Dakota. With two one-megaton explosions per silo, and two for the base itself, it is clear that a vast area of North Dakota would be destroyed, even if every warhead landed exactly on target."

The city council realized that crisis relocation was fantastic, explaining to people that the enormous amount of radiation would prevent meaningful movement, that available fallout sheltering facilities in Grand Forks allocated eight square feet to each person and even that space was poorly ventilated and inadequately supplied. Said the council:

> After carefully examining the evacuation plans proposed by state and Federal Emergency Management officials, the Grand Forks City Council, along with a large number of municipal governments throughout the United States, con-

cluded that such evacuation planning was unrealistic and would, at best, only raise false hopes. The Crisis Relocation plan offered to Grand Forks calls for travel to Jamestown. Jamestown, however, is exposed to the same grave risks as the rest of North Dakota. . . . Although there is some comfort in the busyness of constructing shelters and devising complex plans and systems, that comfort is dangerous. Such activities promote the illusion of protection against nuclear war.

Thus, nuclear civil defenders faced a formidable problem, one that to them was considerably more daunting than that of surviving nuclear war: neither the people nor the governments closest to the people shared their definition of reality. Yet real defense, as well as political expediency, would require considerable commitment from state and local governments, not to mention the people being defended.

In response to this frustrating problem, the idea of dual- or all-hazards planning arose and was given an institutional founding. This institutional mooring allowed war-making organizations to attempt to foist their missions and goals upon local communities and states.

It's not difficult to find references for some conception of all-hazards planning as far back as the early 1950s. Like flexible response, the idea of at once preparing and planning for floods and nuclear catastrophe was not new. One of the fathers of disaster research is E. L. Quarantelli, who helped found the Disaster Research Center, first located at Ohio State in the early 1960s and moved to the University of Delaware in 1985.[45] He notes that the early days of disaster research were dominated, indirectly, by the practical aims of defense needs, with most funding coming from places such as the Army Chemical Center, the Federal Civil Defense Administration, and the Office of Civil Defense Mobilization.[46] The first mention of dual-use thinking happened in 1949 when the Army Chemical Center approached NORC at the University of Chicago, the eventual result of which was a research proposal that said:

> [I]t is felt that empirical study of peacetime disasters will yield knowledge applicable to the understanding and control, not only of peacetime disasters, but also of those which may be anticipated in the event of another war.[47]

Quarantelli notes that the proposal mentions such a dual emphasis several times. Yet it is not until the advent of FEMA that "dual-hazards

planning" becomes a Concept, and one used in the ongoing battle between the federal government on the one hand, and state and local
governments on the other. An idea without an institutional home is
not an idea that matters.

Dual use had the blessing of major civil defense people, including
Defense Secretary James Schlesinger:

> Civil defense readiness generates, as a bonus, an improved
> capability on the part of a State or local government to con-
> duct coordinated operations in the event of peacetime emer-
> gencies. If State and local governments are prepared to deal
> with the worst of all possible situations—a nuclear emer-
> gency—it is a reasonable assumption that these govern-
> ments can handle lesser emergencies . . . effectively and ef-
> ficiently. But should a State or local government turn a blind
> eye to the nuclear attack aspect of civil preparedness, its
> ability to respond to a lesser disaster becomes question-
> able.[48]

Federal incentives to prevent local blindness included "matching
funds to support salaries and administrative costs of State and local
personnel engaged in emergency planning; the national warning and
emergency communications systems; the State and local emergency operating centers; and the national network for emergency public information designed to acquaint officials and the citizens at large on the
steps they should take in an emergency to reduce loss of life and property."[49] Loans, grants, and surplus property also flowed to places willing to engage in civil defense. In early 1972 the Defense Civil Preparedness Agency started throwing resources at states and localities. Staff
specialists, disaster relief, money, construction and maintenance of
emergency operating centers were the main resources, all of which
started to be made available for tornadoes, floods, and hurricanes.
Schlesinger himself notes, for example, that personnel and equipment
were made available to states after Hurricane Agnes in 1972. There are
many other examples.

Dual-hazards planning got renewed life with Jimmy Carter and the
reorganization of the civil defense establishment into FEMA, which
lives today. The Defense Civil Preparedness Agency director in 1979,
in hearings that would result in the death of his organization, said that
the administration's civil defense program would now heavily emphasize crisis relocation and dual-hazards planning "so that whatever capability we are developing could have a peacetime application."[50] Cri-

sis relocation planning was emphasized in the Carter Administration's D-Prime program. The idea was to first put in place relocation programs around "counterforce" areas, to create plans especially for the major metropolitan areas, and to begin micro-plans for thousands of relocating places and host areas. Matching funds for state and local government, of course, would be increased. By the early 1980s FEMA moved from funding local "training and education" at 100 percent to a 50/50 arrangement. But, said FEMA, "the funds must be used primarily for attack preparedness purposes but may be used for emergency preparedness support as well."[51]

Let me now make more explicit the connection between this telescoped history of civil defense and fantasy documents. The plan to win a nuclear war has through the years—especially after weapons delivery systems got more accurate—implied an obligation to "protect" publics with various civil defense schemes. Federal organizations tried to prevail on states and localities to share their definition of this obligation. Yet this effort to diffuse war strategy—which would have nuclearized localities—was thwarted by states and localities at nearly every turn. Some of that local resistance was undoubtedly populist wisdom, to some extent perhaps "experts" and elites became so insulated from seriously contradictory points of view that they started to believe their own fantasies. Whatever the case, there was a serious lack of connection between vision and priority. Local governments and publics were not buying into the game. Some of the resistance undoubtedly sprang from the prosaic, ever-present fiscal squeezes in which state and local governments seem to find themselves.

In any case, we do know that the rhetoric of the federal nuclear establishment shifted from a sharp distinction between nuclear war (and hence civil defense) and other kinds of calamities (and hence disaster rescue), on the one hand, to a merging of these two types of threats. Asserting the apparent affinity between nuclear war and nonwar disasters made preparing civil defense the proper way to prepare for floods and tornadoes. It was the audience's resistance that led to a strong change in the rhetor's utterances. The meaning of symbols (here, civil defense plans) can follow from the interaction between elite interests and popular distrust. Dual-hazards planning normalizes the risk of nuclear disaster by putting it into the same category as a big fire or even a metropolitan rush hour. The affinity smoothes out the rougher edges of annihilation, creating a manageable risk in place of an overwhelming uncertainty.

Power and Rhetoric

Fantasy documents represent a paradox of knowledge. High technology centralizes resources such as capital, technology, and knowledge in production and distribution systems that, most of the time, give us great volumes of high quality goods. Nuclear power and oil production are prime examples; international intelligence and organized crime surveillance are others. The paradox is that the qualities that make such systems high producers also lead them to fold in on themselves. Increasingly beyond the control of those who are best positioned to control them, these systems are almost entirely beyond the reach of outsiders, expert or otherwise. While wisdom and safety are not guaranteed by democracy, in general sociotechnical systems are safer if they are open to scrutiny from without. At the very least, more open systems must have more developed procedures for accountability and this increases the likelihood that their masters can be pushed to admit the limits of their knowledge and control.

In *The Anti-Politics Machine* James Ferguson tells of a rural development project in Lesotho called Thaba-Tseka. It was similar to a thousand other Third World projects, including its failure to achieve official goals. But, Ferguson argues persuasively, "[I]t would be a mistake to make too much" of that failure,[52] because Thaba-Tseka had effects that reached far beyond those intended by the planners. For the planners, increasing agricultural production was the goal, and the only one they would use to judge whether or not they had succeeded. But from a larger view the effect of expanding the government, which was directly attributable to the massive expenditures in the project and how those expenditures were doled out, was certainly an outcome that benefited many groups. More money was spent on infrastructure than would otherwise have been the case, the state was strengthened, and a not insignificant number of people found tangible prosperity in the project. Most important was that the planning process was technologically infused, which entailed a technical language that depoliticized poverty and suffering. A project that had as its official goal the reduction of misery would have been a much greater failure than Thaba-Tseka.

Ferguson emphasizes the unintended consequences of intentions and plans. Though the idea has a long history, much social theory, especially in sociology, has lost the insight that a lot of what happens is in fact unintended. From the various forms of radical theory through psychology and into economics we see enormous amounts of attention and assumption built on intent. Yet it is rarely the case that people sufficiently control their own lives or the environments in which their lives are embedded for intent to tell us much about how society works. Even the most powerful of actors, say bankers with political and military connections, rarely command enough foresight and cunning that we would build explanations for their behavior by asking, "What did they mean to have happen?" We'd likely end up with very bad social theory indeed.

Turning this lesson to the present task, there is little that we can understand about either the production or the consequences of fantasy documents by focusing on the intentions of individual planners or those who direct the planners. We can conclude, we should conclude, that often enough the planners are earnest souls trying the best they can to carry out their assignments. We can say, too, that some of the planners are cynical or even conniving. But what, then, do we have? A deeper understanding, perhaps, of what makes those individuals work as they do, but our understanding of how organizations use the plans isn't similarly deepened. Even less do we understand how organizations create symbols, how they manipulate information without history, or how they seek to control the uncontrollable. Intent, as a category of explanation, is mostly vacuous.

The development of political rhetoric, and the development of plans as forms of rhetoric, occurs in the interactional moments of social conflict. The apparent affinities we are concerned with all arose amidst opposition to elite representations of reality. I doubt that fantasy documents are ever simply produced and then either simply believed or disbelieved by those they are intended to convince. Instead, they emerge piecemeal, by degrees and not fully in the control of those who produce them, out of power struggles between organizations and variously organized publics.

Persuading people, and their local and state government organizations, that nuclear civil defense was feasible required them to cooperate, to share the vision of the experts and bureaucrats, to behave in concert with an externally defined standard of acceptable risk. But people did not cooperate. That resistance gave rise to the apparent affinity of dual-hazards planning.

Persuading people that Long Island could be evacuated swiftly and safely required people to believe that organizations could have a well-developed understanding of psychology and sociology; further, they had to believe that that knowledge would remain valid in an extreme emergency. For without such knowledge LILCO would have to admit that it could not control a massive evacuation. But people did not believe them. That protest would be answered by the apparent affinity that equated commuting with flight from atomic catastrophe.

Persuading people that it was possible to effectively control a massive oil spill demanded that people trust official projections of capabilities, technologies, and knowledge that had never before been demonstrated. But people did not trust them. Out of that distrust came the apparent affinity that small spills on closed waters were the same as big spills on open waters.

We have seen that the audiences for fantasy documents can be the general public, social protest groups, or formal organizations. In all those cases we see that fantasy documents reflect efforts to convince others that what they claim is relevant experience *really is* relevant experience. These interactional moments, these stories of social conflict over the control of futures, these struggles over material resources and cultural symbols, are what give fantasy documents their hue and character. Power and organizational interests are thus indispensable in the development of rhetorics of risk.

Producing Expertise

Colin Gray, long-time contributor to theories and debates about international relations, says of nuclear war something that's apt for all three of the main cases in this book:

> There are no true experts, only specialists, on nuclear war: no one has been there. Knowledge of weapons design and even of nuclear weapon effects (in many instances the knowledge is extrapolative and theoretical—scaled up from very limited test data) is not the same as knowledge of the interaction in combat of two independent wills, either using nuclear weapons or fighting under the shadow of possible or probable nuclear use. . . . War is different from all other conditions.[53]

And yet it did *seem* that there were experts in nuclear civil defense, nuclear evacuation, and major oil spills. Experts were integral players in fashioning the apparent affinities that were so crucial in effecting uncertainty-to-risk transformations. I'm not sure that experts *had* to make the transformations, but they did and probably because technical expertise is highly esteemed in modern society. If you want to convince others that you know what you're doing, and thus should have control over what you would like to control, it's best to appeal to the esoteric knowledge of highly trained shamans. But how do you get technical expertise without benefit of nuclear wars, civilian nuclear evacuations, or successful oil spill response?

The expertise must be manufactured. This process involves two major steps. First is the task of producing esoteric knowledge, or at least the appearance that there are things to be known that only a select few can rightly know. Second is the task of muting competing voices. When the legitimacy of expert status is hotly contested it is more difficult to draw boundaries around esoteric knowledge.

To produce the appearance of expertise is difficult but not impossible. We know that all real experts draw on some body of research, technical documents that contain their esoteric knowledge. But with fantasy documents there is no real research at hand for that purpose. In "research" on nuclear civil defense the main way of creating those documents was the self-referential report. There was a small handful of consulting organizations and research firms that produced simulations and extrapolations. Those simulations and extrapolations were usually made with huge assumptions, the most prominent being that 80 percent of the population would survive. There were almost no data in any of them. They were, indeed, fanciful stories that the contractors told those who had the power to let out contracts.[54] And the research cited in any report was made up of research produced by other, similar contractors. None of the work, probably, could have passed any rigorous review by outsiders. It is from such documents that assumptions of preparation time and evacuation proposals enter the documentary lore, later to become "facts" or "findings" from previous research. They become the micro-fantasies in the larger fantasy documents. Such reports have served the purpose, however, of producing a body of knowledge, a pile of paper, to which subsequent experts can point in an appeal to experiential knowledge.

For Shoreham the main way to manufacture expertise was to appeal to the vast amount of research on natural disasters. Since there *are* bona-fide academic experts in natural disasters, they were available for hire, too. A huge part of the Shoreham saga, as I've indicated, was carried out in courtrooms. So it was important for LILCO to hire professors to argue its case. (Shoreham's opponents hired professors too, and for the same reason. But the opponents did not themselves create a fantasy document, so I'm not concerned with them here.) Professors always refer to and contribute to established stocks of knowledge. As well, they are the very embodiment of expertise. We have a lot of experience, and fairly solid social science, on natural disasters, including the social factors that make them consequential, the immediate organizational and community reactions, and patterns of recovery (or not). By the very act of modeling evacuations (the models don't have to be formal, mathematical models), the professors make the claim that they are predictable, patterned. The models themselves come to have enormous rhetorical value, not because of their specific predictions or even whether they're right. They take on rhetorical value merely by existing, their presence some kind of testimony that the thing being modeled is tractable. After all, credible experts don't model that which they do not understand, do they? And if so, then it is possible to plan them to a degree high enough to ensure their effectiveness.

For major oil spills, networks of experts (on small spills and on environmental regulations) were already in place. As important, there were already in place actual environmental regulations. Those regulations established a set of standards that could be referred to as authoritative knowledge. So people who knew the regulations were the de facto experts. In that way, lawyers, executives, and other bureaucrats—rather than, say, seamen or oil spill response crews—came to proclaim oil spill response as their proper domain.

Muting Other Voices

But there were challenges to the self-created experts. Those challenges were important because they were the source of the particular fantasies proffered by the organizations involved. As well, expertise doesn't function as efficiently as experts and organizations would like it to when there is disagreement over the domain of knowledge to which experts claim exclusive ownership. An expert can't ply her craft if others don't agree with her claim to expert knowledge. As people become increasingly literate about accidents, hazards, and disasters (a common occurrence with local risk disputes), they become increasingly skeptical about the objectivity and disinterestedness of expertise. For legitimacy doesn't automatically follow from expertise. Indeed in the cases of fantasy documents, organizations tried to *first* establish their ownership of the knowledge domain, trying to elicit, along the way, legitimation for those claims. In many areas of modern life what we see is the true creation of expertise, which has the (sometimes unfortunate) side effect of freezing nonexperts out of the decision loop. When lawyers sue you, you have no choice but to engage your own lawyers and put yourself in their hands. They know the rules, they command the law, they are the experts. In the cases presented here, however, that process was reversed: organizations *first* tried to freeze others out of the decision loop, which would have the effect of putting their own experts in control of the fantastic knowledge. Expertise can't function in the midst of seething social conflict. Competing voices must first be muted.

By degrees, in the Shoreham case, LILCO asserted its federally mandated right to choose risks faced by the public. LILCO, and its federal supporters, ultimately failed, obviously, and one of the reasons for that was that it could not establish its experts as the ones with legitimate control over knowledge of risk and danger. Since the nuclear power game was (and is) structured to favor nuclear proponents (those who contest nuclear power are called "intervenors"; even the name suggests unwanted participants in the decision-making process), the only real weapon available to state and local governments was the refusal to participate in emergency preparedness planning and exercises. Key Congresspeople fairly represented the positions of the Nuclear Regulatory Commission, FEMA, and other Shoreham supporters when they said, "[We] do not believe that the State and local government entities should be permitted to veto the operation of commercial nuclear facilities simply by refusing to participate in the preparation, exercise, or implementation of such plans."[55]

The nuclear civil defenders also failed to some degree, although not nearly to the extent that LILCO did. They failed in the sense that state and local governments never really shared the defenders' definition of danger. The main problem was simply that civil defense cost too much money for a long-term and dubious benefit.

But civil defense agencies did enjoy *some* degree of success, and one of the reasons for that was they were able to create expertise. Various organizations through the years claimed jurisdiction over the very idea of knowing how to protect people from massive, unprecedented catastrophe. Opposing voices were dismissed as dilettantish, as not *truly* knowing the issues involved. It would only follow, then, that such contributions would be minor. Consider, for instance, some typical hearings before the House of Representatives' Military Installations and Facilities Subcommittee of the Committee on Armed Services in 1981.[56] All the people on the subcommittee, and all the witnesses save one, were solidly behind the concepts of civil defense and dual-hazards planning. The lone critic, noted physician Irwin Redlener, tried to make the point that "we haven't involved enough people with enough expertise to make the conclusion that the CIA and FEMA seem to feel is a definite conclusion, that trying to evacuate our population center is the way to go." A FEMA official was brought in to comment:

> It's unfortunate that more people do not have the opportunity to study all those questions in depth as we have tried to do in FEMA. I am sure Dr. Redlener does not spend 100 percent of his working time on this subject, nor do I. I would like to point out also that these are not FEMA conclusions. These are conclusion of many, many qualified experts, Federal agencies, private consultant firms, and highly qualified people throughout the United States.

Representative Don Mitchell (of New York) blasts Redlener's "defeatist, naive thinking" and appeals to our sense of patriotism when he says that the Soviets have a civil defense program, so we are at a disadvantage. And, after all, "our *experts* tell us we can survive."[57]

The story of expertise concerning Alaskan oil is a bit different. For in Alaska nearly everyone favored oil development, other than a few environmental groups. The key moment in writing the oil industry's fantasy documents for major oil spills came when Congress effectively bypassed the 1969 National Environmental Policy Act's requirement for considering environmental impacts. Had NEPA been adhered to, the alternative to a pipeline-tanker system—a pipeline from the oil fields through Canada to the Midwest—would have looked considerably more attractive. For political and economic reasons, though, the Canadian alternative was never seriously considered. Also, through the years, as I noted in previous chapters, a few voices in Alaska's Department of Environmental Conservation pressed Alyeska and the oil industry to develop safer oil delivery systems. At critical moments, Alyeska claimed those voices had no authority or meaningful expertise to influence oil development and transport. The muting of opposing voices in Alaska was largely a story of preemption. Compared to the cases of civil defense and Shoreham, there wasn't as much public wrangling over who had a right to proclaim with authority over safety and danger.

Meaningful science, meaningful prediction, and meaningful expertise are predicated on experience, conceptualization, and understanding. Since these attributes are missing when it comes to nuclear war, science and prediction can easily overextend themselves in the service of political commitment and organizational routine. All studies and simulations of how a nuclear war would be carried out—and this applies to all sides of the issue—are premised on assumptions. This is not special; all studies and all arguments need assumptions. The problem with nuclear war planning and civil defense is that the assumptions take on added importance. Beyond that, without any evidence or data directly relevant to the empirical question of nuclear war it is a misnomer for those working in such fields to speak of "conclusions" or "findings." There are none. In fact, "studies" of war planners and post-Armageddon rebuilders are more accurately seen as edicts and parables from high priests of a secular, but nonetheless quite strong, religion.

Once social struggles are settled, or at least mostly settled, an area comes under the symbolic control of an expert, or set of experts. Thereafter, there often arises a cautious acceptance of the experts. It is cautious because of the insider-outsider status that's created when experts interact with nonexperts. It's accepted, more or less, because people do value professional knowledge. Shoreham's opponents learned the lessons of how expertise is created fairly early in the game and thus fought their battles with their own notions of expertise. They developed a network of professors and professional risk assessors who claimed to know that Long Island couldn't be evacuated and that no organization was smart enough to control the massive evacuation that would be required.

Once expertise is established, by which I mean once a set of people or organizations successfully claims jurisdiction over esoteric knowledge, conversations over safety, development, and even justice become cast in technical terms. With expertise, at least in principle, any given question can be addressed in at least apparently factual terms of right and wrong: do we have enough engineering here? Is the structure strong enough? What about the backup systems?

Before expertise is established, though, there are usually social struggles over who has the right to set the terms of discussion. Those struggles tend to become invisible over time, receding into the collective memory so that it appears natural that nuclear experts should know best about the risks of nuclear power, or that oil engineers should know the key issues regarding oil transport, and so on. What gets muted in those processes are different ways of defining the social good. Perhaps it would have been best had oil not been developed at all in Alaska, or perhaps it would have been safer had the Alaskan or federal government or even native Alaskans controlled that development. Perhaps all the money spent trying to convince Americans to support nuclear civil defense would have been better spent on local schools, or on eradicating nuclear weapons in the first place. I'm not saying those alternatives definitely *would* have been better. I don't know that's so. My point is rather that the symbolic apparatus of numbers, of arcane terms, and of debates and arguments that only insiders can understand, all confer surplus capacity to frame who can and who cannot be considered expert. The rhetoric of technical expertise is a dominant one in many major disputes in modern society, and that rhetoric tends to rule out certain kinds of vocabularies. Those vocabularies—of community, democracy, decentralization of decision-making power—are more overtly political than the ones typically employed by technical experts. But they are no less real.

Creating expertise is only partly a matter of making knowledge. It is also a matter of making quiet alternative definitions of knowledge. Experts and expertise are hardly natural phenomena but are socially and politically constructed out of power struggles, clashes of moral vision, and organizational power.

6

Organizations, Symbols, Publics

Planning processes and plans are usually thought of as blueprints for action. Most of the time, they are. But under some circumstances the amount of actual guidance such planning, and plans, can provide is fairly trivial. In those cases, the plans are still useful, but not so much as blueprints for action. Rather they are useful as symbols of expertise and competence. In this way, fantasy documents *do something*—they persuade, they assuage, they insulate.

Organizations are good at solving a lot of problems at one time. At least, they are better at it than other actors such as individuals, groups, or communities. It is true that organizations cause many of our most pressing troubles, but they are also best equipped to gather together resources, divide up tasks, and match resources to tasks in productive ways. Organizations, for all their faults, are smarter than individuals. But organizations are not infinitely smart. The very properties that make them smarter than individuals—their size, their authority, and most of all their ability to splinter problems—also entail limits to intelligence. The same things that make organizations smart also make them dumb. For example, organizations can be structured so that they actually compromise intelligence by promoting what Diane Vaughan, in *The Challenger Launch Decision,* calls "structural secrecy." This is when organizations become so complicated that almost everyone is kept in the dark about what is going on.

Organizations also sometimes tend to push the people who occupy their offices to define problems and solutions in familiar terms, rather than in terms that might actually solve the problem at hand. This means that how organizations see problems and solutions (and thus plans for such) usually develops from routines which themselves develop in response to previously encountered problems. Those routines, those visions, are not always the most appropriate ones to apply to problems. In those cases where the gap between problem and solution becomes quite wide, we see fertile ground for growing fantasy documents.

Fantasy documents tend to arise when there is no meaningful history to draw on in fashioning an appropriate solution to a problem. The basic thing that fantasy documents symbolize is control—control of the untoward, control of danger, control of catastrophes. But before organizations, their experts, and the people at the top who try to direct organizations can claim they are able to control any kind of problem, they must first make the problem into something that *can* be solved.[1] That is, they must transform uncertainties into risks. The uncertainty-to-risk transformation can be quite functional, in the sense that the calculations that effect the transformation are grounded in real knowledge of problems of the same type. But the transformation can also be strategic, the calculations not based so much in knowledge but in the claim to others that it is possible to control the uncontrollable. In such instances it may not be possible to make a real uncertainty-risk transformation but it nevertheless remains important that the calculations *appear* to do so. That's what apparent affinities do.

Most available scholarly and popular literature on disaster response and organizational effectiveness is concerned with making organizations work better, or respond better, or plan better. But much of this book is about how organizations create the categories *in the first place*. As they create those categories they fashion a language with which to speak about uncertainty. The creation of that language, in a sense, creates the very problem to which they will be called upon to respond. I don't want this claim to sound too radical. Nuclear meltdowns aren't socially constructed. They are products of social interaction, certainly, because elites, experts, and organizations created nuclear power, thus creating the very possibility of a meltdown. But my point is different: by making the claim that a civil defense problem is like evacuating a small town or even a large city, risk managers claim that something with which we have absolutely no experience belongs in the same genre as something with which we are quite familiar. The managers are assuming away too many aspects of the problem. By claiming that, after all, Washington, D.C., evacuates within a few hours every day around 5 o'clock in the afternoon, experts are involved in the social construction of danger. The very act of planning is an assertion of expertise, at once a claim to authoritative knowledge about the future and a promise that the organization is sufficiently strong and wise to make that future secure.

Rhetoric and the Public

Plans are a form of language, a way of conveying a message about something. That "thing" might be a claim about what will happen tomorrow (e.g., an appointment book), or it might be a claim by experts that they command superknowledge that enables them to make decisions about a very vague future (e.g., the U.S. Department of Energy's plans to bury high-level radioactive waste safely). Whether trivial or important, instrumental or symbolic, plans, like other forms of language, must be directed at someone else and that someone must understand what is being communicated if the plan is to be more than gibberish. So rhetoric is inherently social because only in interaction can meaning be created.

Fantasy documents are tools of persuasion designed to create the impression of expertise for certain audiences.[2] The rhetorics that organizations use to convince their audiences of certain positions are not randomly chosen. There are both forces from within organizations and pressures from organizations' environments that restrict the range of vocabularies that they will draw on to make a case about some task domain.

Internally, the languages that organizations use are often generated by professionals—professional planners, accountants, managers, risk assessors, etc. While professionals usually know the bounds of their knowledge, professionals are trained to *be experts* about particular domains of knowledge. It's not just that technical knowledge is imparted to professionals in the course of their training but that a posture, a culture, is imparted to them too. This culture of control is quite aggressive in drawing boundaries that say who is in and who is out, and thus in drawing boundaries about power and rights to make decisions. Professional planners and managers make choices about important matters—that is their ideology and mandate, and the main justification for doing what they do. It is just not in the nature of professional managers to abjure difficult, even impossible, choices.

This is so even though managers and organizations often enough avoid responsibility for some problems. Sometimes, for instance, lawyers will advise managers *not* to transform some uncertainty into risk. They do this to avoid legal assertions of responsibility, as when tobacco executives said they had no evidence that cigarettes were dangerous. That managers are sometimes actively ignorant does not mean they shy away from making hard choices.

Professional training and socialization are important in understanding the rhetoric and languages used in fashioning and selling fantasy documents. But there are equally strong pressures on organizations to talk a certain way that emanate from outside organizations, in their environments. *Environment* is not a concept you see much in the scholarly literature on rhetoric. In sociology it refers to the larger contexts of behavior. It refers, especially, to other actors outside an organization that might be important for that organization's functioning: competitors, regulatory agencies, social movement organizations, and so on. In writings on rhetoric, though, the closest one comes to this idea is the notion of *audience.* Yet the relationship between speaker and audience has rarely been addressed in any thorough way.[3] Thinking about that relationship suggests that some nontrivial part of the character of fantasy documents corresponds to the structure of an organization's environment. Rhetors construct their sales pitches so they'll be relevant to actors in the environment. This leads them to adopt categories of language, and in particular apparent affinities, that draw from languages of other groups. You don't talk about justice and social welfare if the other key components of your audience are defense organizations, courts, and foreign spy agencies. The relationship between the organization that creates a fantasy document and the audiences to whom the fantasies are addressed shapes the character of the document that's produced.

And it matters how people actually tell their tales. Famed and controversial economist Donald McCloskey speaks of "implied" audiences in the field of economics, and argues that what the rhetor *thinks* is the audience determines the rhetorical tool that will be used.[4] More concretely, economists can talk about their subjects in terms of mathematics or abstract curves or statistics that presumably represent behavior. Or, they can talk of the same things as matters of trust, or they can use fables and parables to illustrate their concepts. But most economists don't think that trust and fables are legitimate ways to talk about their subject and so an author would appear quite foolish to submit a paper for publication in, say, the *American Economic Review* that relied on them. Or, negatively, consider the case of EPA and the state health department scientists at Love Canal. Those scientists were sent to argue to nonexperts that the probability of real danger was quite low. They were put on a stage in an auditorium filled with angry parents and denizens. Being on stage asserts a position of privilege and superiority about risk and danger. They prepared technical presentations with detail about issues of considerable significance to *them*, and not their audience. To paraphrase but not misrepresent what happened, the experts said "There's not much to worry about. Trust us, we know best because we're smarter than you are about these things." Both things were probably true. But the point is that such a message did more than just fall on ears deafened by sounds of coughing children and gurgling ooze seeping up in people's backyards (more valid indicators of trouble, to the parents, than anything in the scientific arsenal). Adopting such a rhetoric helped drive a wedge between scientists (and the organizations they worked for) and the public they were supposed to protect.

Scholars of rhetoric call this "constitutive," by which they mean that the words make the situation.[5] That's an overstatement, because it implies that if people but talked in different ways their relationships would change. That may be true in extreme situations—think of an American and a Russian trying to communicate—but most situations aren't extreme. Still the idea is useful because it directs our attention to the environment. As planners, elites, and others who make claims of expertise say their words, they help to create the very audiences they have in mind. This is like business scholar Karl Weick's notion of enactment in which actors think and behave in ways that make their ideas come to be reality. Thus the *idea* of the audience, constructed by the speaker, becomes important in shaping how something is defined.

That organizational planning is often isomorphic with properties of the environment does not mean that "people" or "the public" get what they want. Planners for nuclear war and evacuations didn't direct their plans at some amorphous public. Opinions of the public are largely organized by other, more powerful actors. In fact, there is no "public" if by that term is implied some force that represents nonpowerful, nonconnected people who somehow influence what organizations do, what leaders think, and what experts say. Rather than the public, it is usually other organizations to whom these organizations (and their experts) are mainly accountable and so it is other organizations toward which action, including planning, is directed.

As a civil defense planning organization makes increasingly refined plans it permits *other* organizations to plan things they want to accomplish more carefully. As oil companies claim on paper that they can manipulate huge quantities of oil, or as the claim is made that Long Island can be safely evacuated, regulatory organizations get what they need to say that the public interest is protected. This is one way that planning is outward looking, interactive, and highly organizational.

The main audiences for the fantasy documents I've considered are as follows:

Catastrophe by Organization Type

Oil Spills	Nuclear Evacuations	Civil Defense
regulators	*courts*	*local and state government agencies*

In the main cases I've examined here the public has been important in the breach, once organizations, for a plethora of reasons, broke open the issue for wider inspection. Organizations created the danger, and organizations challenged those who created the danger. It is Organizations that made the plans, and that lost or won the battle to define "the problem" in one way rather than another. The story of fantasy documents is largely the story of organizations.

Why Do They Do It?

But why would they do it? Why are these otherwise generally intelligent people willing to tolerate such a massive disconnect between what they say and what they can know or do? One possibility is that they are lying. If fantasy documents are simply lies, the answer to the question "Why do they do it?" will be quite different than if they are not.

THE QUESTION OF DECEPTION

Lying is not rare. In the Vietnam War U.S. defense officials repeatedly claimed the war was winnable and that in fact the U.S. was winning, knowing for quite some time that neither was true. For forty years nearly four hundred black men were told by prestigious U.S. government officials, physicians, and nurses that their syphilis was untreatable—Bad Blood they called it, using a colloquial term familiar to poor blacks in the South. Even with the advent of penicillin *and* knowledge of how syphilis ran its course, the men (and their families) were lied to by the very organizations charged with protecting them. In the 1950s the Atomic Energy Commission, shouldering the impossible responsibilities of both developing and regulating nuclear power, systematically lied about the dangers of nuclear testing. During the presidential campaign of 1964 Lyndon Johnson lied to the American public.[6] He knew Americans didn't want to go to war in Vietnam and he led them to believe that he would prevent it, yet all along he was making plans to escalate bombing campaigns. He had the knowledge, and the requisite deceptive skills, to shape public discussion (or nondiscussion) of peace. After the meltdown of Chernobyl, Soviet officials failed to convey to the world early enough the magnitude of the disaster (lying by omission) and tried to create the impression that the situation was under control. The 1980s saw loud talk of "supply side" rhetoric, which concealed business interests and shaped political argument about economic possibilities and government responsibilities.[7] Deliberate lies are important, and we need more journalistic exposés and more academic treatment of them.

But lies are of a different genre than most fantasy documents. With deliberate deception the deceivers command information sufficient to know they are lying. The basis of fantasy documents is not knowledge but lack of knowledge. To deceive deliberately requires a degree of cunning and a command of information that is not in evidence in the cases reviewed here. The logic of my argument, moreover, goes against the deception thesis: the organizations don't know enough to create effective plans, so how could they know enough to lie and cover up?

Fantasy documents, however, usually *are* deceptive in their *effects*. This makes them even more dangerous than outright lies. All you need to rebut lies are knowledge and the wherewithal (e.g., money, opportunity, political clout) to argue with the deceiver. Fantasies are more elusive than that. They are harder to combat. And their production is more complex. Fantasy planning is more than ruse, more than a shell game in which the handler of the shells, a practiced trickster and deliberate deceiver, separates fools from their money. The deception theory holds that planners and organizational masters are fully rational, decidedly cunning, and completely in control of organizations. But leaders are rarely that competent.

To deceive deliberately is to try to convince others to accept a definition of reality that you do not yourself share. Fantasy documents are attempts to create a reality that all will share. I once spoke at an invitation-only Louisiana Governor's Oil Spill Conference. The audience was equal parts oil industry representatives and environmental regulators. My message was similar to what I've said here about responding to large oil spills: it can't be done so let's stop pretending that it can. I think it was an important message to deliver, but it went over like a lead balloon. Later, outside the building and well away from anyone else, a representative from the American Petroleum Industry (which represents oil and gas companies to the public) said to me in a hushed tone: "Those were very provocative remarks you made this morning, and although I don't agree with your political tone, you're probably right." He continued, "I'm not sure that political arrangements around oil would change if everyone agreed with you, but the discussion would probably be more honest." I explained to him that I thought a more honest discussion would benefit everyone involved, including the industry. His reply: "But we're about to spend 800 million dollars on a national spill response system, so we kind of have to believe it will do some good." Earlier at that same conference, an official from New York's Department of Environmental Conservation looked me in the eye and, dripping with sarcasm, informed me that "[w]e don't need anyone telling us we shouldn't be doing contingency planning." I thought it was precisely the regulators who needed to hear the message, because they were the ones representing themselves as the oil industry's watchdog. Be that as it may, the remarks from both people are fascinating (sans the sarcasm). They do not suggest a pack of liars but more prosaically just people with jobs to do. Their job was to create a reality in which everyone would act as if contingency plans for major oil spills were meaningful representations of organizational capabilities. Believing in the plans was part of believing in their jobs. Believing otherwise was out of the question.

Yet this judgment must be qualified. Fantasy documents lead organizations to believe their own constructions of reality, ignoring or neglecting experience that may contradict those representations. In fact, fantasy documents generally are not wholly disbelieved, since they are not cynical attempts to deceive. Some plans were in place, but none of the following were believed to be credible possibilities: Three Mile Island, Chernobyl, Bhopal, the *Challenger,* and *Exxon Valdez.* But neither can fantasy documents be wholly believed, as the extreme improbability of the events they claim to cover precludes the certainty required for true belief. Fantasy planning proffers a quite unrealistic view or model of organizations. The model entails the fantasy that everything will work right the first time, that every contingency is known and prepared for. When LILCO created its emergency organization—Local Emergency Response Organization, LERO—it created an organization that was even more complex and bureaucratic than its own organization, and expected it to work. The plans, buttressed by many experts, including the Federal Emergency Management Agency and the Department of Energy, allowed leaders to make bold promises that their organization could control a massive evacuation.

Pondering the inner thoughts of the planners leads us down the wrong road. At the end of that road is only a morass of ideology, imputed motives, and confusing ideas. Do they mean to lie? What are they really trying to do? What do they think is so important that they would build these elaborate facades with nothing behind them? And so on. How in the world would we decide such things? We could conduct hundreds or thousands of psychoanalytic-type interviews trying to delve deeply into the motivations of planners. Perhaps we would discover some deep-seated psychological urge to plan. "Aha!," we exclaim, "we have finally got to the root of the urge to control the uncontrollable."

Such a project wouldn't tell us much about how organizations work. It might tell us about the individuals' lives but nothing whatever about the important questions. The theory of planning-as-deception attributes to individuals more control than they usually have. In spite of the claims of some leaders, in spite of popular beliefs, and in spite of the understandable urge to assign responsibility, the fact is that the world is too complex, and organizations too recalcitrant, for even the most cunning of individuals to control them. The problem with conspiracy theories is not that conspiracies do not happen but that individuals rarely command sufficient resources to make them happen.

If there is little we can say, or wish to say, about the intentions and abilities of individuals, there is still much to say about how and why organizations construct fantasy documents. There is also much to say about the effects of those fantasies.

PSYCHOLOGICAL NEED AND PATHOLOGY

One answer to the question "Why do they do it?" revolves around individual psychology. Perhaps there's some deep-seated psychological need in the modern mind that makes it revolt against ambiguity and uncertainty. Or maybe we're just crazy. Robert Jay Lifton, noted psychiatrist and frequent political commentator, advanced this theory in some 1982 congressional hearings on civil defense and limited nuclear war.[8] He was testifying about possibilities of nuclear war civil defense when he said,

> [P]olitical and military leaders have great difficulty in accepting an inability to control or limit a situation. . . . They therefore evolve, and the rest of us share, the illusion of limit and control, though that actuality—that possibility—is not

there. Out of that illusion of limit and control evolve the endless scenarios of limited nuclear war.

Lifton (and others echoed him) added that thinking that nuclear war could be limited, or controlled, was quite probably psychotic. He referred to notions of preparation and evacuation as "paranoid delusion."[9] Psychiatrist Jeffrey Klugman added that it is fine to plan for natural disasters like floods or tornadoes, and it's even fine to plan for unnatural disasters like power plant accidents, but to plan for nuclear war is tantamount to fostering a psychotic denial in our citizenry and our government.[10] "Civil defense," he said with no hint of ambiguity,

> is a psychological defense. Its most important function is to contribute to the system of belief that allows most citizens, including public officials, to deny the realities of nuclear war, and to avoid the anxiety of thinking about the deaths of ourselves and our families, the destruction of our Nation and of our civilization, the possibility of extinction of humanity, and even the possibility of the end of all life.[11]

But psychological explanations of big institutional problems fail us at crucial points, though it's hard not to share Lifton and Klugman's moral outrage. The psychological-need theory too easily maps properties onto organizations that belong only to individuals. There are too many networks, too much power, too much social interaction in formal organizations for there to be a simple correspondence between them and individuals. Even if we put every individual in an organization on the therapist's couch and subjected each of them to a full psychological workup, which would undoubtedly convert them to the Lifton-Klugman view, we still wouldn't have a good theory of how an organization works. The theory says that leaders who lack a compulsion to control would act differently were they put in high decision-making positions. But imagine a CEO of Exxon, who lacked this little piece of psychosis, saying out loud that his company couldn't respond productively to a humongous oil spill. It wouldn't work. There are too many other forces impelling assertions of control, forces that originate in organizations. Organizations are just too powerful in modern society for individualistic analysis to tell us much about how they operate.

POLITICAL PALLIATIVE

Another answer to the question "Why do they do it?" makes a lot more sense than a psychological one. This view recognizes the symbolic nature of fantasy documents and would see such planning, and indeed large amounts of official behavior, as a political palliative.

Probably the key thinker about symbolic politics has been political theorist Murray Edelman, whose books and articles through many years have made major contributions to how we think about how political policies are formulated and how they operate. The main idea here is that the chasm between what officials do and what they say comes from their need or desire to protect their interests, shielding what they are really up to from outside scrutiny. The policies and plans may fail, or make no difference at all, but the words are palliative because they offer the public soothing solutions to difficult problems. "Symbolic reassurance," says Edelman, "of most of the population encourages a quiescent stand in the face of problems and grievances that might otherwise invite resistance."[12] In *The Symbolic Uses of Politics* Professor Edelman tells us that "through language a group can not only achieve an immediate result but also win the acquiescence of those whose lasting support is needed."[13] Official language is the main focus of this work, and the key task is to decode the political interests that are hidden by words.

By the time Edelman wrote the sequel to *Symbolic Uses* he had become even more concerned with language as the key collection of symbols used in political struggles. The sequel is entitled *Constructing the Political Spectacle*, and in it Edelman says that "[P]olitical language discloses the realm of the ambiguous and the domain in which rationalizations of self-interest become the definition of the 'public interest.' "[14] Edelman seems to mean that the words and kind of language that people use to persuade others reflect social conflict. The argument seems correct, to me, about two things. It is right to claim that national-level actors nearly always wrap "the national interest" around self-interest. It is certainly helpful to analyze patterns of language use among powerful elites, and to speculate about the interests such patterns might reveal. The argument is also right to direct our attention to potentially strong connections between rhetoric and power. In all the cases I've talked about in this book, "national interest" is a phrase that elites often use to convince others that everyone is in the same political boat.

Nils Brunsson has a somewhat different explanation for the frequent lack of connection between organizational talk and action, though it resonates with Edelman's perspective. In this view, plans and policies solve problems but not necessarily the problems they claim to address. This would be true of Edelman too, where the problem being solved is that of public scrutiny and real democracy (troublesome concerns for elites). Brunsson's telling is different in his claim that plans and policies regarding high uncertainty resolve *competing* demands. He argues that "insoluble problems are a splendid vehicle for the reflection of many ideas and values."[15]

Brunsson's typology of organizations identifies "action" organizations where "talk and decisions are instruments for coordinating action which leads to products." In "political" organizations, though, pressures from an organization's environment create inconsistencies which push leaders to "talk in a way that satisfies one demand, to decide in a way that satisfies another, and to supply products in a way that satisfies a third."[16] Political organizations are particularly "eager to reflect ideas on a widening range of topics."[17]

In other words, action organizations actually produce useful things but political organizations produce rhetoric, in response to outside pressures. Political organizations are indeed the organization of hypocrisy. "Hypocrisy," Brunsson says, "may be the answer to the problem of the inconsistent norms which face the organization."[18] Decoupling action from decision is thus a solution, not a problem. It is a solution in the sense that it secures and maintains "external legitimacy and support in an environment where inconsistent norms obtain."[19]

The insights from these authors, and others inspired by them, highlight important aspects of political action and decision that are otherwise easily missed. Symbolism and language are key parts of all social life, and there's no good reason to ignore how they work in the political realm. The way Edelman focuses on whom the audience is for official talk, including plans, is a much-needed, interactive corrective to a lot of political thought that presumes one-way communication. And both authors lead us to look for powerful interests in the languages that elites and organizations use to justify what they do.

The problem with such explanations is that they don't sufficiently distinguish function from cause. Civil defense certainly does fit with the war-fighting ideology, the idea that waging and winning nuclear war is a meaningful topic to talk about. But I find it exceedingly difficult to square the image of a fairly large collection of political and military elites conspiring effectively to dupe the public with what countless studies and exposés have taught us: controlling massive bureaucracies is beyond the political skill and cognitive abilities of any one or collection of people. There's just not enough competence at the highest levels of government to pull it off.

There are problems specific to each theory, too, that limit their applicability to fantasy documents. The main problem with Brunsson's theory is there is too much environment. The main problem with Edelman's theory is there is too little organization. Brunsson's "political organizations" seem constantly buffeted by pressures from without, apparently spending nearly all their energies responding to those pressures. The environment demands, the organization responds. There isn't enough of what Karl Weick calls "enactment," the process whereby organizations actively manage their own realities.[20]

There are no organizations in Edelman's palliative politics, and, more generally, there's too much emphasis on language in the theory. There are also no professional experts. There are, instead, only elites whose interests are served when the public is disenfranchised. One reason organizations are important is that they make elite positions possible in the first place. The interests, influence, and information available to elites do not become disconnected from the organization that produced their positions, so analyses of key actions that neglect organizations leave out the context of power. As well, experts are professionals of varying stripes and we know that they often have distinctive outlooks on how the world works. In the cases here, organizational forces, and professional outlooks, have been crucial in shaping how problems are conceived and how plans have been constructed.

The palliative politics theory has a black box problem, in which the inputs and outputs are clear but the mechanisms of production are vague. On the input side of the box are the political interests of the powerful, and on the output side are the words they use to hide those interests. But organizations and experts occupy the box in the middle and to miss them is to miss how fantasy documents are made. Yet there is no obvious reason organizations and professions *couldn't* be part of such a theory.

The larger problem is the overvaluing of language. By arguing that the public is "in touch" with political choices "only through the symbols that engage it," Edelman implies that those who really are in touch do *not* deal in symbols. The problem with concentrating so strongly on language is that doing so leaves us bereft of an answer to the question "Where do these symbols come from?" Answering that question demands that we look to the histories of social conflict that are back of the production of fantasy documents.

This is a larger problem in much of social theory. Talk about *talk,* the analysis of rhetoric, discourse about symbols, and theories of lan-

guage too often become unmoored from social life. The basic insight
of the sociology of knowledge—that there are connections between
ideas and structural positions—seems to get lost when people write
about talk and symbols. Perhaps the lure of dissecting forms of speech
and communication becomes too distracting; or perhaps the task of
specifying the connections between social structure and ideas becomes
too daunting. Yet to fail to attend to such connections, however banal,
is to grant undue efficacy to fruitless reifications. Words, ideas, language, and symbols certainly constrain thought and shape terms of
debate but they do not themselves act. Language does not itself command power and establish dominion over things and people. To lose
the actor in social analysis is to lose the point; to focus on symbols,
rhetoric, and such *in and of themselves* is to relinquish any meaningful
claim to knowledge about why social action happens. When social theory entirely neglects organizational actors—at least in most political
dramas in the modern day—it does worse than miss the point, because
it renders rhetorical analysis into mere mental provocation, curious
perhaps but of limited capacity to say much about how the world
works. Since words don't act, saying that they do leads to explanations
of behavior that attribute motive and meaning to that which cannot
have it. Neglecting the social structures in which language and lives
are embedded rules out, by fiat, fundamental forces of modern society.

In the end, we are left with no way to adjudicate between multiple
realities; to say that things are what they are *merely* because of how
they are or are not *named* is to carry social constructionism into places
it doesn't belong. You can call a peanut butter and jelly sandwich Eggs
Benedict all day long and it won't change a thing. You could define a
peanut butter and jelly sandwich as gourmet food or as some taboo-
ridden evil substance, or you could *rename* it Eggs Benedict, but the
thing is still on the table and it still looks and tastes just as it did before
your mental experiment. Failing to recognize the limits of social constructionism and symbolic analysis empties them of analytic concision
and theoretic utility.

Managerial Imperative

The Environment

For quite some time, scholars have been working on the myriad ways
that organizational environments set limits on what organizations, and
managers, can do. This point is often neglected or ignored altogether

by popular management books that insist on the primacy of sagacious and clever leaders. In the main cases I've talked about here, environmental factors certainly played, and continue to play, important roles in pushing organizations to create fantasy documents. For big oil spills, atomic energy evacuation, and nuclear civil defense there have always been a complex of organizational and political forces demanding that something be done.

The only thing that oil companies fear more than nationalization of their assets in non-U.S. countries is regulators. So when EPA, state departments of environment conservation, or other such organizations declare publicly their expectations that there must be plans and resources in place to respond effectively to a major spill, the oil companies tend to comply. They often do so unwillingly, complaining about their woefully over-regulated status, but eventually they deliver what is expected of them. In Alaska, we saw how Exxon and its brethren fought tooth and nail first not to prepare a contingency plan and then not to prepare a worst-case scenario and a plan for that scenario.

These regulators, incidentally, are what corporate representatives mean when they talk about the "demanding public." There is in fact no demanding public if by that is meant the everyday person-in-the-street somehow forcing executives to accede to their unreasonable expectations.

Regulators, too, figured prominently in the story of the great evacuators of Long Island. But there state-level political organizations were also quite hostile to LILCO, the Nuclear Regulatory Commission, and the Federal Emergency Management Agency. Although formally regulators, the NRC and FEMA were usually very strong supporters of the nuclear industry. But unlike the oil industry's situation, there were indeed well-organized groups of Long Islanders who belonged to local protest groups that clamored for better planning; their expectations were destined to close down the Shoreham power station. Once state- and county-level politicians saw how much popular criticism there was on Long Island, and that it was fairly well organized, they threw their political organizations into the fray. One might also add the major banks and insurance companies to this list of organizations toward whom LILCO was directing its fantasies.[21]

Identifying the relevant environment for civil defenders is a bit more difficult, partly because responsibility for nuclear civil defense passed through many organizations after World War II. Difficult but not impossible. Declaratory nuclear policies were meant to persuade both

American and foreign audiences that nuclear elites both controlled the nuclear weapons and fully understood the technologies at their disposal. Behind the rhetorics of official policy stood an industry—a set of organizations concerned with producing a certain type of product—that was largely obscured from public view. This is not to say that the translucent curtain pulled in front of nuclear war planning was the result of a cunning conspiracy. It would be ludicrous to think that a cabal could control so much over so long a period of time. Nevertheless, the fact is that the policy arguments and political talk about nuclear weapons and nuclear warfighting were carried on in one way, while nuclear war planning was carried on in quite another. Specifically, the war makers always planned to strike first and strike hard, while most of the official talk has been that an American nuclear launch would only be retaliatory.

Nonetheless, Soviet, and later Chinese, nuclear war–making organizations were major audiences for America's *war plans.* At home, local and state governments would become the major audiences for America's *civil defense plans.* The aim, beginning especially in the early 1970s, was to convince those organizations that they should invest resources in plans that federal agencies would create. As I said, state and local governments never really got on board, but that's not the point. The point is that civil defense contingency plans were targeted toward various, organizational, parts of the planners' environment.

This book's main cases have several characteristics in common, and I would expect to find these characteristics in other instances of fantastic claims of controlling the uncontrollable. First, the environments were very relevant to the planning organizations and thus to some nontrivial degree the character of the fantasies was determined outside the planning organization. This is important because—and this is the second common characteristic—the environments toward which the planning organizations were oriented were comprised of other organizations. Organization theorists speak of "isomorphism," by which they mean that organizations tend to look alike. Indeed one of my messages is that the way rhetorics of public, political life are constructed emerges from organizations taking each other's needs and concerns into account. This side-glancing helps produce organizational isomorphism. There isn't much space for people not connected to and served by powerful organizations to have their interests reflected in those rhetorics. Finally, by looking to organizations' environments we see that all the cases share the attribute that their plans result from (sometimes intense) social conflict. In part, fantasy documents originate in power struggles between organizations.

Professions

Scholars have trouble figuring out how best to think of the question "Who controls organizations?" Some approaches hold that leaders matter a great deal, that in fact they have sufficient cognitive capacity, and power, to steer organizations as an airline pilot would direct an aircraft. Such ideas are received most warmly in business schools and radical conspiracy theories. Other approaches deny much efficacy to leaders at all, in effect flattening organizations as if all positions were interchangeable. Those ideas are at home mostly in sociology departments.

There is a middle way, more reasonable for its complexity if less soothing in its political message. This is a view that sees organizations as things that leaders *try* to control and direct and for their efforts they often succeed. But they are often not successful, for two main reasons. First, leaders do not usually have the cognitive capacity to know all that their organizations are doing, an idea stressed a long time ago by Herbert Simon but one that has been incorporated into only a small handful of theories.[22] Second, leaders often do *not* command sufficient power (or authority) to effectively control organizations. Instead, sheer routine, or the power of internal interest groups, or even the influence of outsiders, circumvents leaders' commands, or shapes those commands so that they conform to pre-existing norms. Organizations, indeed, are less like jets that respond to pilots' commands than they are like hot air balloons that pilots gently nudge in one general direction or another, depending on what the weather will allow. The weather—or environment, as organizational scholars call it—is often inclement or even hostile, which has important implications for leaders' abilities to lead and direct.

The idea that leaders nudge heavy objects in hostile environments suggests some observations that help explain why elites construct and promote fantasy documents. There is an imperative of action attached to managerial positions: if leaders do not convince others that they are leading, or trying to lead, their environments are likely to select them out. Leaders don't always have to *actually* lead, if by lead we mean construct a coherent vision for an organization, infuse employees with enthusiasm for that vision, and then push the organization, wisely, deliberately, in a good direction. But others do have to think that they lead; otherwise attacks and assaults from those within and without the organization will almost certainly lead to a fall from grace, or at least from the top of the organization.[23]

So it would be wrong to say that the environment is fully responsible for the production of fantasy documents. If popular management books tend to neglect the environment, a large part of social science neglects individuals. Individuals did matter in my main cases—as occupants of professional positions. Specifically, *managers* matter a great deal in creating fantasy documents.

FAILURE IS NORMAL   If you spend any time at all reading about organizational failures you start to see how utterly prosaic such things are. We mostly take for granted that everyday, run of the mill organizational life is mundane, barely worth comment because it is, well, boring. That's one reason so much writing on the sociology of organizations is uninteresting—it's about the unremarkable, the routine, the normal. But when it comes to breakdowns and disasters, or potential breakdowns and disasters, it's almost natural to think that they're outside the realm of usual organizational life. They are, after all, *accidents*. Their specialness leads us to make special theories for them.

The problem is that failure and accidents aren't special. In fact, it is normal for organizations to fail. Universities don't educate. Churches don't save souls. Hospitals cause illness. Banks go bankrupt. Police departments become corrupt. If failure and disaster are normal rather than aberrant then there's little reason to search for distinctive properties of organizations in failure. We should, instead, look to the same properties that make organizations so effective so much of the time: their capacity for splitting problems, for flattening individual characteristics, their conformity to the demands of their environments, their ability to create their own environments.

Plans do a number of things for managers. Plans are, at bottom, a set of promises to others about what managers can control, and what the future will be, which good managers are supposed to be able to foresee. Thus organizations always have a stake in establishing their competence—i.e., creating or eliciting legitimacy—for controlling the future. Plans, or the act of planning, thus become a rhetorical sign of competence. Civil defense was a talisman, a rabbit's foot. LILCO's evacuation plan was a worry stone, a sign that trouble was contained.

Oil spill contingency plans are a protective shield, a proclamation that the managers are on the job and fulfilling their responsibilities.

When there's no history to draw upon to gauge what kinds of actions would be recognizable as leadership, and if thus there's no practicable way to tell whether managers are indeed managing, then what? Faced with such massive uncertainty about what they're supposed to do, leaders turn to something they *do* know well. One such thing is the kind of training people receive, whether formal training as in disciplinary schooling or informal as in the historical accumulation of on the job training. This seems to account for why, throughout the Cold War, high-level military officers were far more likely than civilians to advocate preventive nuclear war against the Soviet Union.[24]

WHAT RISK MEANS TO MANAGERS   One of the mainstays of managerial training is a bias against the notion of an insurmountable obstacle. Imagine the following scenario, which is not fanciful—I was there. At a meeting of chemical process engineers—people responsible for conceiving and managing safety operations for chemical manufacturing plans—there arises the question "What are the mechanisms through which production pressures are exerted on people?" The real-life scenario is described in which the CEO orders an increase in production. The responsibility for meeting the CEO's goal and ensuring that it is met *safely* falls to the area manager. The area manager is constantly short of money and is being squeezed at every turn for cost savings and increases in profit rates. What does the area manager say? The most likely response, all the process engineers agree, is "can do." It would barely occur to them, or the area manager, to say otherwise.

To managers, "risk" means something quite different from what it means to most people, or to classical decision theory. To managers, risk is not simply a calculated probability that will be coolly decided on. It is instead an opportunity to *do something*. Indeed for managers a key risk is the risk of failing to manage.

A bit of uncertainty, in the sense that I've defined it, is present in managerial choice, but managers distinguish between uncertainty and chance. Zur Shapira is a management scholar who has studied managers' conceptions of risk.[25] For managers, he finds, "risk taking is an endeavor where a manager can use his *judgment*, exert *control*, and utilize *skills*."[26] Managers, in other words, manage. It is in their very structural nature to deny insoluble problems. One of Shapira's managers says that "risk is calculable uncertainty, which can be manipulated by the person involved with the situation."[27] Though this manager thinks there is something about risk that could be coolly calculated, the interesting thing about his view is that it is something he *could control.*

Naturally, Shapira found some differences in personal orientations toward risk and uncertainty, however defined, but here I'm more interested in the overall orientation: the managers he interviewed tried to control the situations they confronted and about the last thing they would ever do is say out loud that they could not, in fact, gain control. This urge goes along with the position they occupy, and while personalities may vary in the degree to which they are comfortable taking chances, managers become similar over time because of their positions. Managers, says Shapira, are "*active* agents who believe that they can use their skills and exert control over decision-making situations even *after* the decisions have been made."[28]

Managers "do not accept the idea that the risks they face are inherent in their situation. Rather, they believe that risks can be reduced by using skills to control the dangers."[29] Nearly three-quarters of the seven hundred managers Shapira studied believed all risks were controllable. Gamblers take risks, in their minds, but managers manage. Robert Jackall points out the irony of managers being responsible for the increasing formal rationality of corporate life, as they import the latest fad and fashion in technical analysis and analytic decomposition. "In trying to come to grips with what seem at times to be incalculable, irrational forces, one must be willing to use whatever tools are at hand," he says.[30] More important here is Jackall's observation that "in an increasingly professionalized managerial environment, to eschew a vocabulary of rationality or the opportunity to routinize decisions when possible, can only make one vulnerable to the charge of 'managing by the seat of the pants.' "[31]

This does not mean that managers are superstitious or irrational, though it often looks like exactly that. Most of the time they are right—most of the time they can do precisely what their beliefs tell them they can do. Otherwise they wouldn't have succeeded long enough to be managers. "Managers," Shapira tells us, "develop in their careers into experienced risk takers."[32] Even when they make wrong decisions, they are right to think that most situations are surmountable, that with enough effort and resources they should be able to figure out the main parameters of a problem.

Where managers' ideas about controllability get interesting (and where they diverge from what economic theory says ought to be true) is in their beliefs about probability and forecasting. "The experience of successful managers teaches them that the probabilities of life do not apply to them," says Shapira.[33] What's not clear is why otherwise intelligent people would think they are so special that they could beat the odds almost all the time. Common sense, and much social theory too, would suggest that when managers are faced with a high-probability, high-consequence event they would: 1) do what they could to lower the chance that the event would happen, 2) lower the chance that the consequences would be bad, or 3) run away from the problem. But that's not what happens. Sometimes they just throw out the estimates that suggest the risk might be too high.

Says one of Shapira's managers: "I always check to be sure that I agree with the parameters. If I don't I will redefine the risk and modify the parameters. . . . [I]f the risk estimates show high risk, I will try to change the scenario into one with less risk."[34] This is one way that managers delude themselves into thinking they can get command of situations. Shapira explains that "professionals and managers alike are confident that, by using their skills to control the situation, they eliminate the risks. Their past experience has apparently boosted their confidence in their expertise in risk taking."[35]

So managers are confident they can control key aspects of a problem, probably even when they shouldn't be. And a central way they exert that control is by defining away the troubling uncertainties. That finding is important because it contradicts how rational models of decision making say managers should and do behave.[36]

Shapira's finding is a specific instance of a more general phenomenon. This is the phenomenon that connects a set of ideas about how the world works with the social position that the person occupies. Poets, novelists, mathematicians, and physicists deal in great uncertainty. Their very craft depends heavily on things existing that can't be controlled or fully predicted. But not managers. The managerial craft depends on the opposite. Controlling things, predicting the future is what managers do; it is *who managers are*. But it is not who managers are because of personality traits or family socialization. It is who managers are because of their professional training and because of the demands of the positions they occupy. Their networks are full of people who predict, manage, control, dominate. How could they be otherwise?

A similar thing happens with other social positions. Rich people tend to believe that they are rich because they deserve it *and* that others not so fortunate deserve *not* to be. This is so even (or especially) when they've inherited their wealth rather than worked for it. Social workers start out their careers to help people but in the real world they run up against the demands of everyday life and often turn into bureaucrats who control rather than help. As lawyers become more successful and move up in their firms, their belief that success depends on merit gets considerably stronger. In fact, in America at least, the more successful people are the more likely they are to think that success goes to the meritorious. Tenured professors almost invariably think that the tenure system is the only way that universities can be organized. Military decision makers, says political scientist Scott Sagan, are "skeptical of non-military alternatives to war" and thus "particularly susceptible to 'better now than later' logic."[37]

The dimensions and qualities of occupational knowledge emanate from social location. People tend to believe about their occupations what their training and social networks say is true. Consider how earthquake experts think.[38] They *know* that their images of the causes of earthquakes are right. In their view, earthquakes are mainly natural occurrences, made into disasters because people move to where earthquakes happen. Yet there are other reasonable ways to conceive what earthquake disasters are. It is not accidental, as it were, that the images held by professional earthquake risk managers appear in a certain way, and not others. Their training and the other people they work with all dictate to them, "this is what an earthquake is." Carol Heimer finds a similar sort of thing in her work on insurance companies. "There is a strong tendency to follow traditions," she says, "whether these traditions are appropriate or not."[39] The chief reason for this is not unreflective habit, but that other actors recognize as legitimate traditional ways of doing things.

Of course the point is not that managers qua experts are irrational but that when they assert that they can control that which cannot be controlled they are doing precisely what the cultural script of *manager* says they should do.

The managerial imperative, then, comes from sources inside and outside organizations. Environments demand rationalistic managerial expertise from those who would control technology and organizations. Managers' training and social networks demand that they represent themselves as controllers, can-do movers and shakers who can look in the face of uncertainty and deny it. Part of managerial competence is precisely to convince others that management is in control. The pressures of the position and of expectations from a rationalistic culture leave managers with little choice but to try to subjugate time, chance, and technical obstacles—the most difficult moments of uncertainty—to schemes of classification and command.

Expert Knowledge

Experts are always important players in risk dramas. The considerable technical details in systems such as nuclear power, chemical waste, and ozone depletion make experts indispensable. More broadly, in these high-stakes, high-danger games *everyone* becomes an expert of some sort of another, or at least tries to make themselves seem like one. Organizational leaders are expert at managing resources, scientists are expert at creating knowledge, technicians are expert at executing complex directives, and, of course, planners are expert at seeing possible futures.

Earlier I said that nearly everyone is an expert in the kinds of risk games I've been writing about. But that was an overstatement. The greater truth is that they all *claim* to be experts at various things (management, science, future telling, and so on). That they claim expertise makes the picture more complex, for simply to assert a claim to something does not guarantee its ownership.

There is an obvious functional need for real expertise in cases of high danger. There's no substitute for a lot of skill when a nuclear plant starts acting up. And yet there is a sense in which expertise is too highly valued in modern society. In Western cultures, and increasingly in non-Western cultures too, expertise is not just something that helps make systems work. It is also *good*. In post-industrial societies that so heavily emphasize knowledge and knowledge production, sheer command of large amounts of information garners respect and admiration, even moral esteem. Few symbols are more powerful in technical disputes than the symbolism of expert knowledge.

Experts are designated as such because they command superior (*superior* means high quantity and high quality) knowledge about something. Superior knowledge, in turn, is based on claims to high-quality experience. Plumbers know vastly more than nonplumbers about soldering pipes together and making water go around corners, because they've fitted pipes to corners and such many times. Mathematicians are experts in the manipulations of arithmetic symbols because they've learned the rules of their trade, and they've applied those rules to problems in the past. Knowledge workers, those who create and diffuse ideas, have special training in thinking and argument.

So experts know a lot of things that other people don't know; and they know those things in different ways than non experts, which means they make their knowledge abstract in ways that most people don't. But what, other than know a lot of things, do experts *do?* And more to the point, what is their place in risk dramas? One view is that they are handmaidens to power, advisors to those who are in positions to make real decisions. From this view, the conceptual distinction between expert and manager corresponds to the concrete workings of the relations between knowledge and decision. In a nuanced analysis of how policy experts work and think, sociologist Steven Brint holds, "Within the American political structure, experts are, for the most part, relatively minor players."[40] Brint's observation, however, appears to apply only to the specific domain of official government policy. He points out that a more subtle and expansive influence of experts is "at the time of the discovery of problems, the founding of institutions, or the inauguration of regulatory proposals."[41]

That's an important point, because when it comes to questions of risk, a common view is that experts and powerful decision makers are dramatically distinct, as the first quote from Brint emphasizes. It follows, again to follow the common view, that the *assessment* of risk is technical and scientific while the *acceptability* of risk is value-laden and political. Put another way, the *facts* of potential danger, in this theory, are objective and could be known without any biases whatever. *Choices* about those facts, however, are inherently full of bias.

We now know the distinction between assessment and acceptability isn't all that helpful, because facts aren't purely objective. Risk assessment is, alas, highly political, especially under conditions of uncertainty. I'll return to this point.

EXPERTS AND PREDICTION

For the moment I want to concentrate on the issue of what experts do. Some experts advise, some collect data, some are more comfortable being in the public eye than others, some use their knowledge for nefarious purposes. Whatever the variation in their training, personal predilections, or relation to power, experts share one attribute: *they predict.* Although they often don't want to accept the responsibility for their predictions—and indeed will usually invoke the handmaiden theory to avoid doing so—they will in fact predict all sorts of things.

Prediction is a form of forward counterfactual thinking, in which complications are assumed away so that the future can be known. And while everyone predicts, just as everyone plans, experts are generally better at it than others. One reason that experts are better than most at predicting is that when they are trained well they are also trained in the *limits* of their knowledge. Careful experts know better than others what they *do not know*.[42] Sociologists of the family may know nothing about the sociology of organizations, but they should be able, if the proper training is in place, to make some predictions about social life in organizations. But good sociologists will be especially careful to emphasize their pointed ignorance about research findings, specific theories, and raging debates in specialized journals.

In general, experts predict well. Weather forecasters may not do a great job of predicting the weather a month or a year in advance, but they do a *reasonable* job on any given day of predicting the weather tomorrow or next week. Certainly, there are times when big weather predictions turn out to be right, as when, for instance, the National Weather Service predicts this or that winter will be mild in the Northeast. But weather is chaotic, so long-term reliable prediction is quite difficult. Two weeks is about the limit of fairly precise forecasting that the Service is comfortable with and even then the predictions are statements of chance rather than certainty.[43] Indeed the Service doesn't try to predict over a whole season but rather to simply give a probability that precipitation (rain or snow) and temperature will be low, high, or about normal. Cognitive psychologists Max Henrion and Baruch Fischhoff explain that "it rains on about 70% of the occasions on which they forecast a 70% probability of rain. They have developed this ability through years of *hands-on experience,* with guidance from computer models, with ample feedback, and within an institution that rewards them for candor (emphasis added)."[44]

It is possible to meaningfully plan and predict when it comes to some hazards. The National Weather Service, the Army Corps of Engineers, and FEMA have developed apparently good models of water and flood hazards in hurricanes.[45]

Philosophers of science, naturally, have given a great deal of thought to the question "What is predictable?" For in considering, for instance, the definition of acceptable science they have had to be quite explicit about what constitutes good theory. And all theories take a stand on the issue of prediction, even if they are not explicit about it. Consider what Mario Bunge in *Causality and Modern Science* has to say. "A theory," he claims, "can predict to the extent to which it can describe and explain."[46] This is a very sensible definition. Yet he makes the point that, strictly speaking, "there is knowledge but not foreknowledge."[47] This is so because of the problem of contingency, or the idea that at any given moment the novel event, the unexpected interaction, can change the course of behavior, even of history.[48] But I find the statement too restrictive. We can't know for sure that the moon will spin about the earth next month, because a comet might knock it off orbit. But it's still a good bet.

Useful though it is, I will leave to philosophy the subtleties of trying to answer the question, "What is predictable?," by reference to the standards of logic and the epistemological principles. Let us look, perhaps more prosaically, at what experts do.

Experts have predicted well on questions of risk and danger. We aren't wholly ignorant about predicting forces that wreak great harm. In September 1984 scientific predictions prompted an evacuation of thirty thousand people from a town in Papua New Guinea, under the threat of a cataclysmic volcanic eruption.[49] Scientists in a local observatory had highly technical sensing equipment and used the Internet to get information about seismic activity from universities. With that information they modeled the likelihood of an imminent eruption. It helped that the mountain cooperated. In 1983 and 1984 it produced ten thousand earthquakes per month, and the ground itself had begun to bulge with magma in key places. At the end of August 1994 a big earthquake struck, and there was a record of seismic activity dating to 1767. So the scientists had palpable indicators on which to base their predictions.

Another example is the devastating 1989 Loma Prieta earthquake in California (7.1 surface wave magnitude), the most damaging quake in the U.S. since the 1906 quake in San Francisco. The U.S. Geological Survey staff knows enough about that earthquake, as well as quakes before it, to say that "events of comparable or greater strength will someday rupture the Hayward and San Andreas faults beneath the most heavily urbanized parts of the San Francisco Bay area."[50] This may sound like predicting that the sun will rise in the east tomorrow, but the Geological Survey is more specific. A 1988 Geological Survey study predicted that the segment of the San Andreas fault that broke "was assigned the highest probability for producing a [magnitude] 6.5 to 7 earthquake of any California fault segment north of the Los Angeles metropolitan area."[51] Not only was Loma Prieta at least somewhat predictable, so were its effects. According to the Geological Survey, "[A]ccounts of the effects of the 1865, 1868, and 1906 earthquakes in the South of Market and Mission districts of San Francisco differ little from what has been written about these areas in October of 1989," when Loma Prieta broke.[52] We can predict with considerable confidence that unreinforced masonry buildings will crumble and that structures built on landfill will topple.[53] The key predictive aid here is long, interpretable history. Technology helps too, because it helps experts understand earth's history. Geologists' strainmeters help them measure how much strain is in a fault. Thus scientists have not only technology with which to gather meaningful data but they can draw on probability theory and mathematics to give them a conceptual frame to organize information into data. Moreover, the theory of plate tectonics allows geologists to model and predict how continents move.

This is not to say that specific earthquakes can now be predicted in a strong sense. In *The Politics of Earthquake Prediction* we find the story of a couple of scientists, working with the theory of general relativity and the theory of tectonics to predict exactly when and where a series of earthquakes would strike Peru.[54] The predictions ended up being wrong, probably because the theory the geologists were working with was highly deterministic (i.e., if *a, b,* and *c* happen then *d* will certainly follow) rather than probabilistic. In any case, the Geological Survey notes that the Loma Prieta case was exceptional rather than usual. And Japan's extensive, and expensive, mosaic of earthquake prediction projects has so far failed to produce reliable signals, or precursors, of quakes.[55] While one of the key researchers in Japan's effort says, "There is a *possibility* of prediction" (emphasis added), establishing the limits of the possible is insufficient for establishing the probability of occurrence. Yet it *does* put it within the realm of possibility.

One conception of "prediction," which accords with common sense and the canons of science, is the very strict one that requires the predictor to specify time, place, magnitude of event. Predicting an earthquake, on this conception, requires the same precision that is possible with, say, specifying the time and location of the rising of the sun each morning. This conception of prediction is useful for many things, including knowing when the sun will rise in the morning, but for social life it's far too strict. Were the requirements for meaningful prediction so rigorous, most of social science would be impossible. We would not be able to say with any legitimate degree of confidence, for instance, that bureaucratic organizations will mold future problems to their routines. Yet this, certainly, is a valid and reliable prediction and an important one too.

In any case, experts can often predict well, and when they do the reason is mainly that they have experience—history—to base their models on. Psychologist James Shanteau is right when he says that "top experts through insights gained from experience know which cues are relevant and which are not."[56] Of course, direct, hands-on experience isn't *always* necessary to make informed decisions. Automobile insurance companies partially base rates for fast sports cars by looking at probabilities of accidents for the entire pool of sports cars, a practice that seems eminently sensible. In the North Sea, insurance companies have puzzled over the problem of how to estimate the risk of rig failure in the absence of meaningful data. They use computer simulations to study wave patterns, they can look to the Gulf of Mexico for similar experiences, they can use probabilistic risk analyses to estimate failure probabilities, and they can depend on expert advice. But all these devices in fact depend on in-genre information if they are to perform well.[57]

WHEN EXPERTS ERR

Of course, experts make a lot of mistakes. Sometimes, they err because the basis of their prediction isn't strong enough. Consider economists. Donald McCloskey argues that economics is more a matter of rhetoric, morality, and literature than science. For McCloskey scientific "rigor" bestows respectability rather than something that disciplines thought. One of McCloskey's strongest claims, though not as thoroughly argued as it might be, is that "prediction is not possible in economics."[58] This heretical assertion is based on the prosaic fact that most economists don't even try to predict; instead, they try to explain things that have already happened.

It may be that the more searching thing to say about predictive economics is that its predictions are so often wrong. The main reason for economics' predictive failure is that economists don't know enough things about the world. For neoclassical economics, when people don't act in accordance with the theory economists are more likely to conclude that something is wrong with the people than with the theory. The thing that would most help develop the predictive capacity of economics would be to find out new, and different, kinds of data about what people think and how they behave.

So sometimes experts err out of ignorance. Experts also err when they project beyond the boundaries of their legitimate domain of expertise. At Yucca Mountain, in Nevada, the U.S. Department of Energy wants to store high-level radioactive waste. But they need to convince Nevadans, most of whom oppose the project, and others that the repository will maintain its integrity for perhaps ten thousand years. When Department of Energy scientists use their experience with recent geologic history (in geology "recent" can mean 100 years) to extrapolate to the year 12,000 they predict far beyond their arena of expert knowledge.[59]

Or, consider the advent of the high-pressure steam engine.[60] When the steam engine was first invented, in the late 1700s, its builders put it together so that it operated under low pressure. When their patent expired in 1800, other builders started to increase the amount of pressure in the engine so that it would go faster. This speedup was like making a new kind of machine, because the knowledge built into the first machine was actually *different* from the knowledge required to make the second operate safely. Nancy Leveson, who designs safety systems for computer programs, says that "the first wide-spread application of the high pressure engine, on steamboats, resulted in frequent and disastrous explosions: passengers and crew were blown up, scalded to death, hit by flying fragments of iron, and blown off steamers to drown."[61]

It wasn't until 1852, when the federal government stepped in to regulate steam engines, that the carnage began to abate. Between 1816 and 1848, Leveson reports, steam engine accidents killed over twenty-five hundred people, injured twenty-one hundred others, and caused three million dollars in property damage.

The problem with steam engines was that people didn't really understand how they worked at high pressure. It took careful thought and analysis to figure out the answer to the steam engine puzzle. But it also took considerable experience with steam engines before experts could make them safe.

Other sources of expert error have to do with the way people think. A long string of studies from psychologists and even engineers shows that experts exhibit systematic judgmental biases.[62] "Anchoring," for instance, is when an initial guess that something will happen influences later guesses, even if new information suggests the first guess was wrong. If the initial estimate is low, later probabilities will tend to be low as well. We can reform the theory, and say that it is not merely new information to which the predictor responds but a broad array of things such as political pressures, organizational demands, and expert ideologies. Recall that experts claimed they could save 80 percent of Americans in the event of major nuclear war. Civil defenders anchored their survival estimate—which never had any evidentiary basis—and it was never revised downward.

Another reason experts make mistakes is that they become bound to the methods of their trade. Consider the U.S. Department of Energy's plan to bury radioactive waste in Yucca Mountain in Nevada. The Department of Energy's experts claim they can keep the waste safe for ten thousand years. Yet the experts, or would-be experts, have chosen to work with certain models, rather than others, because those models are *workable* and not because they are the best models.[63] It's not that the risk assessors are lazy but that their professional gaze is severely narrowed by the methods they use to answer the question "Is the Yucca repository a safe thing to plan for?" It seems that the methods themselves help to predetermine the answers that the assessors find.

Experts make mistakes for many reasons, then, but the hardest reasons to pin down are those that emanate from institutional contexts. Most expertise regarding risk is situated in complex organizations.[64] That means that experts often make their judgments *for* organizational purposes. This is not to say that experts simply make up a judgment to suit someone else's interests, but it does mean that expert judgment is often subject to pressures that vary across social contexts. For example, experts often make judgments about the safety of some system, *later* to follow those decisions with formal risk analyses; scientists are also sometimes highly selective in quoting research that supports their own institutional interests.[65]

Ann Langley, a business scholar, conducted a study in which she found a strong association between the character of an organization's structure and how formal analyses were used.[66] She argued that traditionally structured bureaucracies are more likely to use formal analyses to gather information and to control subordinates, while organizations with relatively more professionals will use them for communicative purposes. I am less concerned with the asserted connection between structure and use of analysis than with the more general observation that social form is systematically connected with the production and use of symbols. Langley notes that:

> At the micro level . . . formal analysis studies are carried out within specific social contexts involving different people linked together in hierarchical relationships: some people request analysis, some do it, and some receive it. [T]he purposes of analysis and the political dynamics surrounding it depend on who does what for whom . . .[67]

A dramatic example of how organizational pressures and institutional arrangements narrow the vision of experts is the destruction of the space shuttle *Challenger*. Diane Vaughan's *The Challenger Launch Decision* shows how a certain world view about danger and safety was created at NASA. NASA was a place that was resource rich, with some of the best experts in the world; it was also a place where mistakes could be highly visible. Thus there were strong incentives to make the space shuttle as safe as possible. But it wasn't. The *Challenger* flight was in fact extremely risky.[68] In hindsight, and highly public hearings, it was obvious that *Challenger* shouldn't have been launched. At the time, though, in the meetings where the series of decisions were made to go ahead with the flight, the choice was less clear. What happened was that NASA management and engineers defined away evidence that suggested the flight was dangerous. Vaughan calls it the "normalization of deviance." Each little decision was probably by itself insignificant, but they accumulated and one moment started to rest on another, and another, until by the time the key question popped up—My God, do you want me to wait until next April to launch?—there was only one answer. This is a process that happens in all sorts of organizations, but the consequences aren't as severe if the product is computer chips or housing loans.

So institutional pressures shape expert judgments by setting the terms by which some knowledge is deemed relevant. This is surprising, because if what experts claim to know were truly objective then all properly trained experts, faced with the same data and employing the same methods, should come up with the same estimates of risk. That they often do not shows how production pressures, power struggles, and political interests sometimes nudge expert judgments in certain directions.

When experts err it is sometimes because they lack data or good theory, sometimes because of narrow training, and sometimes because of professional ideologies. Experts also err simply, importantly, because like most of us, they work for organizations.

Ending Reflections

Our risky systems require a logic that leads to all sorts of failures. We increasingly depend on systems that have catastrophic potential. A few actively oppose those systems, and a common response to that opposition is to produce plans that promise personnel, equipment, and organization that will respond effectively to severe emergencies. Sometimes, we see fantasy plans cropping up after dramatically public accidents. After a Valujet airplane crashed into the Everglades in 1996, killing 110, there were calls from some quarters that the Federal Aviation Administration have a "zero annual accident rate." Positive responses to such entreaties are well-intentioned but seriously misguided, because they proffer promises that can never be kept.

Fantasy documents also emanate from systems that are either new (such as nuclear power) or newly scaled up (oil shipments from the Alaskan slope), and where, therefore, the historical record is absent or unrepresentative. This absence removes what might otherwise work as a reality check, because we do not know how such a system will behave under stress. Moreover, even if we had some experience with the behavior of comparably risky systems, the plans must be designed to cover a wide range of particular accidents, and each accident may be different enough to be off the plan's map. This leads to the absence of a second reality check: each accident is unique, and plans cannot cover everything.

Let us be clear that the production of fantasy documents is not merely a product of private industry. Far from it. Regulatory agencies seem to be just as willing as for-profit corporations to make promises beyond their reach. As unwittingly false promises, fantasy documents are decidedly not the result of capitalism. They are just as likely to show up in societies that are less capitalistic than the United States.

Fantasy documents are tools of persuasion. One important consequence of fantasy documents is that they license persuasion of employees. The employees, of course, want to believe that it is impossible for their Russian reactor to explode, for the booster rocket joints to fail, and so on. The organization encourages them to believe so with the fantasy documents. Thus, the people with the most experience with the organization they give their lives over to are not encouraged to bring that experience to bear upon the credibility of the fantasy document.

Normalizing Danger

A short while ago I claimed that experts tend to face down impossible problems. This does not mean they are as willing to accept responsibility for impossible consequences. Fantasy documents normalize danger by shielding elites and organizations from responsibility and by creating the impression that the worst case has been fully considered, and is covered. Of course, we all overpromise sometimes and organizations are often taken to task for it, so it may seem insignificant to draw attention to this aspect of fantasy documents. But it *is* significant, because once the fantasy is created, and some measure of legitimacy garnered for it, it sets the terms of debate over important issues.

Notice that this view of planning, predicting, and promising means that fantasy documents are much more than just lies. They can preclude some thoughts from ever arising, stifling objections to potentially dangerous or corrupt actions. They can so shape the context in which arguments occur that those who would criticize the fantasizers are, by default, extremists. They rule in and rule out as relevant who has wise things to say about nuclear Armageddon. They make it seem irrational to oppose a nuclear power plant. These shaping effects happen because the documents provide the categories available with which to talk about corporate power, government neglect, and the consequences of huge catastrophes for people's lives, their communities, and their environments.

Another consequence of fantasy documents is that they may well increase the danger from the systems they represent.[69] Once a plan is constructed and credulously presented, an organization becomes even more committed to it. Plans and policies name the problems they're supposed to solve, and that naming can easily constrict the range of vision about how systems work. If the naming is the correct one, then the constriction is an efficient way to rule out irrelevancies. But if the naming is incorrect, then important ways in which things can go awry will be neglected or ignored. With high-technology systems that are very resource intensive—and that therefore have strong vested-interests—it seems more likely that the naming will be incorrect than correct.

These observations suggest a few policy implications of my analysis. Because they tend to close off discussion, we may need regulations to pry open such systems. We might require systems with catastrophic potential to demonstrate that they've considered alternative interpretations to their version of how systems might break down, and how best to respond to those breakdowns. One of the key things that planning processes do is project a built-in theory about how organizations work, and also of how people think and behave. We might very well want to require our agents of protection to incorporate the knowledge of social and organizational scholars into those plans.

When fantasies are proffered as accurate representations of organizational capabilities, we have the recipe not only for organizational failure but for massive failure of the publics those organizations are supposed to serve. Fantasy documents normalize danger by allowing organizations and experts to claim that the problems are under control. Complex, highly interactive systems increasingly insinuate themselves into society. The justifications that attend those systems often mask the failures we need to see more clearly. In these ways, fantasy documents can contribute to increased danger by decreasing vigilance and diminishing the capacity for organizational learning.[70]

In addition, relying on what are most likely bad plans can lead to lower emphasis on prevention. The earnest belief that it really is possible to protect Americans when the bombs start to fall could lead to diminished caution in high-tension international conflict. The conviction that there is sufficient protection for huge numbers of people who might have to flee Long Island could foster a false sense of security that the evacuation could not be controlled. The faith that ten or twenty million gallons of oil *can* be corraled and collected could permit organizations not to prepare for other contingencies that *could* actually matter for people and their environments.

Let me put those ideas in a different way. To admit you probably can't evacuate twenty miles or fifty miles around a nuclear plant leads not only to ideas about closing nuclear plants but to other ideas about political negotiation and responsibility. To admit that civil defense plans probably wouldn't matter much at all leads to great emphasis on conventional war or even political negotiation. To admit you can't do a thing to contain huge amounts of oil on open waters leads to discussions about safer technology, conservation, and alternative energy sources.

Since the acceptability of risks is fundamentally a negotiated process, to take the fantasy out of fantasy documents would lay bare the political arrangements that underlie all decisions about important choices. While we would not want to consider policies and regulations that would stifle creativity—and fantasy documents are certainly instances of creativity—we might very well want to devise ways to bias processes of political and technical decision making in ways that favor extant, rather than imagined, bodies of knowledge. Such a thing would have to be done carefully, else we simply move the locus of decision making from creating apparent affinities to legitimating what is considered acceptable knowledge. The idea would be to break open technical arguments so that a wider and deeper array of voices would be heard. As policies and choices develop, we may wish to insist that all parties justify more carefully than usual the evidentiary claims they use to establish expertise.

Fantasy documents can function as shields, protecting organizations from outside scrutiny, keeping at bay mettlesome citizen groups, media vultures, and other inefficient, democratic forces. By representing as fact something that is chiefly opinion, organizations present themselves as keepers of safety and calm. Not quite guardian angels, they are the white knights of risk standing ready to put themselves between any fire-breathing threat and the innocents who would otherwise be sacrificed. But that of course is a bag of symbolic tricks. Organizations are much more likely to put others, not themselves, at risk. In fact, organizations never really love and protect people. They aren't designed to do that, and it is only in the breach—usually when some outside agent forces the matter—that organizations earn their knighthood.

And yet I don't think representations of super-competence and super-caring are real conspiracies to dupe the public. More often, fantasy documents are moments of self-deception. I think that elites generally understand that they benefit from the way that fantasy documents stifle broad-based discussions about why decisions are made as they are, how resources are allocated, and what difference it would make if other choices and allocations were to come about. But those are *effects* of fantasy documents; only rarely are they the intentions. The reason is simple: the managers and experts who create fantasy documents don't have sufficient knowledge or experience to effectively organize and execute the kind of conspiracy that would be necessary.

But the construction of fantasy documents is not random. If they aren't designed conspiratorially, they *are* designed to persuade, because regulators, lawmakers, and the opponents of whatever system is being defended must be assuaged as much as possible. To the extent that fantasy documents are believed by people outside of organizations, they can lead to a misplaced sense of complacency. The leaders and experts, after all, have said they are on top of things, and that they are looking out for everyone's interests. It's also not uncommon to hear the ringing rhetoric of patriotism trotted out to justify dangerous systems. This is some sort of dual protection for organizations—we have a plan and the ultimate mandate. Not only do we have a plan, but a deep moral obligation to protect ourselves against the Russians or the Arabs, or whatever evil foreign threat is at hand.

One problem with the complacency that fantasy documents facilitate concerns the loss of institutional trust when things go wrong. Organizations sometimes make excessive claims, and then can't live up to their promises. Publics are often baffled and angered when organizations seem incapable of adequate response. When the often substantial gaps between what organizations *say they can do* and what they *can actually do* become public, institutional legitimacy is threatened and the probability of popular distrust increases.

This is an example of *social liquefaction.* Liquefaction is when the ground becomes highly fluid in an earthquake; it usually happens on landfill or where the water table is high, and the soil can become so saturated with water that it becomes unstable. The result can be catastrophic if buildings or other life-supporting structures are built on it. Social liquefaction happens when organizations and their leaders can't live up to their claims, promises, or plans. The bonds of institutional trust between people and organizations are often quite tenuous, easily broken by the slightest act of misfeasance, malfeasance, or recreancy.[71]

Fantasy documents are often cast in technical language, the language of "experts," an efficient language for those familiar with it but an exclusive one for those who are not. In fact, there is a sense in which all the fantasy documents I've been talking about would be gibberish to most people. Oftentimes core issues of fantasy documents are discussed in the realm of formal modeling, mathematics, and other highly technical languages.

But there are other possibilities, other languages that would convey different sorts of things. Other languages could be used to talk about nuclear war, perhaps ones that revolve around issues of morality, which would entail talk of right and wrong; or a language of social science, which would entail talk of social order and organizational behavior under ambiguous conditions; or a language of aesthetics and literature, which would entail talk of individual-level horror and stories of misery. The same can be said of cleaning up huge oil spills and evacuating Long Island. One consequence of conducting debates over the efficacy and certainty of contingency plans for such horrors is that most people can't participate in the discussion. These are more instances of the unorganized shouldering the consequences of decisions made by others.

Fantasy documents use apparent affinities to transform uncertainty into risk. They symbolize rationality and control. In the short run, fantasy documents protect organizations, and their putative masters, in the occasional battles they must wage against those who may not share their interests. But they do us no service, as a society, because they truncate meaningful learning about what we don't know. By holding forth chimerical images of the future they create false expectations about wisdom and ignorance. I can not say how we might change the managerial imperative that leads otherwise intelligent people to assert groundless expertise and competence. But I doubt that the categories of argument, the organizational skill, and the bold vision required for that change will originate in the government and corporate organizations that govern our lives.

The antithesis of a fantasy document is the forthright admission that risk and danger are being created. Attending such an admission would be an honest assumption of the costs of creating danger, as well as an honest appraisal of the uncertainties our organizations create. One such cost is simply taking full responsibility for putting people at risk. We don't have many leaders like that. We don't have many organizations that would vault people like that to positions of leadership. And organizations don't generally exist in environments that would permit that sort of candor. More's the pity. Society would be safer, smarter, and fairer if our organizations and their masters could admit their limitations, declaring frankly that they can not control the uncontrollable.

NOTES

Chapter One

1. See Elliott Jaques, *The Measurement of Responsibility.*

2. One thing the book is not: a basic work in how to characterize and explain rhetoric *per se.* Some scholars make a fine living in that pursuit, and while I find much of the work on Rhetoric without institutional sensibility, I leave critical evaluation of that work to others (see, for instance, Edwin Black's *Rhetorical Questions*).

3. Some of these come from a fine article by Thomas F. Homer-Dixon ("On the threshold") on environment and social conflict.

4. For other arguments about the influence of organizations, see James Coleman's *Power and the Structure of Society* and *The Asymmetric Society.* For an argument that runs strongly counter to my view, see James Jasper's *The Art of Moral Protest.*

5. Of course, the very properties that make organizations good solutions to big problems can become dysfunctional. Size and splintering can lead to disconnects between subunits so that one department doesn't get the information it needs from another (this was an important factor in the *Challenger* accident; Vaughan, *The Challenger Launch Decision*). Superior resources can lead to institutionalized arrogance, so that officials systematically neglect bad news (Clarke, "The disqualification heuristic"). As well, tradition, habit, and inertia can prevent officials from pursuing innovative solutions. But I'm in no way saying organizations are the *perfect* or even optimal response when big problems arise. They are, however, more often than not, the *only* response.

6. Stinchcombe, *Information and Organizations,* p. 5.

7. Perrow and Guillen, *The AIDS Disaster,* p. 130.

8. Ibid., p. 133.

9. See, e.g., the discussion in Perrow, *Complex Organizations,* pp. 120–27; see also the wonderful chapter 4 of Jackall's *Moral Mazes: The World of Corporate Managers.*

10. *Organizations,* p. 137.

11. Frank Knight, *Risk, Uncertainty, and Profit,* p. 210.

12. I make no claim that Knight's is an ultimate, set-in-stone distinction, only that it's a useful one. Later conceptions of "uncertainty" rest on highly subjective notions of probability, so that, for instance, if someone holds a low degree of confidence in their predictions or beliefs we can speak of relatively high uncertainty. This elaboration is important for economic theories of choice un-

der uncertainty (on which see the synthetic review by Hirschleifer and Riley, "The analytics of uncertainty and information—an expository survey"), but need not concern us here.

13. See Mark Dowie's "How Ford put two million firetraps on wheels."

14. From another view, a main reason that the report was done in the first place was the sparse experience with reactor failures. So it's also true to say that Rasmussen was oversold as having accomplished the task of knowing the probabilities of failure when its results were simply intelligent guesses.

15. See, for instance, Martha Feldman's *Order without Design* and her article with James March, "Information in organizations as signal and symbol."

16. There *is* recognition that this happens among some urban planners. For an example, and also an analysis of connections between rhetoric and urban planning, see James A. Throgmorton's *Planning as Persuasive Storytelling*, especially chapter 2, "The argumentative or rhetorical turn in planning." Institutional theory in the sociology of organizations also lays heavy emphasis on the symbolism of strategies, structures, and programs (e.g., Powell and Dimaggio's *The New Institutionalism in Organizational Analysis*).

Chapter Two

1. Duncan Campbell, *War Plan UK*, p. 22.

2. Campbell demonstrates that the British public has always looked upon nuclear civil defense as chimerical and that the historical legacy of British civil defense is in controlling labor strikes.

3. Public Service Electric and Gas, Emergency Preparedness Group, Nuclear Department, P.O. Box 236, Hancocks Bridge, NJ 08038.

4. Torrey Canyon story taken from Jeffrey Potter, *Disaster by Oil, Oil Spills: Why They Happen, What They Do, and How We Can End Them*, chapter 1.

5. Union oil well from Elizabeth R. Kaplan, "California: Threatening the Golden Shore," p. 4. Alaska Oil Spill Commission, Final Report, p. 86. NB: great variation in estimates are the rule for well blowouts; they are *very* hard to measure. Arrow: should be changed to 2.5 million gallons. National Research Council, *Oil in the Sea: Inputs, Fates, and Effects*, p. 376. Argo Merchant, *Oil in the Sea*, p. 376. Amoco Cadiz, *Oil in the Sea*, p. 562. NB: 1 ton = 7.5 barrels, 1 barrel = 42 gallons. *Oil in the Sea*, p. 567. Alaska Oil Spill Commission, Final Report, p. 86. *New York Times*, 27 June 1989, A12.

6. I mean here only containment and cleanup, not rescuing a vessel or trying to prevent a vessel from breaking up.

7. E. J. Tennyson and H. Whittaker, *The 1987 Newfoundland Oil Spill Experiment*.

8. Oil Spill Intelligence Report, 26 October 1987, p. 2.

9. Some of this section comes from an article Charles Perrow and I wrote called "Prosaic organizational failure," *American Behavioral Scientist*.

10. *New York Times*, 4 June 1994.

11. *New York Times*, 13 October 1994; Dismantling of the Shoreham Nuclear power plant is completed.

12. *New York Times*, 4 April 1994, p. 24.

13. Nuclear Regulatory Commission, Emergency planning proceeding, p. 100.

14. Federal Emergency Management Agency, Post exercise Assessment.

15. Nuclear Regulatory Commission, Regarding Contention EX 50, p. 50.

16. FEMA, Post exercise assessment, p. 29.

17. An instrument that measures and indicates the amount of x-rays or radiation absorbed in a given period.

18. FEMA, Post exercise assessment, p. 105.

19. Ibid., p. 111.

20. Nuclear Regulatory Commission, Regarding Contention 20, p. 101.

21. FEMA, Post exercise assessment, p. 116.

22. Ibid., p. 136.

23. Ibid., p. 139.

24. Ibid., p. 138.

25. On the good Dr. Brill see NRC, Regarding Contention 20, pp. 161–69.

26. Nuclear Regulatory Commission, Emergency planning contentions relating to the February 13, 1986 exercise, p. 113.

27. The following quotes are from Defense Civil Preparedness Agency, *Guide for Crisis Relocation Contingency Planning,* pp. 3–7.

28. The genesis of the Post Office's plan was in the Carter Administration. This is true of many nuclear things, including strategic targeting, civil defense, and plans to fight a long nuclear war, that we often attribute to the Reagan Administration.

29. General Manager, Prevention and Planning Division, Jerry Jones (1983). Emergency Preparedness Planning Postal Hearings 1983.

30. Ibid., p. 11.

31. I'm not only paraphrasing individual testimony but stringing together testimony from several different individuals. The meaning of the testimony is not compromised.

32. Emergency Preparedness Planning Postal Hearings, pp. 13–14.

33. Ibid., p. 17.

34. Ibid., p. 18. Even this seems overstated. Judging by the size of the black dot, Miami is a very high-risk area, and radiation would likely spew across the Everglades. While northern Minnesota is indeed dot-free, North Dakota, right next door, is full of ICBM silos and other military-relevant targets and so is considerably blackened. The Senator may be right about some parts of the Rockies.

35. Ibid., p. 18.

36. Randolph Lanari, *Minnesota Population Protection Procedures,* p. 4.

37. Ibid., p. 14.

38. Defense Civil Preparedness Agency, Information Bulletin No. 306, p. 8.

39. See Federal Emergency Management Agency, Oversight: will US nuclear attack evacuation plans work?; Franklin, "Festival rings with ridicule of civil defense plan"; Beres, "Surviving nuclear war."

40. FEMA, Oversight, p. 25.

41. Ibid.

42. Charles Henderson and Walmer E. Strope, *Crisis Relocation of the Population at Risk in the New York Metropolitan Area.*

43. P. D. LaRiviere and H. Lee, *Postattack Recovery of Damaged Urban Areas.*

44. FEMA, Oversight.

45. Ibid., pp. 5–6.

46. Beres, "Surviving nuclear war," p. 45.

47. FEMA, Oversight, p. 862.

48. Ibid., p. 817.

49. Ibid., p. 772.

50. Hearing before the House Committee on Armed Services, 97th Congress, 1st session, March 1982.

51. See 1983 Emergency Preparedness Planning Postal Hearings; FEMA, Oversight; and Carsten Haaland, with Conrad Chester and Eugene Winger, Oak Ridge National Laboratory, *Survival of the Relocated Population of the U.S. after a Nuclear Attack,* Final Report, June 1976, ORNL-5041.

52. Leaning and Keyes, Introduction to *The Counterfeit Ark,* p. xix, who quote Estes, Testimony before the Senate Committee on Armed Services, 97th Congress, 1st session, 30 March 1981, p. 4382.

53. FEMA Acting Associate Director John W. McConnell, Hearing before the House Committee on Armed Services, 97th Congress, 1st session, March 1982, p. 783, emphasis added. McConnell was acting associate director for Plans and Preparedness.

54. Leaning and Leighton, "Do those who know more also know more about how much they know?" p. 3.

55. See Beres, "Surviving nuclear war," p. 78.

56. For work relevant to the panic issue, see Quarantelli and Dynes' "Response to social crisis and disaster" and Kreps' *Social Structure and Disaster.* And on problem of disrupting moral order see Kai Erikson's *Everything in Its Path* and *A New Species of Trouble.*

57. Conahan, Letter to Sala Burton.

58. GAO, Nuclear weapons, p. 29.

59. Ibid., p. 30.

60. Guy Oakes, *The Imaginary War: Civil Defense And American Cold War Culture.*

61. See, for example, the collections of articles in Grinspoon, *The Long Darkness,* and Peterson, *The Aftermath.*

62. My colleague Carol Heimer thinks dreams may profitably be seen as "very first drafts of plans." This possibility, I think, is a chapter in a different book.

Chapter Three

1. Readers interested in the philosophy of prediction should see the celebrated, if dense, *Fact, Fiction, and Forecast* by Nelson Goodman. I'm not concerned here with the formal logic of connecting prediction, knowledge, and experience, but how well, in practical terms, we have done it and the differences between that and the symbolism of grand claims of control.

2. Jastrow et al., in *Scientific Perspectives on the Greenhouse Problem,* present

a reasonably persuasive case that the probability of a greenhouse effect is low. It is a book by very famous scientists that sets out to stick close to the evidence and to be clear about what is and is not known. It drifts, however, into political denunciation of "public hysteria" and such, familiar epithets to readers of technology studies, science studies, and the like. Conservative politicians are given reasonable-sounding quotes while those on the other side are painted in near-red stripes. For a much more balanced assessment, see Schneider's *Global Warming: Are We Entering the Greenhouse Century?* a book that, although published by the Sierra Club, is very careful in placing the uncertainties in their larger contexts, specifying, for instance, how far off the mark someone *might* be to conclude that the temperature rise of the last 100 years is the result of greenhouse gases. Schneider is, nonetheless, quite uncertain about the models and what to conclude from them.

3. Jastrow et al., *Scientific Perspectives*, p. 6.

4. Ibid., p. 13.

5. Yet, if you were to judge the importance and frequency of organizational failure by how much academic attention the subject gets you would think we live in a nearly perfect world, because there is so little of it. One exception to the general lack of attention is an edited volume of the *American Behavioral Scientist* 1996, volume 9, number 8, all of which is devoted to organizational failures of one sort or another. This issue is reprinted and expanded in Anheier's, *When Things Go Wrong.*

6. My account is based on Hugh W. Stephens, "The Texas City disaster."

7. Ibid., p. 196.

8. Zelinsky and Kosinski, *The Emergency Evacuation of Cities*, p. 236.

9. Marples, *The Social Impact of the Chernobyl Disaster*, p. 31.

10. Zelinsky and Kosinski, *Emergency Evacuation*, p. 237.

11. Ibid., p. 238.

12. Marples, *Chernobyl*, p. 114.

13. Ibid., p. 115.

14. Ibid., p. 31.

15. Ibid., p. 31.

16. I do not dispute that panic was a fully rational response, only that uncontrolled flight is quite rare in the annals of evacuation histories.

17. NTSB, Hazardous materials release following the derailment of Baltimore and Ohio Railroad Company train no. SLFR, p. 1. See also Tom Coakley and Ray Flack, "Evacuees return home after acid smothered," *Denver Post*, 4 April 1983, p. 1+.

18. NTSB, Miamisburg report, p. 7.

19. Ibid., p. 38.

20. Romano, "State's disaster plan failed 'the acid test.' "

21. Ibid., p. 1.

22. Ibid., p. 7.

23. Ibid.

24. Ibid.

25. White et al., *The Livingston Derailment*, p. 1; I'll refer to this report at the Livingston Report.

26. NTSB, ICA derailment.

27. Much damage was done, and much fear was created, but none so significant as the discovery, two weeks into the cleanup operation, that a tankcar containing perchloroethylene—a very toxic chemical—had ruptured and all its contents spilled. Although cleanup operations are not really my main concern here, it's worth pointing out that the PCE was a major development in the Livingston drama, indeed extending the cleanup by nearly two years. Heavy rains drove the chemical deep into the ground, where it began to move in a huge swale. At first mitigation efforts were directed at digging up all the dirt that might have been contaminated, but that effort failed. In the end, permanent wells and huge sump pumps were sunk into the ground on the hope that most of the chemicals could be captured.

28. Livingston Report, p. 38.

29. Ibid., p. 50.

30. Ibid.

31. Ibid., p. 5.

32. Ibid., p. 38.

33. All was not perfect, of course. These assessments are relative to other, similar disasters.

34. Louisiana's oil refineries explode and its chemical plants breach containment with some frequency, so the claim that Livingston was the state's "worst" accident is damning indeed.

35. Russell Dynes, a longtime contributor to research on disasters, notes that the centralized, military style organization of emergency services is contradicted by research on disaster response ("Disaster reduction" and "Community Emergency Planning"). For instance, community emergency planning usually recommends highly centralized control of resources after disasters, but the research shows that members of the public are usually quite resilient.

36. This crash is another instance in which the NTSB finds human error is a sufficient explanation of the disaster, while production pressures are neglected (though, notably, tight scheduling in bad weather at National Airport *are* mentioned). The first officer remarked, "[T]his is a losing battle here on trying to deice those things, it (gives) you a false feeling of security that's all that does." The captain responded, "That, ah, satisfies the feds" (NTSB, *Air Florida Inc. . . . ,* p. 18). And flight crews couldn't see the length of the runway because of heavy snow. NTSB concludes the first officer wasn't assertive enough, which may be true, but misses the point that the airport probably should have been closed and never asks why the airlines would be flying in the first place. On the ideology of human error see Perrow (*Complex Organizations*), Tasca (*The Social Construction of Human Error*), Clarke ("The wreck of the *Exxon Valdez*"), and Clarke and Short ("Social organization and risk").

37. NTSB, Air Florida, Inc. collision.

38. Emergency Preparedness Hearings, 1982, p. 325.

39. Both quotes in NTSB report, Air Florida, Inc. collision, p. 79.

40. Ibid., p. 77.

41. Zelinsky and Kosinski, *Emergency Evacuation*, pp. 28–35.

42. Ibid., p. 33.

43. NTSB, Hazardous materials accident report, p. 3.

44. Ibid., p. v.

45. Ibid., p. 66.

46. Don Terry, "2 tank cars stir fears at scene of derailment," *New York Times,* 2 July 1992, A12.

47. Myers, "Thousands evacuate twin ports . . . ," p. 1A.

48. Ziegler et al., "Evacuation from the nuclear technological disaster," pp. 1–16.

49. See Katz, *Life after Nuclear War,* appendix A, for a good summary of these issues.

50. Flynn and Chalmers, *The Social and Economic Effects of the Accident at Three Mile Island,* pp. 28, 34.

51. Ziegler et al., "Evacuation from the nuclear technological disaster," p. 3.

52. Flynn, "Local public opinion," p. 151.

53. McCaffrey, *The Politics of Nuclear Power,* p. 96.

54. Interestingly, widespread panic is not the pattern following any type of disaster, whether it be tornado, hurricane, or massive bombing (the firebombing of Tokyo was an exception). Even events such as the fire at the Beverly Hills Supper Club and the stampede at the Who concert, which are commonly thought of as examples of panic, were not (see Johnson, "Panic and the breakdown of social order"). The pattern, in fact, is one of terror, accompanied by a moment of stunned reflection, or even anomie, followed by fairly orderly response. Even in the horrors chronicled by the Strategic Bombing Survey, cities burn, bodies explode, houses fall down and still people do not panic (see Janis, *Air War and Emotional Stress;* Hersey, *Hiroshima;* U.S. Strategic Bombing Survey, pp. 94–97 and SRI, 1:93–97). Graphic stories of firebombs and especially nuclear attack in Japan demonstrate unparalleled horror and excruciating anguish, but no panic. Resignation, depression, lethargy, yes, but no panic.

55. Dennis Mileti and John Sorenson, "Determinants of organizational effectiveness in responding to low probability catastrophic events"; the quotes in this paragraph are on pages 2–4.

56. My comments here are in no way critical of the newsletter or the center. Indeed the center gave me a grant to do research in Alaska on the Exxon oil spill, and I wouldn't have been able to do the work without that support.

57. Carley and Harrald, "Hurricane Andrew response," p. 2.

58. See Goldberg, "Thick smoke clears town" (chemical plant explosion); *(New Orleans) Times Picayune,* 7 May 1990 (flood); *Atlanta Journal and Constitution,* 13 May 1990 (flood); Warren and Pierre, "Broken gas pipe forces hundreds to flee in LaPlace"; Chapple, "Chemical truck blaze routs 700 at Covington."

59. Surro, "A line of cars 50 miles long."

60. The same can be said, incidentally, about planning and cost-effectiveness. Zelinsky and Kosinski (p. 300) conclude that: "we are incapable of answering the question as to whether evacuations are generally cost-effective. A case-by-case approach is the only viable strategy, and at best we can offer only guesses about certain individual events. Thus there cannot be much dispute that some of the major wartime evacuations—Leningrad, USSR, Germany II, and Japan, and Chernobyl as well—were paying propositions however huge

the expenditures involved. On the other hand, one may argue plausibly for either side of the argument in cases such as Mississauga, Three Mile Island, and some of the Gulf Coast hurricanes. . . . [T]here is no consistent answer to the question of the value of evacuations, whether measured in human lives and suffering or the accountant's balance sheet. Variability from event to event is enormous."

Chapter Four

1. Some of the material in this chapter comes from my articles "Oil spill fantasies" and "The disqualification heuristic."

2. See, using different logics, M. Meyer, *Limits to Bureaucratic Growth,* and Arthur Stinchcombe, *Information and Organizations.* Guy Oakes, in *The Imaginary War,* talks about breaking down the civil defense problem into smaller parts and says this "reductive analysis was one of the basic premises of the Cold War conception of nuclear reality" (p. 81). I've no quarrel with his point other than that such analysis is common to *all* problem solving.

3. William James held with the most emphatic of italics and capitals that *"Association . . . is between* THINGS THOUGHT OF—*it is* THINGS, *not ideas, which are associated in the mind.* We ought to talk of the association of *objects,* not of the association of *ideas" (The Principles of Psychology,* p. 554). A few pages earlier he claimed that "To be found *different,* things must as a rule have some commensurability, some aspect in common" (p. 528). What Professor James does not tell us is how things are thought similar if not with ideas, and what he misses is that standards of commensurability are neither self-evident nor objectively given.

4. Shrivastava, *Bhopal,* p. 53.

5. Vaughan, *The Challenger Launch Decision,* p. 148. Vaughan's chapter 4 is especially good on how experience that suggested danger was "normalized."

6. Both quotes from Vaughan, *Challenger,* p. 149.

7. Davis, *Lawrence and Oppenheimer.*

8. National Research Council, *Oil in the Sea;* also, "The rash of tanker spills is part of a pattern of thousands a year," *New York Times,* 29 June 1989, A20.

9. The difficult ecological irony is that we can decrease the risk of huge spills by increasing the number of containment compartments in large ships but doing so would increase the risk of small spills from overflowing, not to mention explosions and increasing burning of fossil fuels to power the vessels. I should point out that Prince William Sound is not the "open sea" but still quite a large body of water, and oil that escapes to large bodies of water becomes impossible to corral.

10. Exxon's plan might be considered a sixth, but it pertained to cleanup rather than immediate spill response.

11. Alyeska Pipeline Service Company, Oil Spill Contingency Plan.

12. Alaska Oil Spill Commission, Spill: The Wreck of the *Exxon Valdez.*

13. Alyeska, Oil Spill Contingency Plan, p. 3.50. This notation indicates section three of the plan, page 50.

14. Ibid., p. 3.51.

15. Ibid., p. 3.53.

16. Ibid.

17. Ibid., p. 3.54.

18. Ibid.

19. Lightering is transferring oil from one vessel to another. Where it is possible, lightering is extremely important, since it can prevent substantial amounts of oil from being released (the *Exxon Valdez* might have lost another forty million gallons were it not for lightering). Lightering is often dangerous, because of fires, explosions, and uncontrollable vessels.

20. Alyeska, Oil Spill Contingency Plan, 3.54.

21. Ibid., 3.56.

22. Ibid.

23. Volmert, Letter to Ernst Mueller.

24. This is from United States of America Nuclear Regulatory Commission, Docket No. 50-322-OL-3, Emergency Planning Proceeding, November 18, 1983; hereafter, NRC, 1983.

25. See Eckstein, *Nuclear Power and Social Power*, chap. 4.

26. NRC, 1983.

27. The quotes in this and the next paragraphs come from NRC 1983, pp. 86–87.

28. United States of America, Nuclear Regulatory Commission, Before the Atomic Safety and Licensing Board, In the Matter of Long Island Lighting Company, Docket No. 50-322-OL-03, Testimony of Kai T. Erikson and James H. Johnson on behalf of Suffolk County Concerning Contention 25—Role Conflict, November 18, 1983, p. 6.

29. They also noted the considerable amount of research from psychologists that shows people are very afraid of radiation risks, which would presumably make them less likely to go gentle into the radiation zone. LILCO subsequently initiated a system of tracking for evacuation workers, whereby they could keep track of their families. But the system would be activated only after people reported for their emergency duties, so it wouldn't resolve the key problem: people not showing up to begin with.

30. Note that this statement suggests LILCO could have made comparisons with *other* nuclear accidents rather than ice storms and commuting. Yet *LILCO* had not had experience with other nuclear accidents, but *had* with ice storms. In addition, nuclear threats, as Kai Erikson argues in *New Species of Trouble*, are much more feared than other threats.

31. The quotes in this paragraph are from NRC, 1983, p. 94.

32. Quotes from here to the end of this section are from NRC, 1983, pp. 96–106.

33. NRC, 1983, p. 100.

34. Rosenberg, "The origins of overkill," p. 29.

35. Part of the reason for the commitment to massive first-strike was that during this time targeting intelligence was at a severe disadvantage, so much so that the CIA was depending on Nazis and World War II maps for targeting purposes. The lack of targeting precision added to the need to deliver huge amounts of explosives to a larger number of places, just to make sure the targets were destroyed. Of course, the main reason for such a commitment was

simply that if the enemy shot first, our weapons would be destroyed. Nuclear weapons inherently entail a use-it-or-lose-it dynamic.

36. Kennedy, The President's Civil Defense Message.

37. Watson, "We couldn't run, so we hoped we could hide," p. 47.

38. Ibid.

39. Yoshpe, "Our missing shield," 389.

40. See, e.g., the history and discussion in Garrett, Civil Defense and the Public.

41. Hearing before the Committee on Banking, Housing, and Urban Affairs, U.S. Senate, 95th Congress, 2d session, 8 January 1979, Washington: USGPO, p. 15.

42. Garrett, Civil Defense and the Public, p. 5.

43. Ibid.

44. We would never expect them to address the issue of whether it would be *worth* staying alive after nuclear war.

45. Let alone a good thing, as in a report from RAND, that held:
But the fact remains that, taken as a whole, resources would have been depleted in smaller proportion than the human population. In this sense, then, nuclear war could be expected to increase per capita wealth. And if circumstances were such that the increased stock of capital per worker could be utilized effectively, higher output per worker would mean that GNP for the nation as a whole would also be higher—on a per capita basis (Hanunian, *Dimensions of Survival,* p. 138).

46. In Yoshpe, "Our missing shield," p. 398.

47. Ibid., p. 417.

48. Quoted in *U.S. Civil Defense Council Bulletin,* p. 1.

49. Garrett, Civil Defense and the Public, p. 9.

50. "Civil defense programs—roles and missions," *Foresight,* January/ February 1975, pp. 2–3.

51. Garrett, Civil Defense and the Public, p. 9.

52. Hearings before the Military Installations and Facilities Subcommittee, p. 869.

53. FEMA, *Oversight,* p. 7; also quoted in Beres, "Surviving nuclear war," p. 84.

54. Guiffrida, Testimony, p. 943.

55. Acting associate director, plans and preparedness, FEMA John W. McConnell, 1982 Committee on Armed Services meeting, pp. 783.

56. Hearings before the Military Installations and Facilities Subcommittee of the Committee on Armed Services House of Representatives, 97th Congress, 1st Session, HR 3519, Title 8, 26 and 27 February 1981, p. 771.

57. Michael Burawoy, *Manufacturing Consent.*

58. For contemporary treatments see Eviatar Zerubavel, *The Fine Line,* Nelson Goodman, *Fact, Fiction, and Forecast,* and the various readings and citations in *How Classification Works,* edited by Mary Douglas and David Hull. For interesting psychology see Alan Collins et al., "Reasoning from incomplete knowledge."

Chapter Five

1. Eliot Freidson, in *Professional Powers,* supports this view, while Mary Bernstein and James Jasper, in "Interests and credibility: whistleblowers in technological conflicts," dispute it. Bernstein and Jasper argue that whistleblowers in the nuclear industry are seen as legitimate to the extent they are *not* connected to organizations. Important though they are, whistleblowers are rare.

2. Some work that's premised on the idea that organizations are central include Short and Clarke, *Organizations, Uncertainties, and Risk;* Perrow, *Normal Accidents;* Sagan, *The Limits of Safety;* and Vaughan, *The Challenger Launch Decision.* Two books that show individuals can be just as central as organizations are Jasper's, *The Art of Moral Protest* and Mazur's *A Hazardous Inquiry: The Rashomon Effect at Love Canal.*

3. On this see Simpson's "Addressing the audience."

4. The National Academy of Sciences (*The Great Alaska Earthquake*) estimates this quake at 8.3. I've seen estimates as high as 9.2.

5. "The disqualification heuristic."

6. Alyeska, *Oil Spill Contingency Plan,* p. 3.50.

7. For much of this history I rely on David McCaffrey, *The Politics of Nuclear Power,* chap. 5.

8. Eckstein, *Nuclear Power and Social Power,* chap. 4.

9. McCaffrey, *The Politics of Nuclear Power,* p. 99

10. Quoted in McCaffrey, op. cit., p. 104.

11. McCaffrey, op. cit., p. 110.

12. Quoted in McCaffrey, op. cit., p. 126.

13. Quoted in McCaffrey, op. cit., p. 128.

14. McCaffrey, op. cit., p. 29.

15. FEMA, *Post Exercise Assessment.*

16. Nuclear Regulatory Commission, Docket No. 50-322-OL-5R, p. 14.

17. Nuclear Regulatory Commission, LILCO's testimony on contentions ex 15 and 16, p. 13.

18. Ibid., p. 14.

19. Ibid., p. 16.

20. Quoted in McCaffrey, *The Politics of Nuclear Power,* p. 131.

21. Quoted in McCaffrey, op cit., p. 132.

22. See the history and copious supporting evidence for this statement in Popkin, "The history and politics of disaster management in the United States," and Sorensen, "Society and emergency preparedness."

23. Popkin, "The history and politics of disaster management"; May, *Recovering from Catastrophes;* Rubin, "Community recovery from a major natural disaster."

24. Oakes, *The Imaginary War,* p. 82.

25. Ibid., p. 82.

26. Garrett, *Civil Defense and the Public,* p. 12.

27. Ibid.

28. George Kennan, in "International control of atomic energy," criticized this practice very early in the arms race.

29. I say this even though a few pages from here I argue that the actual war planners—in the early days this meant top military men—planned only massive first-strikes. It is not the only contradiction in the realm of things nuclear.

30. Writings on nuclear strategy are legion. Some helpful ones are Colin S. Gray, *Strategic Studies and Public Policy: The American Experience; Strategic Nuclear Targeting*, edited by Desmond Ball and Jeffrey Richelson; *The Use of Force: International Politics and Foreign Policy*, edited by Robert J. Art and Kenneth N. Waltz.

31. In Pringle and Arkin, SIOP, p. 115.

32. Ibid.; see also Rosenberg, "The origins of overkill."

33. Desmond Ball, "Counterforce targeting: how new? how viable?"; also Scott Sagan, *Moving Targets*.

34. Ball, "Counterforce targeting."

35. The NCA is comprised of the President, Secretary of Defense, and their deputized alternatives plus successors.

36. In Sagan, *Moving Targets*, pp. 42–43.

37. Both quotes from SRI, 1:19.

38. The point here is not that they might have been wrong about the horrors but that they were trying to create demand for their product.

39. Scott, "Public reaction to a surprise civil defense alert . . ."

40. Weart, "History of American attitudes . . .," p. 25.

41. See Garrett, *Civil Defense and the Public*, p. 4.

42. Kreps, *Social Structure and Disaster*.

43. Garrett, *Civil Defense and the Public*, p. 5.

44. See Grand Forks City Council, "Nuclear war in Grand Forks?"

45. Quarantelli, "Disaster studies."

46. Quarantelli also notes the secret research done by some members of the sociology department at the University of Oklahoma in the early 1950s on such things as troop behavior "in the field exposed to an atom bomb test explosion in a Nevada exercise" (Ibid., p. 292). That research, classified at the time, contributed to the collective behavior field in sociology.

47. Quoted in Quarantelli, op. cit., p. 289.

48. "Civil defense programs—roles and missions," *Foresight*, January/February 1975, pp. 2–3.

49. Yoshpe, "Our missing shield," p. 418.

50. Ibid., p. 454.

51. On February 26 and 27, 1981, H.R. 3519, Title 8, To authorize appropriations for such fiscal year for civil defense, and for other purposes, 97th Congress, p. 867.

52. Ferguson, *The Anti-Politics Machines*, p. 254.

53. Gray, *War, Peace, and Victory*, p. 109.

54. Civil defense was also something of a boon to social science, perhaps along the lines that Reagan's Strategic Defense Initiative was for physics: see, for instance, the interesting "Theories of social change and the analysis of nuclear attack and recovery" by Neil Smelser, the papers by Smelser and Sidney

Winter Jr. in "Vulnerabilities of social structure," edited by Vestermark, and especially Kenneth Boulding's "A pure theory of death."

55. Quoted in McCaffrey, *The Politics of Nuclear Power*, p. 127.

56. On February 26 and 27, 1981, HR 3519, Title 8, To authorize appropriations for such fiscal year for civil defense, and for other purposes, 97th Congress, p. 770.

57. This and the previous quote, respectively, are from the document cited in notes 51 and 56, pp. 770–71.

Chapter Six

1. This is probably a distinctly modern response. In the Trobriand Islands, at least in Malinowski's day, natives invoked magic under conditions of high danger and high uncertainty. "We find magic wherever the elements of chance and accident," he wrote, "and the emotional play between hope and fear have a wide and extensive range. We do not find magic wherever the pursuit is certain, reliable, and well under the control of rational methods and technological processes" (Malinowski, *Magic, Science, and Religion,* pp. 139–40). Magic is not, however, an option available to modern managers.

2. Planning and creating apparent affinities might all be analyzed, with some profit, as tropes. Types of tropes include metonymy (where one thing stands for another), synecdoche (substituting parts for wholes), metaphor (using one idea to illustrate another), and irony (using transliteral meanings). I don't mean this book to be a contribution to rhetorical analysis, however, and that's why I've not much labored in the sometimes fertile, sometimes florid fields of rhetorical literature.

3. An exception is Simpson's, "Addressing the audience."

4. In *The Legacy of Kenneth Burke,* edited by Herbert W. Simons and Melia Trevor; see also McCloskey's books, *The Rhetoric of Economics* and *If You're So Smart.*

5. See, for an untypically clear example, James A. Throgmorton's "Planning as a rhetorical activity."

6. An interesting discussion of this episode, and other things too, is Sissela Bok's *Lying: Moral Choices in Public and Private Life,* pp. 170–75.

7. Fred Block's *Revising State Theory* shows more generally how certain economic rhetorics mask business interests in the formation of public policy.

8. FEMA, Oversight, p. 9.

9. Ibid.

10. Ibid., p. 59.

11. Ibid., p. 51.

12. Edelman, "The social psychology of politics," p. 244.

13. Edelman, *The Symbolic Use of Politics*, p. 114.

14. Edelman, *Constructing the Political Spectacle*, p. 237.

15. Brunsson, *The Organization of Hypocrisy*, p. 23.

16. Ibid., p. 27.

17. Ibid., p. 23.

18. Ibid., p. 172.

19. Ibid., p. 188.

20. Weick, *The Social Psychology of Organizing.*

21. For evidence and argument on the power of investment organizations in shaping the corporate landscape, see Beth Mintz and Michael Schwartz's *Power Structure of American Business,* Kevin Delaney's *Strategic Bankruptcy,* Rick Eckstein's *Nuclear Power and Social Power,* Davita Glasberg's *The Power of Collective Pursestrings.*

22. See Scott Sagan's *Limits of Safety,* Charles Perrow's *Normal Accidents,* and Marshall Meyer's *Limits to Bureaucratic Growth.*

23. For likely scenarios see Meyer and Zucker's *Permanently Failing Organization.*

24. In "The perils of proliferation," political scientist Scott Sagan points out that the prevailing view is that military officers are no more or less likely to advocate war than civilians. Sagan argues convincingly that that argument applies to "war in general" rather than preventive war, and he has considerable direct evidence to support his contention.

25. Zur Shapira, *Risk Taking.*

26. Ibid., p. 48.

27. Ibid., p. 49.

28. Ibid., p. 73; my emphasis.

29. Ibid., p. 73.

30. Jackall, *Moral Mazes,* p. 76.

31. Ibid.

32. Shapira, *Risk Taking,* p. 81.

33. Ibid., p. 127.

34. Ibid., p. 75.

35. Ibid., p. 82.

36. For psychological experiments on preferring certain outcomes with modest gains to uncertain ones with large gains, see Kahneman et al., *Judgment under Uncertainty.* See Kahneman and Lovallo, "Timid choices and bold forecasts," for some arguments about the broader applicability of those findings; see also the terrific review article by Hickson, "Decision-making at the top of organizations." More general statements about this phenomenon are in Dalton's *Men Who Manage,* Alvin Gouldner's *Patterns of Industrial Bureaucracy,* Peter Blau's *The Dynamics of Bureaucracy,* MacCrimmon and Wehrung's *Taking Risks: The Management of Uncertainty.*

37. Sagan, "The perils of proliferation," p. 76.

38. Robert A. Stallings, *Promoting Risk: Constructing the Earthquake Threat.*

39. Heimer, "Allocating information costs in a negotiated information order," p. 406.

40. Brint, *In an Age of Experts,* p 137.

41. Ibid., p. 139.

42. But see the learned Jerome Ravetz's ("The sin of science") argument that modern science has a bias against admitting the limits of what is known and can be known.

43. William K. Stevens, "Is a bitter winter on the way?" *The New York Times,* 11 December 1994, p. E3.

44. In Henrion and Fischoff, "Assessing uncertainty in physical constants," p. 791.

45. See Sorensen, "Society and emergency preparedness," pp. 248–49.

164. Bunge, *Causality and Modern Science*, p. 307.

47. Ibid., p. 308.

48. Steven Jay Gould, *Burgess Shale* (*Wonderful Life*, NY: Norton, 1989).

49. See Kerr, "In New Guinea, eruption forecasting scores a success."

50. USGS Staff, "The Loma Prieta, California, earthquake: an anticipated event," p. 286; see also the companion article by Lindh, "Earthquake predictions come of age."

51. USGS, p. 286.

52. Ibid. See also Holzer, "Predicting earthquake effects."

53. In the case of the Marina district, which suffered enormous fire damage, the fill was put there partly to house the Panama-Pacific International Exposition, a key theme of which was to celebrate San Francisco's recovery from the 1906 disaster.

54. Olson, Podesta, and Nigg, *The Politics of Earthquake Prediction*.

55. See Normile, "Japan holds firm to shaky science." Predicting natural events is neither mystical nor chimerical, at least in nonmagical cultures. In September of 1994 thirty thousand residents in Papua New Guinea evacuated hours before a potentially devastating volcanic eruption. Certainly, predicting such eruptions is not as developed as predicting when the sun will rise tomorrow, but there have been several notable successes (Kerr, "In New Guinea").

56. Shanteau, "How much information does an expert use? Is it relevant?" p. 83.

57. Heimer, "Allocating information costs in a negotiated information order" and "Substitutes for experience-based information"; see also March, Sproull, and Tamuz, "Learning from samples of one or fewer." Heimer does not think they are always good predictors of the future; quite the contrary. My point is merely to note the general problem of using information to reduce uncertainty and to observe that such reduction is most successful when based on highly relevant experiential data.

58. McCloskey, *If You're So Smart*, p. 15.

59. Shrader-Frechette, "Risk estimation and expert judgment."

60. On this history see Leveson, "High pressure steam engines and computer software," paper presented to the International Conference on Software Engineering, Melbourne, Australia, 1992.

61. As usually happens, the blame was on operators for not running the engines properly.

62. Freudenburg, William R. "Perceived risk, real risk," Lichtenstein and Fischhoff, "Do those who know more also know more about how much they know?" other psychological cites; Apostolakis, "The concept of probability in safety assessments of technological systems."

63. Shrader-Frechette, *Burying Uncertainty*, especially chaps. 1 and 6.

64. See Dietz and Rycroft, *The Risk Professionals*, for an excellent example.

65. E.g., Mazur, "Disputes between Experts"; Shrader-Frechette, *Burying*

Uncertainty; Freudenburg, "Nothing recedes like success?"; Stallings, *Promoting Risk.*

66. "In search of rationality."

67. Ibid., p. 626.

68. All space flight is risky but for reasons not relevant here the *Challenger* flight was more risky than normal, as Vaughan documents.

69. This view contrasts sharply with that of James March and his colleagues, in "Learning from samples of one or fewer," who see such speculation and projection as a way to learn from scarce experience. That argument neglects the rhetorical character of fantasy documents and thus their use as tools in political conflict.

70. On the problem of vigilance see Freudenburg's "Nothing recedes like success?"

71. Freudenburg, "Risk and recreancy."

BIBLIOGRAPHY

Addington, Larry H. "The policy of the United States on nuclear weapons, 1945–1985." In *Arms Control and Nuclear Weapons: U.S. Policies and the National Interest,* ed. W. Gary Nichols and Milton L. Boykin, 41–49. Westport, CT: Greenwood Press, 1987.

Alaska Oil Spill Commission. Spill: the wreck of the *Exxon Valdez,* Final Report, Juneau: State of Alaska, February 1990.

Alyeska Pipeline Service Company. Oil Spill Contingency Plan, Prince William Sound, January 1987.

Anheier, Helmut K., ed. *When Things Go Wrong: Failures and Breakdowns in Organizations.* Thousand Oaks: Sage, 1998.

Apostolakis, George. "The concept of probability in safety assessments of technological systems." *Science,* 7 December 1990, 1359–1364.

Arkin, William M., and Richard W. Fieldhouse. *Nuclear Battlefields: Global Links in the Arms Race.* Cambridge, MA: Ballinger Publishing, 1985.

Art, Robert J., and Kenneth N. Waltz, eds. *The Use of Force: International Politics and Foreign Policy.* 2d ed. New York: University Press of America, 1983.

Atlanta Journal and Constitution. "7,000 ordered to evacuate as flood risk grows," 13 May 1990, A4.

Ball, Desmond. "Counterforce targeting: how new? how viable?" *Arms Control Today* 11, no. 2 (1981): 1–9.

Ball, Desmond Ball, and Jeffrey Richelson, eds. *Strategic Nuclear Targeting.* Ithaca: Cornell University Press, 1986.

Beres, Louis René. "Surviving nuclear war: U.S. plans for crisis relocation." *Armed Forces and Society* 12, no. 1 (1985): 75–94.

Berger, Peter L., and Thomas Luckmann. *The Social Construction of Reality: A Treatise in the Sociology of Knowledge.* Garden City, NY: Anchor Press, 1967.

Bernstein, Mary, and James M. Jasper. "Interests and credibility: whistleblowers in technological conflicts." *Social Science Information* 35, no. 3 (1996): 565–589.

Bielby, William, and Denise Bielby. " 'All hits are flukes': institutionalized decision making and the rhetoric of network prime-time program development." *American Journal of Sociology* 99, no. 5 (1994): 1287–1313.

Black, Edwin. *Rhetorical Questions.* Chicago: University of Chicago Press, 1992.

Blau, Peter. *The Dynamics of Bureaucracy.* 2d ed. Chicago: University of Chicago Press, 1969.

Block, Fred L. *Revising State Theory: Essays in Politics and Postindustrialism.* Philadelphia: Temple University Press, 1987.

Bok, Sissela. *Lying: Moral Choices in Public and Private Life.* New York: Vintage Press, 1989.

Boulding, Kenneth. "A pure theory of death: dilemmas of defense policy in a world of conditional viability." In *Behavioral Science and Civil Defense,* ed. George W. Baker and Leonard S. Cottrell, Jr., 53–59. Washington, DC: USGPO, 1962.

Brint, Steven. *In an Age of Experts: The Changing Role of Professionals in Politics and Public Life.* Princeton: Princeton University Press, 1994.

Brunsson, Nils. *The Organization of Hypocrisy: Talk, Decisions, and Actions in Organizations.* New York: Wiley, 1989.

Bunge, Mario. *Causality and Modern Science.* 3d ed. New York: Dover Publications, 1979.

Burawoy, Michael. *Manufacturing Consent: Changes in the Labor Process under Monopoly Capitalism.* Chicago: University of Chicago Press, 1979.

Campbell, Duncan. *War Plan UK, London: The Truth about Civil Defence in Britain.* London: Burnett Books, 1982.

Carley, Kathleen, and Jack Harrald. "Hurricane Andrew response." *Natural Hazards Observer,* November 1992, 1–3.

Carrier, G. F., F. E. Fendell, and P. S. Feldman. Firestorms. Defense Nuclear Agency, 15 April 1982.

Chapple, Charlie. "Chemical truck blaze routs 700 at Covington." *The (New Orleans) Times Picayune,* 1 January 1989, A1.

Chiles, James R. "How we got ready for a war that was never fought." *Smithsonian,* September 1988, 175–204.

Clarke, Lee. "The wreck of the *Exxon Valdez.*" In *Controversies: Politics of Technical Decisions,* 3d ed., edited by D. Nelkin, 80–96. Beverly Hills: Sage Publications, 1992.

———. "The disqualification heuristic: when do organizations misperceive risk?" *Research in Social Problems and Public Policy* 5 (1993): 289–312.

Clarke, Lee, and Charles Perrow. "Prosaic organizational failure." *American Behavioral Scientist* 39, no. 8 (1996): 1040–1056.

Clarke, Lee, and James F. Short Jr. "Social Organization and Risk: Some Current Controversies." *Annual Review of Sociology* 19 (1993): 375–399.

Coakley, Tom, and Ray Flack. "Evacuees return home after acid smothered." *Denver Post,* 4 April 1983, 1+.

Cockburn, Andrew. *The Threat: Inside the Soviet Military Machine.* New York: Random House, 1983.

Coleman, James. *Power and the Structure of Society.* New York: Norton, 1973.

———. *The Asymmetric Society.* Syracuse: Syracuse University Press, 1982.

Collins, Alan, Eleanor Warnock, Nelleke Aiello, and Mark Miller. "Reasoning from incomplete knowledge." In *Representation and Understanding: Studies in Cognitive Science,* ed. D. G. Bobrow and A. Collins, 383–415. New York: Academic Press, 1975.

Conahan, Frank C. Letter to Sala Burton, Ronald V. Dellums, and Don Edwards, 10 February 1987.

Dalton, Melville. *Men Who Manage.* New York: Wiley, 1959.

Davis, Nuel Pharr. *Lawrence and Oppenheimer.* New York: Simon and Schuster, 1968.

Defense Civil Preparedness Agency, Department of Defense. *Guide for Crisis Relocation Contingency Planning,* CPG 2-8-1, USGPO, October 1976.

————. Information Bulletin No. 306, USGPO, April 25, 1979.

Delaney, Kevin J. *Strategic Bankruptcy: How Corporations and Creditors Use Chapter 11 to Their Advantage.* Berkeley: University of California Press, 1992.

Douglas, Mary, and David Hull, eds. *How Classification Works.* Edinburgh: Edinburgh University Press, 1992.

Dietz, Thomas, and Robert W. Rycroft. *The Risk Professionals.* New York: Russell Sage Foundation, 1987.

Dowie, Mark, "How Ford put two million firetraps on wheels." *Business and Society Review* 23 (fall 1977): 46–55.

Drabek, Thomas. "The evolution of emergency management." In *Emergency Management: Principles and Practice for Local Government,* ed. Thomas E. Drabek and Gerard J. Hoetmer, 3–29. Washington, DC: International City Management Association, 1991.

Duluth News-Tribune. "Spill refugees recount their experiences," 1 July 1992, 1A.

Dynes, Russell R. "Disaster reduction: the importance of adequate assumptions about social organization." *Sociological Spectrum* 13 (1993): 175–192.

————. "Community emergency planning: false assumptions and inappropriate analogies," *International Journal of Mass Emergencies and Disasters* 12, no. 2 (1994): 141–158.

Eckstein, Rick. *Nuclear Power and Social Power.* Philadelphia: Temple University Press, 1997.

Edelman, Murray. *The Symbolic Uses of Politics.* Urbana: University of Illinois Press, 1967.

————. *Constructing the Political Spectacle.* Chicago: University of Chicago Press, 1988.

————. "The social psychology of politics." In *The Dynamics of American Politics,* ed. Lawrence C. Dodd and Calvin Jillison, 234–251. Boulder: Westview Press, 1994.

Emergency Preparedness in the Washington Metropolitan Area Hearings, Oversight Hearings before the Subcommittee on Government Operations and Metropolitan Affairs of the Committee on the District of Columbia, House of Representatives, 97th Congress, 2d session, 2 February and 5 May 1982, Washington, DC: USGPO, 1983.

Emergency Preparedness Planning of United States Postal Service, Hearing before the Subcommittee on Postal Personnel and Modernization of the Committee on Post Office and Civil Service, House of Representatives, 97th Congress, 2d session, 12 August 1982, p. 4. Washington, DC: USGPO, 1983.

Erikson, Kai. *Everything in Its Path: Destruction of Community in the Buffalo Creek Flood.* New York: Simon and Schuster, 1976.

————. *A New Species of Trouble: Explorations in Disaster, Trauma, and Community.* New York: W. W. Norton, 1994.

Federal Emergency Management Agency. Oversight: will US nuclear attack evacuation plans work? 97th Congress, 2d session, 22 April 1982.

———. Post exercise assessment: February 13, 1986, Exercise of the Local Emergency Response Organizations (LERO), as specified in the LILCO Transition Plan for the Shoreham Nuclear Power Station at Shoreham, New York, 17 April.

Feldman, Martha S. *Order without Design: Information Production and Policy Making*. Stanford: Stanford University Press, 1989.

Feldman, Martha S., and James G. March, "Information in organizations as signal and symbol." *Administrative Science Quarterly* 26 (1981): 171–186.

Ferguson, James. *The Anti-Politics Machine: "Development," Depoliticization, and Bureaucratic Power in Lesotho*. Cambridge: Cambridge University Press, 1990.

Finesilver, Sherman G. *Timely Tips When Disaster Strikes in Earthquakes, Hurricanes, Floods, Storms, and Nuclear Attack*. Denver: Howard Warren Publishers, 1969.

Flynn, Cynthia B. "Local public opinion." In *The Three Mile Island Nuclear Accident*, ed. Thomas H. Moss and David L. Sills. *Annals of the New York Academy of Sciences* 365 (1981): 146–158.

Flynn, Cynthia B., and J. A. Chalmers. The social and economic effects of the accident at Three Mile Island, NUREG-CR-1215, Washington, DC: USGPO, 1980.

Franklin, Ben A. "Festival rings with ridicule of civil defense plan." *New York Times*, 30 May 1982, B2.

Frederick, Chuck. "Railroaded again." *Duluth News-Tribune*, 2 July 1992, 10A.

Fredrickson, Tom. "Potential nightmare turns into smooth evacuation." *Duluth News-Tribune*, 1 July 1992, 6A.

Freidson, Eliot. *Professional Powers: A Study of the Institutionalization of Formal Knowledge*. Chicago: University of Chicago Press, 1986.

Freudenburg, William. "Perceived risk, real risk: social science and the art of probabilistic risk assessment." *Science*, 7 October 1988, 44–49.

———. "Nothing recedes like success? risk analysis and the organizational amplification of risks." *Risk* 3, no. 1 (1992): 3–35.

———. "Risk and recreancy: Weber, the division of labor, and the rationality of risk perceptions." *Social Forces* 71, no. 4 (1993): 909–932.

Freudenburg, William, and Susan K. Pastor. "NIMBYs and LULUs: stalking the syndromes." *Journal of Social Issues* 48, no. 4 (1992): 39–61.

Garrett, Ralph L. Civil Defense and the Public: An Overview of Public Attitude Studies. Research Report No. 17, Washington, DC: FEMA, 1976.

General Accounting Office. Nuclear winter: uncertainties surround the long-term effects of nuclear war, GAO/NSIAD-86-62, March 1986.

———. Nuclear weapons: emergency preparedness planning for accidents can be better coordinated, GAO/NSIAD-87-15, February 1987.

Giuffrida, Louis. Testimony before the House Committee on Armed Services, Military Installations and Facilities Subcommittee, 97th Congress, 2d session, 12 March 1982.

Glasberg, Davita Silfen. *The Power of Collective Pursestrings: The Effects of Bank*

Hegemony on Corporations and the State. Berkeley: University of California Press, 1989.

Goldberg, David. "Thick smoke clears town." *Atlanta Journal and Constitution,* 10 May 1991, F1.

Goodman, Nelson. *Fact, Fiction, and Forecast.* 4th ed. Cambridge: Harvard University Press, 1983.

Gouldner, Alvin. *Patterns of Industrial Bureaucracy.* Glencoe, IL: Free Press, 1954.

Grand Forks City Council. Nuclear war in Grand Forks? 1983.

Grange, The Honorable Mr. Justice Samuel G. M. Report of the Mississauga Railway Accident Inquiry. Hull, Quebec, Canada: Minister of Supply and Services, Canadian Government Publishing Center, 1981.

Gravelle, Julie. "EPA workers on scene of spill." *Duluth News-Tribune,* 1 July 1992, 8A.

———. "Wash veggies, shower, and then don't worry." *Duluth News-Tribune,* 1 July 1992, 8A.

Gray, Colin S. *Strategic Studies and Public Policy: The American Experience.* Lexington: University Press of Kentucky, 1982.

———. *War, Peace, and Victory: Strategy and Statecraft for the Next Century.* New York: Simon and Schuster, 1990.

Grinspoon, Lester, ed. *The Long Darkness: Psychological and Moral Perspectives on Nuclear Winter.* New Haven: Yale University Press, 1986.

Gusfield, Joseph, *The Culture of Public Problems.* Chicago: University of Chicago Press, 1981.

Hanunian, N. Dimensions of survival: postattack survival disparities and national viability, RAND Corporation, Santa Monica, CA, RM-5140-TAE, November 1966.

Hassard, John. "Maintaining perceptions: crisis relocation in the planning nuclear war." In *Civil Defense: A Choice of Disasters,* ed. John Dowling and Evans M. Harrell, 85–104. New York: American Institute of Physics, 1987.

Hearings before the Military Installations and Facilities Subcommittee of the Committee on Armed Services, House of Representatives, 97th Congress, 1st Session, H.R. 3519, Title 8, 26 and 27 February 1981.

Heimer, Carol A. "Allocating information costs in a negotiated information order: interorganizational constraints on decision making in Norwegian oil insurance." *Administrative Science Quarterly* 30, no. 3 (1985): 395–417.

———. "Substitutes for experience-based information: the case of oil insurance in the North Sea." In *Organization Theory and Project Management,* chap. 3. Bergen: Norwegian University Press, 1985.

Henderson, Charles, and Walmer E. Strope. Crisis Relocation of the Population at Risk in the New York Metropolitan Area, DCPA Contract No. 01-76-C-0308, Project No. 5591, SRI International, USGPO, September 1978.

Henrion, Max, and Baruch Fischoff. "Assessing uncertainty in physical constants." *American Journal of Physics* 54, no. 9 (1986): 791–798.

Hersey, John. *Hiroshima.* New York: Alfred A. Knopf, 1985.

Hickson, David J. "Decision-making at the top of organizations." *Annual Review of Sociology* 13 (1987): 165–192.

Hirschleifer, Jack, and John G. Riley. "The analytics of uncertainty and information—an expository survey." *Journal of Economic Literature* 17 (1979): 1375–1421.

Holzer, Thomas L. "Predicting earthquake effects—learning from Northridge and Loma Prieta." *Science,* 26 August 1994, 1182–1183.

Homer-Dixon, Thomas F. "On the threshold: environmental changes as causes of acute conflict." *International Security* 16, no. 2 (1991): 76–116.

Jackall, Robert. *Moral Mazes: The World of Corporate Managers.* New York: Oxford University Press, 1988.

Jaques, Elliott. *The Measurement of Responsibility.* Cambridge: Harvard University Press, 1956.

James, William. *The Principles of Psychology.* New York: Henry Holt and Company, 1893.

Janis, Irving Lester. *Air War and Emotional Stress.* New York: McGraw-Hill, 1951.

Jasper, James M. *The Art of Moral Protest: Culture, Biography, and Creativity in Social Movements.* Chicago: University of Chicago Press, 1998.

Jastrow, Robert, William Nierenberg, and Frederick Seitz. *Scientific Perspectives on the Greenhouse Problem.* Ottawa, IL: Marshall Press, 1990.

Johnson, Norris R. "Panic and the breakdown of social order: popular myth, social theory, empirical evidence." *Sociological Focus* 20, no. 3 (1987): 171–183.

Joint Committee on Defense Production, Congress of the United States. Civil Preparedness Review, Part II, Industrial Defense and Nuclear Attack, 95th Congress, 1st Session, Washington, DC: USGPO, 1977.

Kahneman, Daniel, Paul Slovic, and Amos Tversky. *Judgment under Uncertainty: Heuristics and Biases.* Cambridge: Cambridge University Press, 1982.

Kahneman, Daniel, and Dan Lovallo. "Timid choices and bold forecasts: a cognitive perspective on risk taking." *Management Science* 39, no. 1 (1993): 17–31.

Kaplan, Elizabeth R. "California: threatening the golden shore." In *The Politics of Offshore Oil,* ed. Joan Goldstein, 3–28. New York: Praeger Publishers, 1982.

Katz, Arthur M. *Life after Nuclear War: The Economic and Social Impacts of Nuclear Attacks on the United States.* Cambridge, MA: Ballinger, 1982.

Kennan, George. "International control of atomic energy." *Foreign Relations* 1 (1950): 37–40.

Kennedy, John F. The president's civil defense message. Speech delivered to U.S. Congress, 25 May 1961.

Kerr, Richard A. "In New Guinea, eruption forecasting scores a success." *Science,* September 1994, 2005.

Knight, Frank H. *Risk, Uncertainty, and Profit.* 1921. Reprint, New York: Kelley and Macmillan, 1975.

Kreps, Gary A. *Social Structure and Disaster.* Newark: University of Delaware Press, 1989.

———. The federal emergency management system in the United States: past and present. Paper presented at the 12th World Congress of Sociology meetings in Madrid, Spain, 1990.

Lanari, Randolph. Minnesota Population Protection Procedures, Division of Emergency Management, Room B5, State Capitol, March 1992.

Langley, Ann. "In Search of Rationality." *Administrative Science Quarterly* 34, no. 4 (1989): 598–632.

LaRiviere, P. D., and H. Lee. Postattack Recovery of Damaged Urban Areas. OCDP Contract, No. PS-64-201, SRI, Washington, DC: USGPO, November 1966.

Leaning, Jennifer, and Langley Keyes. Introduction to *The Counterfeit Ark* ed. Leaning and Keyes, xvii–xxv. Cambridge, MA: Ballinger Publishing, 1984.

Leaning, Jennifer, and Matthew Leighton. "The world according to FEMA." *Bulletin of the Atomic Scientists* 39 (1983): S2–S6.

Leveson, Nancy. High pressure steam engines and computer software. Paper presented to the International Conference on Software Engineering, Melbourne, Australia, 1992.

Lichtenstein, Sarah, and Baruch Fischhoff. "Do those who know more also know more about how much they know?" *Organizational Behavior and Human Performance* 20 (1977): 159–183.

Lindh, Allan G. "Earthquake predictions come of age." *Technology Review,* February/March 1990, 43–51.

MacCrimmon, Kenneth R., and Donald A. Wehrung, with W. T. Stanbury. *Taking Risks: The Management of Uncertainty.* New York: Free Press, 1986.

Malinowski, Bronislaw. *Magic, Science, and Religion, and Other Essays.* Garden City, NY: Doubleday, 1954.

March, James G., and Zur Shapira. "Managerial perspectives on risk and risk taking." *Management Science* 33, no. 11 (1987): 1404–1418.

March, James G., and Herbert A. Simon. *Organizations.* 2d ed. Cambridge: Blackwell, 1993.

March, James G., Lee S. Sproull, and Michal Tamuz. "Learning from samples of one or fewer." *Organization Science* 2, no. 1 (1981): 1–13.

Marples, David R. *The Social Impact of the Chernobyl Disaster.* New York: St. Martin's Press, 1988.

May, Peter J. *Recovering from Catastrophes: Federal Disaster Relief Policy and Politics.* Westport, CT: Greenwood Press, 1985.

Mazur, Allan C. "Disputes between experts." *Minerva* 11, no. 2 (1973): 243–262.

———. *A Hazardous Inquiry: The Rashomon Effect at Love Canal.* Cambridge: Harvard University Press, 1998.

McCaffrey, David P. *The Politics of Nuclear Power: A History of the Shoreham Nuclear Power Plant.* Boston: Kluwer Academic Publishers, 1991.

McCloskey, Donald N. *The Rhetoric of Economics.* Madison: University of Wisconsin Press, 1985.

———. *If You're So Smart: The Narrative of Economic Expertise.* Chicago: University of Chicago Press, 1990.

McMurty, R. Roy. Derailment: The Mississauga Miracle, Ontario, 1980.

Meyer, Marshall W., with William Stevenson and Stephen Webster. *Limits to Bureaucratic Growth.* New York: W. de Gruyter, 1985.

Meyer, Marshall W., and Lynne G. Zucker. *Permanently Failing Organization.* Newbury Park: Sage Publications, 1989.

Meyers, John. "Rail veteran says crew not at fault." *Duluth News-Tribune,* 2 July 1992, 10A.

Mileti, Dennis S., and John H. Sorensen. "Determinants of organizational effectiveness in responding to low probability catastrophic events." *Columbia Journal of World Business* 22, no. 1 (1987): 1–9.

Mills, C. Wright. *The Causes of World War III.* New York: Simon and Schuster, 1958.

Mintz, Beth, and Michael Schwartz. *The Power Structure of American Business.* Chicago: University of Chicago Press, 1985.

Molotch, Harvey L., and John R. Logan. *Urban Fortunes: The Political Economy of Place.* Berkeley: University of California Press, 1987.

Mission Research Corporation. Public Safety Support of the Crisis Relocation Strategy, Final Report, Vol. 1: Research, MRC Report #7442-6-476, Santa Barbara, CA 93102, 1976.

Mulford, Charles L., and Gerald E. Klonglan. "The local coordinator: all hazards planning." *Foresight,* July / August 1974, 12–13.

Myers, John. "High pressure kept benzene cloud from dispersing." *Duluth News-Tribune,* 1 July 1992, 8A.

———. "Thousands evacuate twin ports after benzene gas blankets area." *Duluth News-Tribune,* 1 July 1992, 1A.

National Academy of Sciences. Emergency Planning and Behavioral Research. Washington, DC: USGPO, 1962.

———. *The Great Alaska Earthquake of 1964.* Vol. 2, *Seismology and Geodesy,* Washington, DC, 1964.

National Research Council. *Oil in the Sea: Inputs, Fates, and Effects.* Washington, DC: National Academy Press, 1985.

National Transportation Safety Board, Air Florida, Inc., Boeing 737-222, N62AF, Collision with 14th Street Bridge nearing Washington National Airport, Washington, D.C., 13 January 1982; adopted 10 August 1982.

———. Railroad accident report—Denver and Rio Grande Western Railroad Company train yard accident involving punctured tank car, nitric acid and vapor cloud, and evacuation, Denver, Colorado, 3 April 1983.

———. ICA derailment, 28 September 1982, Final Report, Washington, DC, 10 August 1983.

———. Hazardous materials release following the derailment of Baltimore and Ohio Railroad Company train no. SLFR, Miamisburg, Ohio, 8 July 1986.

———. Hazardous materials accident report, derailment of Burlington Northern freight train no. 01-142-30 and release of hazardous materials in the town of Superior, Wisconsin, 30 June 1992, PB94-917003, NTSB / HZM-94-01; March 1994.

New York Times. "Uranium shipment ends Shoreham reactor's nuclear life," 4 June 1994, 24.

Newhouse, John. *War and Peace in the Nuclear Age.* New York: Alfred A. Knopf, 1989.

Nitze, Paul. "Atoms, strategy, and policy." *Foreign Affairs* 34, no. 2 (1956): 187–198.

Normile, Dennis. "Japan holds firm to shaky science." *Science*, 17 June 1994, 1656–1658.

Nuclear Regulatory Commission. Before the Atomic Safety and Licensing Board, in the Matter of Long Island Lighting Company, Shoreham Nuclear Power Station, Unit 1, Docket No. 50-322-OL-3, Emergency planning proceeding, testimony of Matthew C. Cordaro, Russell R. Dynes, William G. Johnson, Dennis S. Mileti, John H. Sorensen, and John A. Weismantle on behalf of the Long Island Lighting Company on Phase II Emergency Planning Contention 25 (Role Conflict), 18 November 1983.

———. Emergency planning contentions relating to the February 13, 1986 exercise, Docket No. 50-322-OL-5, In the Matter of Long Island Lighting Company, Shoreham Nuclear Power Station, Unit 1, United States of American Nuclear Regulatory Commission, Before the Atomic Safety and Licensing Board, 1 August 1986.

———. Before the Atomic Safety and Licensing Board, Docket No. 50-322-OL-5, Regarding Contention EX 50—Training of Offsite Emergency Response Personnel, 20 March 1987.

———. Before the Atomic Safety and Licensing Board, Docket No. 50-322-OL-5R, In the Matter of the Long Island Lighting Company, LILCO's testimony on Contention EX 50, 20 March 1987.

———. Before the Atomic Safety and Licensing Board, Docket No. 50-322-OL-5, In the Matter of Long Island Lighting Company, LILCO's testimony on Contentions EX 15 and 16, 6 April 1987.

———. Before the Atomic Safety and Licensing Board, Docket No. 50-322-OL-5R, In the Matter of the Long Island Lighting Company, Regarding Contention 20, Fundamental Flaws in LILCO's Training Program, 2 February 1989.

Nye, Joseph S., Jr. *Nuclear Ethics*. New York: Free Press, 1986.

Oakes, Guy. *The Imaginary War: Civil Defense and American Cold War Culture.* New York: Oxford University Press, 1994.

Olson, Richard Stuart, Bruno Podesta, and Joanne M. Nigg. *The Politics of Earthquake Prediction*. Princeton: Princeton University Press, 1989.

Perrow, Charles. "The organizational context of human factors engineering." *Administrative Science Quarterly* 28, no. 4 (1983): 521–41.

———. *Normal Accidents: Living with High-Risk Technologies*. New York: Basic Books, 1984.

———. *Complex Organizations: A Critical Essay*. 3d ed. New York: Random House, 1986.

Perrow, Charles, and Mauro F. Guillen. *The AIDS Disaster: The Failure of Organizations in New York and the Nation*. New Haven: Yale University Press, 1990.

Peterson, Jeannie, ed. *The Aftermath: The Human and Ecological Consequences of Nuclear War*. New York: Pantheon, 1983.

Pipes, Richard. "Why the Soviet Union thinks it could fight and win a nuclear war." In *U.S.–Soviet Relations in the Era of Détente*, 135–170. Boulder: Westview Press, 1981. Originally published in *Commentary* 64, no. 1 (1977): 21–34.

Popkin, Roy S. "The history and politics of disaster management in the United States." In *Nothing to Fear: Risks and Hazards in American Sociology*, ed. Andrew Kirby, 101–129. Tucson: University of Arizona Press, 1990.

Powell, Walter W., and Paul J. DiMaggio, *The New Institutionalism in Organizational Analysis*. Chicago: University of Chicago Press, 1991.

Powers, Thomas. "Choosing a strategy for World War III." *Atlantic*, November 1982, 82–110.

———. "Nuclear winter and nuclear strategy." *Atlantic*, November 1984, 53–64.

Pringle, Peter, and William Arkin. *SIOP: The Secret U.S. Plan for Nuclear War*. New York: W. W. Norton, 1983.

Quarantelli, E. L. "Disaster studies, an analysis of the social historical factors affecting the development of research in the area." *International Journal of Mass Emergencies and Disasters* 5, no. 3 (1987): 285–310.

Quarantelli, E. L., and Russell R. Dynes. "Response to social crisis and disaster." *Annual Review of Sociology* 3 (1977): 23–49.

Ravetz, Jerome R. The sin of science: ignorance of ignorance, Knowledge: creation, diffusion, utilization, 1993, 15(2): 157–165.

Romano, Jay. "State's disaster plan faced 'the acid test.' " *New York Times*, 21 March 1993, 1, 7.

Rosenberg, David Alan, The origins of overkill: nuclear weapons and American strategy, 1945–1960, International Security, 1983, 7(4): 3–69.

Rubin, Claire B. "Community recovery from a major natural disaster." Boulder: University of Colorado, Institute of Behavioral Science, 1985.

Sagan, Scott D. *Moving Targets: Nuclear Strategy and National Security*. Princeton: Princeton University Press, 1989.

———. *The Limits of Safety: Organizations, Accidents, and Nuclear Weapons*. Princeton: Princeton University Press, 1993.

———. "The perils of proliferation: organization theory, deterrence theory, and the spread of nuclear weapons." *International Security* 18, no. 4 (1994): 66–107.

Scanlon, T. Joseph. "Toxic chemicals and emergency management: the evacuation of Mississauga, Ontario, Canada." In *Coping with Crises: The Management of Disasters, Riots, and Terrorism*, ed. Uriel Rosenthal, Michael T. Charles, and Paul T. Hart, 303–323. Springfield, IL: Charles C. Thomas, 1989.

Scheer, Robert. *With Enough Shovels: Reagan, Bush, and Nuclear War*. New York: Random House, 1982.

Schlesinger, James R. "Civil defense programs: roles and missions." *Foresight*, January/February 1975, 2–3.

Schneider, Stephen H. *Global Warming: Are We Entering the Greenhouse Century?* San Francisco: Sierra Club Books, 1989.

Scott, William. Public reaction to a surprise civil defense alert in Oakland, California, Federal Civil Defense Administration (circa 1956, no date given on the document).

Shanteau, James. "How much information does an expert use? Is it relevant?" *Acta Psychologica* 81 (1992): 75–86.

Shapira, Zur. *Risk Taking*. New York: Russell Sage Foundation, 1995.

Short, James F. Jr., and Lee Clarke, eds. *Organizations, Uncertainties, and Risks.* Boulder: Westview Press, 1992.

Shrader-Frechette, Kristen S. "Risk estimation and expert judgment: the case of Yucca Mountain." *Risk* 3 (1992): 283–315.

———. *Burying Uncertainty: Risk and the Case against Geological Disposal of Nuclear Waste.* Berkeley: University of California Press, 1993.

Shrivastava, Paul. *Bhopal: Anatomy of a Crisis.* Cambridge, MA: Ballinger, 1987.

Simons, Herbert W., and Melia Trevor, eds. *The Legacy of Kenneth Burke.* Madison: University of Wisconsin Press, 1989.

Simpson, Ruth. "Addressing the audience: conceptions of audience in theories of rhetoric." Sociology Department, Rutgers University, 1994.

Smelser, Neil J. Theories of social change and the analysis of nuclear attack and recovery, Human Sciences Research, McLean, VA, report to Office of Civil Defense, Department of Defense, 1967.

Sorensen, John H. "Society and emergency preparedness: looking from the past into the future." In *Nothing to Fear: Risks and Hazards in American Sociology,* ed. Andrew Kirby, 241–260. Tucson: University of Arizona Press, 1990.

Stallings, Robert A. *Promoting Risk: Constructing the Earthquake Threat.* New York: Aldine De Gruyter, 1995.

Stanford Research Institute. Impact of air attack in World War II: selected data for civil defense planning, Division III: social organization, behavior, and morale under stress of bombing, vol. 1: public attitudes and behavior, prepared for the Federal Civil Defense Administration, Washington, DC, 1953.

———. Impact of air attack in World War II: selected data for civil defense planning, Division III: social organization, behavior, and morale under stress of bombing, vol. 2: organization and adequacy of civilian defenses, prepared for the Federal Civil Defense Administration, Washington, DC, 1953.

Stephens, Hugh W. "The Texas City disaster." *Industrial and Environmental Crisis Quarterly* 7, no. 3 (1993): 189–204.

Stinchcombe, Arthur L. *Information and Organizations.* Berkeley: University of California Press, 1990.

Sullivan, Roger J., Winder M. Heller, and E. C. Aldridge, Jr., Candidate U.S. Civil Defense Programs, System Planning Corporation, Defense Civil Preparedness Agency, March 1978.

Surro, Roberto, In Texas, a line of cars 50 miles long, New York Times, 26 August 1992, D20.

Tasca, Leo, The Social Construction of Human Error, Ph.D. dissertation, State University of New York–Stony Brook, 1989.

Tennyson, E. J,. and H. Whittaker, The 1987 Newfoundland Oil Spill Experiment, Proceedings, Eleventh Arctic and Marine Oil spill Program Technical Seminar, June 7–7, 1988.

Throgmorton, James A. "Planning as a rhetorical activity." *Journal of the American Planning Association* 59, no. 3 (summer 1993): 334–346.

———. *Planning as Persuasive Storytelling.* Chicago: University of Chicago Press, 1996.

Times Picayune (New Orleans). "Fierce rains, rising rivers hit La., Texas," 7 May 1990, A1.

Timmerman, Peter. The Mississauga train derailment and evacuation: November 10–17, 1979, Event Reconstruction and Organizational Response, Publications and Information, Institute for Environmental Studies, University of Toronto, Toronto, Canada, May 1980, Pub. No. ERR-6.

Tompkins, Phillip K. "On risk communication as interorganizational control: the case of the aviation safety reporting system." In *Nothing to Fear: Risks and Hazards in American Sociology*, ed. Andrew Kirby, 203–239. Tucson: University of Arizona Press, 1990.

Tompkins, Phillip K., and G. Geney. "Communication and unobtrusive control in contemporary organizations." In *Organizational Communication: Traditional Themes and New Directions*, ed. R. McPhee and P. Tomkins, 5–26. Newbury Park: Sage Publications, 1985.

United States Strategic Bombing Survey. Field report covering air-raid protection and allied subjects in Nagasaki, Japan, Civil Defense Division, 11–16 November 1945, published 1947.

United States Geological Survey Staff. "The Loma Prieta, California, earthquake: an anticipated event." *Science*, 19 January 1990, 286–293.

United States House of Representatives. Environment, Energy, and Natural Resources Subcommittee of the Committee on Government Operations, FEMA, Oversight: will US nuclear attack evacuation plans work? 22 April 1982.

United States Civil Defense Council Bulletin. Federal civil defense agency continues peacetime disaster aid to communities, 1976.

US Defense Civil Preparedness Agency. Significant events in the United States civil defense history, 1972.

United States Strategic Bombing Survey, Physical Damage Division. Effect of the incendiary bomb attack on Japan. Washington, DC: USGPO, 1946.

Vaughan, Diane. *The Challenger Launch Decision: Risky Technology, Culture, and Deviance at NASA*. Chicago: University of Chicago Press, 1996.

Vestermark, S. D., Jr., ed. Vulnerabilities of social structure: studies of the social dimensions of nuclear attack, Human Sciences Research, McLean, VA, report to Office of Civil Defense, Department of Defense, 1966.

Volmert, Lawrence E. Letter to Ernst Mueller, ADEC Commissioner, 22 April 1982.

Warren, Bob, and Robert E. Pierre. "Broken gas pipe forces hundreds to flee in LaPlace." *The (New Orleans) Times Picayune*, 25 October 1991, B1.

Watson, Bruce. "We couldn't run, so we hoped we could hide." *Smithsonian*, April 1994, 46–57.

Weart, Spencer. "History of American attitudes to civil defense." *Civil Defense: A Choice of Disasters*, ed. John Dowling and Evans M. Harrell, 11–32. New York: American Institute of Physics, 1987.

Weick, Karl E. *The Social Psychology of Organizing*. Reading, MA: Addison-Wesley, 1979.

———. "The collapse of sensemaking in organizations: The Mann Gulch Disaster." *Administrative Science Quarterly* 38, no. 4 (1993): 628–652.

White, LuAnn E., Sharon F. Bock, and Andrew J. Englande. The Livingston derailment, a report for the Office of Health Services and Environmental

Quality, Department of Health and Human Resources and the Department of Environmental Quality, State of Louisiana, 1984.

Wolensky, Robert P., and Kenneth C. Wolensky. "Local government's problem with disaster management: a literature review and structural analysis." *Policy Studies Review* 9, no. 4 (1990): 703–725.

———. "American local government and the disaster management problem." *Local Government Studies*, March/April 1991, 15–32.

Yoshpe, Harry B. Our missing shield: the U.S. civil defense program in historical perspective. FEMA 1981.

Zelinsky, Wilbur, and Leszek A. Kosinski. *The Emergency Evacuation of Cities: A Cross-National Historical and Geographical Study.* Savage, MD: Rowman and Littlefield, 1991.

Zerubavel, Eviatar. *The Fine Line.* New York: Free Press, 1991.

Ziegler, Donald J., Stanley D. Brunn, and James H. Johnson. "Evacuation from the nuclear technological disaster." *Geographical Review* 71 (1981): 1–16.

INDEX

Agnew, Spiro, 106
AIDS (acquired immunodeficiency syndrome), 9–10
Air Florida No. 90, crash of, 58–59, 178n36
Air Force (U.S.), 39–40, 67
airplanes: crashes of, 58–59, 60, 63, 166, 178n36; design of, 66, 72; in evacuation exercise, 26–27, 34
air raid sirens, testing of, 121
Alaska: environment of, 80; expertise in, 132; oil spill in, 19–20, 23; social conflict in pipeline issue in, 104–9. *See also* Alaskan Pipeline; *Exxon Valdez* (tankship); Prince William Sound; Valdez (Alaska)
Alaska Department of Environmental Conservation (ADEC), 79–80, 107–9, 132
Alaskan Pipeline: alternatives to, 105–6, 132; contingency plans and, 19, 76–81, 106–9; Environmental Impact Statement for, 105–6; opposition to, 43, 106; transportation issues for, 71–72, 104–6. *See also* Alyeska Pipeline Service Company
Alaska Regional Oil and Hazardous Substances Pollution Contingency Plan, 76
Alert America (federal program), 118
Alyeska Pipeline Service Company: audience for plans of, 41; claims of, 19; contingency plan of, 76–81, 106–9; distrust of, 128; failure of, 43; regulators' conflicts with, 107–9, 149; responsibility of, 76
American Behavioral Scientist (journal), 177n5
American Petroleum Industry, 141–42

American Trader (tankship), 21
ammonium nitrate fertilizer, explosions of, 48–49
Amoco Cadiz (tankship), 21
anchoring, concept of, 163–64
Anheier, Helmut K., 177n5
apparent affinities: absent for routine events, 98–99; concept of, 14, 71–73; creation of, 73–74, 99–100, 118, 127–28, 136, 171; for evacuations, 74, 87–90, 95, 113–14, 117, 128, 136; in nuclear power plant evacuation plans, 73–74, 83, 87–90, 128, 129; for nuclear war, 93–97, 123–25; in nuclear war civil defense plans, 73–74, 93–97; in oil spill cleanup plans, 74–75, 81–82, 107–9, 128; in problem solving, 71, 73–74; psychology of, 180n3; rationale for, 87–88; success of, 97, 98
Argo Merchant (tankship), 21
Arkin, William, 184n31
Army (U.S.), 39–40, 61, 123
Army Corps of Engineers (U.S.), 159
Arrow (tankship), 21
Art, Robert J., 184n30
Artificial Island (N.J./Del.), evacuation plan for, 18–19
Asselstine, James, 64
Association of American Railroads, Bureau of Explosives, 55
Atlantic Ocean, oil spills and, 21–23
atomic bomb: staged explosion of, 121; troop behavior and, 184n46. *See also* nuclear war
Atomic Energy Act, 116
Atomic Energy Commission, 12, 109, 113, 140. *See also* nuclear power plants; Nuclear Regulatory Commission; nuclear war